Masterpieces
of Ancient Greek Literature
Part III

Professor David J. Schenker

THE TEACHING COMPANY ®

PUBLISHED BY:

THE TEACHING COMPANY
4151 Lafayette Center Drive, Suite 100
Chantilly, Virginia 20151-1232
1-800-TEACH-12
Fax—703-378-3819
www.teach12.com

ISBN 1-59803-279-8

David J. Schenker, Ph.D.

Associate Professor and Chair of Classical Studies,
University of Missouri-Columbia

David J. Schenker is Associate Professor and Chairman of the Department of Classical Studies at the University of Missouri-Columbia. He has been interested in classical literature at least since he was six years old, when his mother took him to see the 1967 production of Aeschylus's *Oresteia* at the Guthrie Theater in Minneapolis. His career took him from Vanderbilt (B.A., 1982); through one year of teaching high school Latin at the Darlington School in Rome, Georgia; to the University of California at Berkeley (M.A., 1985, and Ph.D. in Classics, 1989). He taught two years at Allegheny College before coming to Missouri.

Professor Schenker was a recipient of the 2006 American Philological Association Awards for Excellence in Teaching. He has also won several teaching awards at Missouri, including the Provost's Outstanding Junior Faculty Teaching Award and the William T. Kemper Award for Excellence in Teaching.

Professor Schenker's primary area of research interest is Greek literature of the 5th and early 4th centuries B.C.E., with a special focus on Plato and the tragedians, especially Aeschylus. He has published articles on these subjects in several academic journals, such as *Classical Journal, Transactions of the American Philological Association*, and the *American Journal of Philology*. From 1999–2005, Professor Schenker served as coeditor of the journal *Classical and Modern Literature*.

Table of Contents
Masterpieces of Ancient Greek Literature
Part III

Masterpieces of Ancient Greek Literature

Scope:

The best of ancient Greek literature retains a freshness and immediacy that reaches far beyond its time and place of creation and speaks to readers and audience members today. In these 36 lectures, we discuss selections from that group of masterpieces, starting in every case with the cultural and historical background of each, then focusing on close readings of the works themselves. A guiding principle throughout is that these are not museum pieces to be venerated because of their age, but works of great literature that remain compelling, meaningful, and enjoyable. The organization of the course is largely chronological; in a few places, we break from that order to bring together works of similar genre.

We begin with definitions of the key words in the title of the course—*ancient*, *Greek*, and *literary masterpieces*—then move into six lectures on Homer's two epics: Lectures Two through Four on the *Iliad* and Lectures Five through Seven on the *Odyssey*. We briefly consider the method of their composition, then move through the epics book by book, highlighting the primary themes and poetic devices of each. the *Iliad* is indeed a moving war story, and the *Odyssey* is full of adventure and intrigue, and that narrative force is enough to qualify these epics as masterpieces. Beyond that, though, they both confront timeless questions and problems that define our human condition. For us, as for the ancient Greeks, these two poems serve as foundation for all that follows.

Lectures Eight and Nine focus on works contemporary, or nearly so, with the Homeric poems: Hesiod's didactic epics *Theogony* and *Works and Days* and the poems, authorship unknown, collectively called the Homeric Hymns. These works are central to our understanding of early Greek myth but can also stand on their own for their literary and artistic value.

In Lectures Ten and Eleven, we cover considerable ground, geographically and chronologically, with a discussion of the large and varied collection referred to as lyric poetry. The richness of this corpus makes generalization difficult: These poems are metrically varied, often reflective rather than narrative, typically fairly short, and intended for a wide variety of purposes and contexts.

Representative authors include Archilochus, Solon, Sappho, and Alcaeus.

A large section of the course, Lectures Twelve through Twenty-Four, covers the drama of 5th- and early 4th-century Athens, both tragedy and comedy. We survey the historical and dramaturgical context of the plays in Lecture Twelve, then devote three lectures to each of the four major playwrights of the period. For Aeschylus, we look at the *Persians* in Lecture Thirteen, then discuss his trilogy, the *Oresteia*, in Lectures Fourteen and Fifteen. For Sophocles, Lecture Sixteen introduces two plays, *Ajax* and *Philoctetes*; then, we go into greater depth with the three plays that center on the story of Oedipus: *Oedipus the King* in Lecture Seventeen and *Oedipus at Colonus* and *Antigone* in Lecture Eighteen. The corpus of extant tragedies by Euripides is larger. We look briefly at *Electra*, *Orestes*, and *Trojan Women* in Lecture Nineteen, then, choosing depth over breadth, we focus on three more of his works: *Medea*, *Hippolytus*, and *The Bacchae* in Lectures Twenty and Twenty-One. Our sole representative of Old Comedy, Aristophanes, takes us into the early 4th century. We discuss the genre in Lecture Twenty-Two, then, in Lectures Twenty-Three and Twenty-Four, look at several of the extant comedies as illustrations of his technique.

We turn next to two historians, with no apologies for including their works as literary masterpieces. Herodotus's *Histories* (Lectures Twenty-Five and Twenty-Six) is, in fact, much more than that. Using the Greek-Persian conflict as an organizing principle, Herodotus gives us an account of his world that is stamped both by Homeric models and by his own particular vision. Thucydides's masterpiece *The History of the Peloponnesian War* does indeed give us a straightforward narrative of the events of that war but also stands, as the author himself claims, as a possession for all time. In Lectures Twenty-Seven through Twenty-Nine, we consider passages from *The History* that illustrate Thucydides's views of the effects of war, international politics, and human nature more generally.

The next three lectures (Thirty through Thirty-Two) bring us into contact with an author who would seem to reject the whole idea of studying literary masterpieces. Plato's characters often speak of the shortcomings of the poets and storytellers, yet the artistry of his own dialogues belies that attitude toward literature. Lecture Thirty introduces the idea of Plato as a literary author, rather than simply a philosopher, with examples drawn from throughout his corpus. We then look in greater detail at two of the most polished of his literary creations, *Symposium* (Lecture Thirty-One) and *Phaedrus* (Lecture Thirty-Two).

Moving into a genre often maligned in Plato's dialogues, we consider, in Lecture Thirty-Three, the literary merits of some of the greatest orators of the 5th and 4th centuries, drawing examples from the speeches of Lysias and Demosthenes.

Thanks in large part to the conquests of Alexander the Great, literary production in the 4th century shifts away from the Greek mainland to the city of Alexandria in northern Africa. In Lectures Thirty-Four and Thirty-Five, we discuss the work of three poets of the Hellenistic Age: one of Callimachus's hymns, Theocritus's pastoral poetry, and the epic of Apollonius.

The final lecture (Thirty-Six) gives us an opportunity to look back at the primary themes and developments raised in the course of the lectures and forward to the influence of these masterpieces, most immediately on the Romans and, through them, on much of the Western world.

Course Notes

All dates in the course are B.C.E. unless otherwise indicated.

All Essential Readings listed after the lectures in this booklet are primary sources. If no Essential Readings are listed for a particular lecture, then no primary sources are required reading for that lecture.

Lecture Twenty-Five
Herodotus I—Introduction to History

Scope:

We shift now from poetry to prose for the next nine lectures, starting with five lectures on history and the two major Greek historians, Herodotus and Thucydides. Herodotus has been called both the Father of History, as the first practitioner of the genre as we know it, and the Father of Lies, for his many so-called digressions and fantastic stories. In this lecture, we first look at the proem of Herodotus's *Histories*, in which he sets out the goals of his history of the Persian Wars, revealing, among other things, his heavy reliance on Homer. Then, using selected passages from throughout the history, we discuss such issues as his use of sources, arrangement of material, and reliance on an overarching view of history. Discussion of Herodotus's historical method raises more general questions about historical objectivity, the relation between history and literature, and the place of the historian in his work.

Outline

I. In this lecture, we move from poetry to prose, starting with Herodotus, the man who has been called both the Father of History and the Father of Lies.

II. We know few details about the life of Herodotus (c. 484–425).

    A. He was born in the city of Halicarnassus on the coast of what is now Turkey.

    B. He traveled widely, to various parts of Persia, to Egypt, and to Babylon.

    C. He lived in Athens for some time.

        1. He is said to have been a friend of Sophocles and to have given public readings in Athens of his work in progress.

        2. He then moved to the Greek colony of Thurii in southern Italy.

III. He describes his work as the publication of his "inquiry," *historie* in Greek, from which we derive the word *history*.

A. Completed during the 420s, the work was later divided into nine books.

B. The first six books take us through the growth of the Persian Empire (with an excursus on Egypt in Book 2) and end with the defeat of the Persians at Marathon, just outside Athens, in 490.

C. The final three books describe the second wave of invasions of Greece, led this time by the Persian king Xerxes, ending with his defeat at Plataea in 479.

IV. The brief proem and the first few chapters of the history outline Herodotus's goals and methods.

A. His goal is Homeric, to preserve the memory of the great deeds of both Greeks and non-Greeks.

B. His discussion of the origins of the East/West conflict tells us much about his use of sources.

    1. The Persians, he says, blame the Phoenicians for starting the conflict by kidnapping the Greek woman Io. The Greeks retaliated by kidnapping the Phoenician Europa. The Trojans then kidnapped Helen, and the Greeks won her back.

    2. In other words, he brings together what we see as the separate realms of myth and history. Mythical accounts have Io and Europa snatched away by Zeus, and we know about Helen.

    3. He also records the Phoenician account: Io was not kidnapped but went willingly.

    4. He offers the two versions of the story but does not judge their accuracy, opting instead to begin with the first Eastern aggression against Greeks, by Croesus the Lydian (c. 550).

C. Herodotus then reveals a cyclical view of events that will guide and inform his history.

    1. He will tell equally about small and large cities, because many of the formerly small have become great and vice versa.

    2. The general principle is that happiness never stays long in one place.

V. Two shorter stories from later in the *Histories* illustrate Herodotus's idea about the inevitable change in human fortunes.

   A. In Book 3, we see that the Egyptian king Amasis was nervous about the unalloyed prosperity of his ally Polycrates (3.40–43).

      1. He persuaded Polycrates to forestall disaster by throwing away some prized possession.

      2. Polycrates threw a valuable ring into the sea, but a fisherman soon brought it back in the belly of a fish, with predictably dire results.

   B. In another story, in Book 7, we hear about a storm in 480 that destroyed some 400 ships from Xerxes's fleet just off the Greek coast.

      1. Herodotus mentions that one Ameinocles, a Greek who lived on the nearby shore, collected great wealth from the shipwreck (7.190).

      2. But even this bit player cannot get away with his good fortune: Herodotus tells us briefly and cryptically that he suffered the calamity of killing his own son.

VI. Several passages from Book 1 illustrate Herodotus's methods.

   A. He explains how the sovereignty in Lydia passed into the family of Croesus by telling the story of Gyges and Candaules (1.7–13).

      1. This early change in Lydian dynasties is hardly essential to an understanding of the Persian Wars, but the story is irresistible.

      2. The king Candaules was so in love with his wife that he felt compelled to show her off, naked, to his favorite bodyguard, Gyges.

      3. The queen realized she was being watched and gave Gyges the option of killing the king or being killed himself. Thus, Gyges, ancestor of Croesus, became king.

      4. Herodotus gives no indication of how he knows this story, and some of the speeches could have been known only by the principals.

5. But the story serves as a good introduction to the intrigue and imperial oddity of Eastern monarchs.

B. The story of Solon and Croesus (1.29–33, 86) is similarly suspect—and useful.

    1. The Athenian wise man and, as we have seen, lyric poet Solon traveled to the court of Croesus at Sardis.

    2. Croesus showed off his legendary wealth, then asked Solon who, in his opinion, was the happiest man he knew.

    3. Solon mentioned first an Athenian, Tellus, who had died gloriously in battle defending his city, then two sons from Argos who had died in an act of devotion to their mother.

    4. To Croesus's outrage, Solon explained that fortunes change, and no one can be considered happy until dead.

    5. Years later, Sardis was taken by the Persians, and Croesus, about to be killed, called out the name of Solon and was saved at the last instant. Only then had he recognized the truth of what Solon said.

    6. The meeting between Solon and Croesus is historically impossible.

    7. But it serves as a perfect introduction to the differences between the East, represented by a king who values wealth more than all else, and an Athenian wise man who recognizes happiness in private citizens and understands the fickleness of fortune.

VII. We can draw some conclusions about Herodotus's goals and his methods.

A. Sometimes he shows an interest in source evaluation, but sometimes not. In any case, he is transparent about the preconceptions that guide him.

B. Herodotus might not meet the standards of a modern scientific historian, but he does achieve his own goals.

C. His primary goal is to preserve the memory of great deeds and ensure that they receive proper glory. He certainly makes events and people memorable.

Essential Reading:

Herodotus, *The Histories*, Book 1.1–86.

Supplementary Reading:

Kurke, "Charting the Poles of History: Herodotos and Thoukydides."

Marincola, "Introduction," in *Herodotus: The Histories*.

Romm, *Herodotus.*

Questions to Consider:

1. Herodotus, it has been said, was too good a historian to let facts get in the way of the truth. What do you think of that statement as it applies both to Herodotus and to other historians?

2. Herodotus was steeped in the literature we have been reading. What influences on his work do you find, from Homer through to the playwrights?

Lecture Twenty-Five
Herodotus I—Introduction to History

Welcome back. We shift now from poetry to prose for the next nine lectures, starting with five lectures on history and the two major Greek historians, Herodotus and Thucydides. Herodotus has been called both the father of history, as the first practitioner of the genre as we know it; and also the father of lies, for his many so-called digressions and fantastic stories. In this lecture, we begin with some notes on the life of Herodotus; then look at the proem, that is the introduction, of his *Histories*, where he sets out the goals of his history of the Persian Wars, revealing among other things his heavy reliance on Homer and Homeric models. Then, using selected passages from throughout Herodotus's *Histories*, we discuss such issues as his use of sources, arrangement of material, and reliance on an overarching view of history. In the next lecture, also on Herodotus, we'll look more closely at some of his narratives of the events of the Persian Wars.

Herodotus was born about 484, died in 425. He was born in the city of Halicarnassus on the coast of what is now Turkey. Now those dates make him too young to have participated directly in the Persian Wars of 490 and then 484–79, but he was close enough to them to have access to eyewitness accounts. We have only a few details about his life. He claims to have traveled widely, to various parts of Persia, to Egypt, to Babylon, and throughout Greece; and he backs up those claims with eyewitness accounts of those areas. Nevertheless there are some scholars who still say he's just making it all up.

We know that Herodotus lived in Athens for some time, where he is said to have been a friend of Sophocles. He seems to have given public readings in Athens of his work in progress. So this history, like the plays we've been reading, and the lyric poetry, and certainly the epic poetry, all of it was intended primarily for performance. One reason for this is that literacy was growing only slowly through the course of the 5th century, so in order to have an audience at all an author would have to recite or perform. Herodotus moved from Athens to the Greek colony of Thurii in southern Italy at some point. That's about all we know and his work gives us no further clues about its author.

So on to the work itself. Herodotus describes his work as the publication of his inquiry; the Greek word for inquiry is *historie*, from which we derive the word history. It was Cicero, the Roman statesman, who called Herodotus the "father of history." Later readers, less pleased with his approaches, his methods, changed that to call him "father of lies." We can weigh those two reactions as we proceed. Herodotus completed his work during the 420s, and it was later divided into nine books. We usually refer to passages from Herodotus by book number and then paragraph within that book. The first six books take us from distant beginnings in the age of myth, through the growth of the Persian Empire, with a long excursus on Egypt in Book 2; and that section ends with the defeat of the Persians at Marathon, just outside of Athens, in 490 B.C.E. The final three books, books 7–9, describe the second wave of invasions of Greece, led this time by the Persian king Xerxes, ending with his defeat at Salamis in 480 and Plataea in 479.

The work starts with a brief proem, an introduction, in which Herodotus introduces himself and the subject of his work. In the first few chapters of the history itself, he then goes on to tell us about his methodology and some of his goals. So let's start as Herodotus himself does, with the proem—here's how he begins:

> Herodotus of Halicarnassus here displays his inquiry, so that human achievements may not become forgotten in time, and great and marvelous deeds—some displayed by Greeks, some by barbarians—may not be without their glory; and especially to show why the two peoples fought with each other.

He starts—as we've seen—by identifying himself and his place of origin. Nothing about Muses here, or a request for their help; this is his work, and he wants everyone to know it. But his goal is Homeric in spirit, to preserve the memory of great deeds and to make sure they're not without their glory, their *kleos*. That was certainly the desire of the Homeric heroes and the Homeric poet. Note here too that Herodotus intends to preserve the deeds not only of Greeks, but of barbarians as well. Now the word "barbarian," our English word, comes from the Greek word *barbaros* and this refers to any non-Greek speaker because someone not speaking Greek sounded like they were speaking gibberish, something like *bar bar bar*, hence the *barbaros*. It's not a necessarily pejorative term. It is a remarkable feature of Herodotus's *History* that he is so open to the customs, practices, the achievements of all he considers, not only the Greeks but these barbarians as well.

In his opening chapters, Herodotus discusses the origin of the conflict between East and West, a sort of global conflict, as he sees it; it's something that led to the more particular wars that he'll describe between the Persian Empire and Greece. This discussion of origins shows us much about Herodotus's use of sources throughout. He says that his Persian sources blame another Eastern people, the Phoenicians, for starting this global conflict by kidnapping the Greek woman Io and taking her off to Egypt. The Greeks then retaliated by kidnapping the Phoenician woman Europa, and taking her back to Greek island Crete. The next step was the Trojans, another Eastern people, kidnapping Helen from Greece, and then in the Trojan War the Greeks came and won her back.

Now the story of Helen and the Trojan War is what we would call myth, rather than history, and the same goes for Io and Europa. Mythical accounts have both Io and Europa being snatched away from their homes not by foreigners, but by the gods, with Zeus central to each story. There's no mention of Zeus here, but a rationalized account of the myths serves as history for Herodotus. Now Herodotus goes on to say that the Phoenician account of all of these events is slightly different from this Persian account that he started with. The Phoenicians say, "We didn't kidnap Io; she came willingly." Still no mention of Zeus.

Now if we leave behind this whole issue of myth as history for a moment, what's noteworthy here is the fact, or at least the claim, that Herodotus has checked not just one, but two sources: first the Persians, then the Phoenicians; and he has presented to us, the readers, what both of these two sources say. Now this is the most we could expect from Herodotus, he had very little precedent to work with. There had indeed been a few before Herodotus to write geographies, or genealogies, works similar to his *Histories* in many ways; but they were few and, as far as we can tell, nowhere near as broad in their scope, nowhere near as concerned with their sources. So, what Herodotus has done, he travels to his sources—as he says— he looks at sites; he asks questions; he checks one oral tradition against another; he sometimes applies his own powers of judgment when there's some discrepancy; and he often leaves the final decision up to us, his audience. Here are all the possibilities: You make your decision.

Rather than judging between these two stories about origins that he's given us, Herodotus goes on to say that he will simply begin with the point that he is sure about—and he says that clearly in this passage:

> So much for what Persians and Phoenicians say; and I have no intention of passing judgment on its truth or falsity. I prefer to rely on my own knowledge, and to point out who it was in actual fact that first injured the Greeks...

We'll soon learn that the man who first injured Greeks is Croesus, the Lydian king, and this was in about 550 B.C.E.; but before he starts in with Croesus, Herodotus continues by telling us more about his particular methodology. He tells us in the passage I'm about to read that he constructs his history with an overall view of the world in mind. He has a cyclical view of events that will guide and inform his history. Here's what he says:

> ...then I will proceed with my history, telling the story as I go along of small cities of men no less than of great. For most of those which were great once are small today; and those which used to be small were great in my own time. Knowing, therefore, that human prosperity never abides long in the same place, I shall pay attention to both alike.

We might wonder whether it's appropriate to begin a history by saying this is the way the world works and this is the way I will fit my history into it, but in any event the sentiment expressed here is not a new one to us in this course. The large are cut down to size. Solon, you might remember in his poetry, wished for prosperity but only in moderation and only obtained with justice, lest the gods get angry. Oedipus was held up as an example of a man who had everything going for him, until all turned sour: Count no man happy until he's dead. This general principle, that happiness never stays long in one place, obviously applies to the whole of the history to the extent that the mighty Persian Empire is brought low by the ragtag group of Greeks who turned them back. But this idea, this cyclical idea, also appears throughout Herodotus's work, in any number of smaller ways.

Let's look at two shorter stories from later in the *Histories* that illustrate on a smaller scale, Herodotus's idea about the inevitable change in human fortunes. In Book 3, as part of his long description of the rise of the Persian Empire, we hear about an alliance between an Egyptian king, Amasis, and Polycrates, tyrant of the island of Samos. Polycrates was remarkably successful in every one of his ventures, winning wars, amassing wealth, and growing ever more powerful. This made Amasis nervous. He sent advice to his ally Polycrates: Never, he said, can anyone be so lucky forever; we all face a necessary alternation of good and bad fortune. Since yours has been so good, you're definitely, obviously, necessarily, heading for a fall unless you do something right now to prevent that. So, he advises Polycrates, find the single object you prize the most and throw it away.

Well Polycrates heard this advice and approved of it. He chose out of all of his extensive treasures that one thing that he valued most—an emerald signet ring as it turns out—and he threw it deep into the sea. A few days later, a fisherman caught an unusually large fish. You can see where this is going. It was so large that he brought it to Polycrates. The fish was cut open and, yes, there was the ring returned to Polycrates. Polycrates told all of this story to Amasis, and Amasis promptly broke off their alliance, he was so certain that Polycrates's continued good fortune would soon be balanced by bad. In fact, we learn that Polycrates's fortunes didn't change right away, but he was indeed eventually murdered, treacherously, and his body was hung out on a cross.

There's another story that illustrates this cyclical turn of history. This one is from Book 7, it's even shorter. In 480, Xerxes's massive fleet, his fleet of invasion to Greece, suffered a severe setback when a storm destroyed some 400 of his ships just off the Greek coast. From this bad fortune for Xerxes, though, one man profited immediately: Ameinocles, a Greek who lived on the nearby shore and who collected great wealth from this tremendous shipwreck. But even this bit player, this guy we hear nothing about anywhere else, even he cannot get away with his good fortune. Here is how Herodotus describes it, about Ameinocles:

> …he subsequently picked up a large number of gold and silver drinking-cups which were washed ashore, and found Persian treasure-chests containing more gold, beyond

counting. This made him a very rich man, though in other respects he proved less fortunate; for he met with the distressing disaster of having killed his son.

It's almost as an afterthought, with no details provided; we learn that not even this poor beachcomber—or this rich beachcomber—can live life with unalloyed prosperity.

Let's go back to Book 1 now, for more examples of Herodotus's historical methods more generally, and two passages illustrate them very well. First the story of Gyges and Candaules, it's a story that gained some degree of notoriety from its use in Michael Ondaatje's novel *The English Patient*, subsequently made into a movie. This story explains how the sovereignty in the kingdom of Lydia had passed into the family of Croesus. How does this fit into the history more generally? Well, Croesus was the first barbarian to subjugate the Greeks, and Lydia will eventually be swallowed up as part of the Persian Empire. So, this early change in Lydian dynasties is hardly essential to an understanding of the Persian Wars, but the story is irresistible, so Herodotus includes it.

The Lydian king Candaules, the story begins, was in love with his wife. So in love that he felt compelled to show her off, naked, to his favorite bodyguard Gyges. Gyges of course resisted this, didn't dare see the queen naked, but Candaules commanded and set up a scheme. Gyges was to hide behind the bedroom door, wait for the queen to come into the bedroom at night, take off her clothes, and then as she was getting into bed, slip out the door unseen after seeing the queen naked. Gyges goes along with it, but the queen realized that she was being watched. She saw Gyges hiding behind the door, but held her tongue. The next day, she confronted Gyges about it, and gave him an option. She said to him, you, Gyges, may either kill the king who clearly set up the whole thing, or be killed yourself. Gyges, Herodotus tells us, chose to survive, and thus he became king. And he was an ancestor of Croesus, the first in that line of Lydian kings.

Herodotus gives us no indication how he knows this story, nothing about sources here, and some of the speeches, as those within the king's bedroom, could have been known only by the principals in the story. But it's a good story; it serves as excellent introduction to the intrigue and the imperial oddity of Eastern monarchs. Greeks would never do something like this.

There's a second story, also in Book 1, the story of the meeting of Solon and Croesus that's similarly suspect, but even more useful for this history. You might recall that Solon, whom we read as a lyric poet, was even more celebrated for his reform of Athenian laws. After those reforms, Solon left Athens and traveled the world. He was welcomed all over as one of the world's wisest men, asked his opinion on any number of matters. Among his many travels, he visited the court of Croesus at Sardis. Now Easterners—all Easterners—were wealthy by Greek standards, but none as wealthy as Croesus—hence the saying to be as wealthy as Croesus. Croesus proudly showed off his legendary wealth to Solon, touring him through his treasuries, showing all that he had, all that he owned; then he brought Solon before him and asked him, who, in his opinion, was the happiest man he knew.

"Well," Solon answered, "that would be the Athenian man named Tellus." "Who? We've never heard of this guy," certainly Croesus hasn't. "Tellus had a comfortable life, fine sons, even grandchildren, and he died gloriously while fighting for Athens, and he was honored with a public funeral." Well, this was not what Croesus wanted to hear, but he says "Okay, who comes in second? Who's the second happiest that you know?" "Well," says Solon, "that would be two young men from Argos, Cleobis and Biton. Their mother was a priestess of Hera, and she was late for a festival in honor of Hera that she had to get to. She needed to be driven there in an oxcart but the oxen were all out in the field. Her two sons agreed to take it upon themselves: They pulled the cart themselves in the place of the oxen and got their mother to the festival. At the festival, the proud mother asked the goddess Hera to give her two sons the greatest blessing possible in return for what they'd done for her. In answer to her prayers, the two boys instantly fell over dead; some idea of what's a part of good fortune. In any event, these boys come in second place for being happiest."

Croesus is now really outraged at this slight, at this unwillingness to recognize his good fortune and his prosperity;. and he says so to Solon:

> "That's all very well, my Athenian friend; but what of my own happiness? Is it so utterly contemptible that you won't

even compare me with mere common folk like those you have mentioned?"

So Solon explains to Croesus that fortunes change, and no one can be considered happy until dead. Here's part of what he says:

> "…whoever has the greatest number of the good things I have mentioned, and keeps them to the end, and dies a peaceful death, that man, Croesus, deserves in my opinion to be called happy. Look to the end, no matter what it is you're considering. Often enough God gives a man a glimpse of happiness, and then utterly ruins him."

Croesus sends Solon away after hearing that, thinking that Solon is not so wise after all. But that's not the end of the story. Years later, the Lydian capital Sardis was taken by the Persians and Croesus himself was taken prisoner. He was tied to a stake and about to be burned. At that moment, Croesus remembered what Solon had said so many years earlier about always looking to the end, about the change of fortunes and there, tied to the stake awaiting his painful death, Croesus moaned out loud three times the name of Solon. The Persian king Cyrus, watching this death of Croesus, was intrigued by this moaning and asked about it. So Croesus told him the story of their meeting, recognizing now how wise Solon had been so many years earlier. As the flames started licking around Croesus's feet, Cyrus the Persian king also recognized the wisdom in Solon's words and started pondering his own mortality, his own changeability of fortune. And he decided to save Croesus from the flames—with the help of a providential rainstorm.

Now this is a good story, as I hope you'll agree, but it is historically impossible, historically impossible that Solon and Croesus ever met. Croesus ruled from 560–546, Solon had reformed the Athenian laws in 594 and we know he was back in Athens after his travels. It seems very probable that Herodotus knew the story was impossible. Why, then, does he include it in his history? Well, for a variety of reasons. In the first place, it does illustrate beautifully this idea of changing fortunes that we talked about already, this cyclical idea, as it's argued by Solon here and then realized by Croesus and even by Cyrus.

In addition, this story serves as a perfect introduction to some of the essential differences between the East and the West. On one we side we have Croesus, the wealthiest of all Eastern monarchs who are famous for being wealthy, and he measures his happiness in terms of that wealth. Look, too, at Croesus's behavior, imperiously ushering Solon through his treasuries and then demanding answers to his questions. That's the East as represented by Croesus. On the other side a representative of Athenian wisdom, a personification, if ever there was one, of moderation in all things. In his reforms of Athens Solon, we might recall, made neither side happy. He didn't seize power for himself when he had the chance; look at those people that he mentioned, Tellus, Cleobis, and Biton. Clearly he values duty to one's city, duty to the gods, duty to family far beyond material wealth. Look too at the way that Solon responds to Croesus. He knew good and well what the rich man wanted to hear, but he wasn't in the least swayed from telling the truth, what he really thought. There's no kowtowing toward the East by this Greek. He is a quintessential Athenian, a quintessential Greek in so many ways, who is opposed then to the quintessential Easterner, Croesus. In the end of this story who comes out on top? It's clearly the Greek, Solon, who's seen as superior. In other words, this story might not be true, but Herodotus is too good a historian to let facts get in the way.

Now we've been talking in this lecture about Herodotus's goals and his methods. Sometimes he does show an interest in source evaluation, offering us a choice of different sources, recognizing his limitations, making sure to list where he gets his information; but sometimes he doesn't do that. We've also seen that he has an overarching view of the cyclical nature of history, and maybe even makes events fit into that view. But at least we can say that Herodotus is transparent about these preconceptions, these prejudices, these biases. Herodotus, thus, would probably not meet the standards of a modern scientific historian, but he does achieve his own goals. His primary goal, remember, is to preserve the memory of great deeds, and ensure that they receive proper glory, and one thing Herodotus certainly does do is to make events and people memorable.

In the next lecture we'll continue with Herodotus, following some of his narratives, tracing with him some of the central events in the Persian Wars.

Lecture Twenty-Six
Herodotus II—The Persian Wars

Scope:

In this lecture, we continue with Herodotus, shifting from his historical methods to his narrative style. Herodotus gives us a detailed account of the main events of the Persian Wars, and we look here at his account of Xerxes's preparations and the battles of Marathon, Thermopylae, and Salamis. But he gives us much more as well, offering cultural background, geographical breadth, and what we consider mythological background to those central events. These so-called digressions often take the form of self-contained stories and are among the most memorable parts of the history. Do they add anything to his overall history? Or does this style lead us to suspect even the most straightforward and seemingly pertinent parts of the history?

Outline

I. The first four books, and part of the fifth, trace the growth of the Persian Empire through several generations of kings and include extended discussion of expeditions to Egypt, Scythia, and elsewhere.

   A. As Herodotus introduces each new region, each part of the world that becomes part of the Persian Empire, he stops to fill in some detail about the customs of those people.

   B. Books 3 and 4 take us into the reign of Darius and his expeditions against India and the Scythians far to the north. Again, there are many more opportunities for ethnography and lists of local customs.

II. We now pick up the narrative with the first clash between Greeks and Persians in the Ionian revolt against Persian rule (5.28–38, 97—6.42).

   A. Greeks living in Ionia, the area along the eastern coast of the Aegean, went to the Greek mainland to find help in their revolt.

1. The Athenians sent 20 ships.
2. The Ionians and the Athenians burned the Persian city Sardis, and the Athenians returned home.

B. The Persians sacked the Ionian stronghold Miletus in 494, and the remaining Ionians fell easily after that.

1. In Miletus, most of the men were killed, and the women and children were sold into slavery.
2. Phrynichus, an Athenian playwright, wrote a tragedy called *The Capture of Miletus*. The Athenians fined him for reminding them of their sorrows and made it illegal to stage the play ever again.

III. The Persian king Darius then sent a force against Greece, using as a pretext the involvement of Greek cities, especially Athens, in the Ionian revolt.

A. The Athenians asked Sparta for assistance, but the Spartans were unable to help because it was against their law to march before the full moon.

B. The Athenians attacked the Persians at Marathon at a run and defeated them.

C. Although they were outnumbered two to one (20,000 to 10,000), only 194 Athenians died compared to 6,400 Persians.

IV. Ten years later, under Darius's son Xerxes, the Persians returned to finish the job.

A. The Persian preparations were undertaken on a magnificent scale (7.20).

1. Ten years earlier, the Persian fleet had been caught in a storm rounding Mount Athos; for this reason, Xerxes had a canal cut through the peninsula that connects the mountain to the shore (7.22–24).
2. Xerxes transported his troops across the Hellespont by means of a bridge of boats. When his first bridge fell apart in a storm, he cursed the sea, whipped it, and threw chains into it (7.33–36).
3. Having thus subjugated both land and sea, Xerxes led an army toward Greece so large that it drained rivers dry

(7.43).

    4. Visions and omens were uniformly unfavorable, but Xerxes ignored them. His Greek advisor, Demaratus, warned that the Greeks, especially the Spartans, would not be overawed by the size of his army, but Xerxes did not believe him (7.102–104).

B. On the Greek side, the Athenians had been building up their naval power.

    1. With profits from a surprisingly productive vein in the silver mines, the Athenian Themistocles had persuaded the city to build ships.

    2. As the Persians approached, an oracle said that the Athenians should trust in their wooden walls. Themistocles interpreted the wooden walls as their ships (7.141), and his interpretation carried the day.

V. The Greeks first took a stand against the Persians at a narrow pass in northern Greece called Thermopylae (7.175), with the navy nearby at Artemisium.

A. The Greek forces at Thermopylae were led by the Spartan king Leonidas and 300 Spartan soldiers (7.202–204).

    1. Xerxes expected the small number of Greeks to run at the sight of his army, but instead, they held the narrow pass against numerous assaults (7.210–212).

    2. A native of the area then told Xerxes about a secret pass over the mountain that would allow him to surround the Greeks (7.213).

    3. Realizing that his forces were being surrounded, Leonidas sent all the Greeks to safety, remaining at the pass with his Spartans.

    4. The slaughter was terrible, and every Spartan died. Herodotus made a point of learning the name of each of the Spartans (7.223–224).

B. The Greek fleet, far outnumbered, held its own against the Persians at Artemisium (8.10–18).

VI. Thanks to Athenian trickery, the Greek fleet defeated the Persians at Salamis, near Athens.

A. The Athenians had abandoned their city; the Persians sacked it and burned the Acropolis (8.50–54).

B. As other Greeks were deciding to take up a defensive position further south, Themistocles sent a secret message to the Persians (8.75–83).

　　1. Pretending to offer help, he encouraged the Persians to blockade the Greek fleet at Salamis, lest it slip from Persian grasp.

　　2. In fact, his goal was to keep the entire navy at Salamis, where the shallows and narrow straits worked to the advantage of the smaller Greek ships.

　　3. As we read in Aeschylus's *Persians*, the Greeks won a decisive naval victory at Salamis (8.84–96).

　　4. After the destruction of the Persian fleet at Salamis, Themistocles laid the foundation for friendship with the Persians, something that would come in handy shortly when he turned out to be a little too clever for the Athenians and had to leave his home city.

VII. The Persians retreated by land to Plataea, north of Athens, where the Greek forces led by the Spartans defeated them soundly (9.61–70).

VIII. What do we make of Herodotus: Father of History? Father of Lies? Maybe both?

A. His use of sources is often exemplary, even by modern historical standards, but he is clearly not limited by those standards.

B. He has strong ideas about the shape of history, and those ideas guide his narrative.

C. In any case, he tells a compelling and a memorable story.

Essential Reading:

Herodotus, *The Histories*, Books 5–9.

Supplementary Reading:

Lateiner, *The Historical Method of Herodotus*.

Luce, *The Greek Historians*, chapters 2 and 3.

Questions to Consider:

1. Compare Herodotus's account of the Persian Wars, and the battle of Salamis in particular, with the version in Aeschylus's *Persians*.

2. On what grounds are we justified in calling this account of the Persian Wars a literary masterpiece?

Lecture Twenty-Six
Herodotus II—The Persian Wars

Welcome back. In this lecture we continue with Herodotus, shifting from his historical methods and goals to his narrative style. Herodotus gives us a detailed account of the main events of the Persian Wars, that's his central subject; and we will look here at some of those accounts, namely: the lead-up to the wars; Persian preparations for the wars; and the battles of Marathon, Thermopylae, and Salamis. But Herodotus gives us much more as well, offering cultural background, geographical breadth, and what we might consider the mythological context for those central events. These so-called digressions focus often on the customs of the various people that Herodotus encounters on his journeys, and they're among the most memorable parts of the entire work. Do they add anything to the overall history? Or does this style lead us to suspect the accuracy of even the most straightforward and seemingly pertinent parts of the history? Those are some questions we might keep in mind as we look at Herodotus in this lecture.

The first four books of Herodotus's *History*, and part of the fifth, trace the growth of the Persian Empire through several generations of kings, and they include extended discussion of Persian contact with Egypt, with Scythia, and elsewhere. Book 1, as we saw in the last lecture, includes Herodotus's introduction, and then follows the career of Croesus, the king of Lydia and the first Easterner, according to Herodotus, who subjugated Greeks. The Persians defeat Croesus, they then add Lydia to their empire, and now that in the course of that activity Herodotus has introduced the Persians, Herodotus can then step back into a discussion of the origins of the Persian Empire. As Herodotus introduces each new region that comes up in his account, each part of the world that becomes part of the Persian Empire for example, he stops to fill in some detail about the customs of those people.

We hear about the Lydians, about the Babylonians, about the Ethiopians, and we have an entire book, Book 2, on the Egyptians. That material on Egypt is particularly interesting for the fact that Herodotus gives so much credit to the Egyptians for being such an absolutely ancient people, so much older in their customs, their practices, their religion, than the Greeks. He's the first to admit that the Greeks owe much to the Egyptians. This has become an interesting argument in terms of the debate about origins of Western culture and Afrocentrism. Herodotus is very clear about this, that Greeks owe much to the Egyptians. The detail that he includes is fascinating. All of the gods started with the Egyptians that the Greeks now recognize many of their religious practices, many of their political practices. Herodotus often editorializes as well, especially with approving comments about what might seem outlandish habits.

After this Book 2 on Egypt, books 3 and 4 take us into the reign of the Persian king Darius, and his expeditions against India and the Scythians far to the north. Many more opportunities here for ethnography and lists of local customs: We learn for example that the semen of the Indians is dark like their skin. We also hear about ants the size of foxes who go out in the desert and dig up gold. The Indians then follow behind those ants and sift out the gold from that sand and then race back to their towns before those huge ants can track them down and kill them: great stories about these various peoples.

Herodotus summarizes his attitude toward all these various customs with a story in Book 3, chapter 38. The Persian king Darius has brought before him certain peoples, and he's asked Greeks what it would take to make them eat the bodies of their dead fathers. Of course these Greeks were outraged, since their practice was to burn the dead. Darius then turned to a group of Indians who were present and asked if they would ever burn their dead fathers' bodies, and they were equally outraged. Their custom was to eat the flesh of the dead. The point here is that customs differ, that everyone thinks their own customs are best, and, as Herodotus says, only a madman would mock the customs of others.

After four books of such sorts of ethnography and history—justified loosely since all of these various places figured in the growth of the Persian Empire—after all of that, the narrative starts moving toward its goal—the Persian Wars with Greece—by describing the first clash between Greeks and Persians in the Ionian revolt against Persian rule. Greeks living in Ionia, that is, the area along the Eastern coast of the Aegean, were under Persian rule at this period, the late 6th century. And in 499, some of those people, some of those Ionians, revolted against the Persian rule and went to the Greek mainland to ask for help. Now, this act of requesting help from those Greek city-states on the mainland allows Herodotus to shift our attention for a moment to the Greek mainland, where he then fills us in on the background of some of these Greek city-states: Sparta, Athens, up to about the year 500. Yes, this is a digression, but it's also a clever way to remind us or to fill us in on what's going on on the other side, even as Persian power is growing.

It's in this section on Sparta and Athens that we get information about the tyranny of Peisistratus and his family in Athens, as well as the democratic reforms instituted by Cleisthenes and others that followed that tyranny. We also learn about political institutions in Sparta such as their double kingship. Now, Thucydides will follow up on some of this, as we'll see soon, correcting what he sees as mistakes in Herodotus's account; but he does give us lots of information, by the way, fitting it in. Back to the story: The Athenians responded to the request for help—this request from the Ionians—by sending a modest force of 20 ships. They joined the Ionians and succeeded in burning down the Persian city Sardis, formerly the capital of Lydia, destroying temples and much else in the process. The Athenians then returned home, but the damage had been done; not only to Sardis, but also to Greek–Persian relations.

The Persians successfully put down the revolt, ending it effectively in 494 by sacking the Ionian stronghold Miletus, a city just north of Herodotus's birthplace, Halicarnassus. Herodotus's description of the fighting at Miletus is indicative of the way he approaches battle narratives in general. There is little information here, not much information about particular strategies or maneuvers. Rather, Herodotus emphasizes the exploits of individuals, unusual events that happened, and the way that the events fit into some sort of predestined or preordained pattern. We hear in this account about the Greek contingent from Samos that deserted, all except 11 ships that stayed to fight at Miletus. The names of the few Samians who stayed were inscribed on a column to commemorate their bravery, and Herodotus says that he's seen that column. We hear about the escape routes of other Greek contingents: One of them was wiped out by natives who were confused and thought that these Greeks were hostile invaders; another group ended up sailing all the way to Sicily and turned to piracy.

Anyway, after this naval victory at Miletus, the Persians killed most of the men of Miletus and sold the women and children into slavery.

Thus, Herodotus says, a prediction was fulfilled. A prediction made by the oracle of Apollo at Delphi, that Miletus would become a prize, her women slaves, and her temples cared for by others.

There was great grief in Athens, Herodotus tells us, at the fall of Miletus. He tells us that the Athenian playwright Phrynichus wrote a tragedy about the end of the Ionian revolt, it was called *The Capture of Miletus*. The tragedy was performed and the Athenians, Herodotus tells us, fined Phrynichus for reminding them of their sorrows, and they made it illegal to stage the play ever again. As we might expect after that sort of reception, that play does not survive.

Moving on. In Book 6, the Persian king Darius sends a force—a military force—against Greece, using as a pretext the involvement of Greek cities, in particular Athens, in the Ionian revolt. Darius was so enraged by the Athenians' involvement in the revolt that he had a servant whose job was to remind him regularly of Athens, to repeat to him, "remember Athens." This Persian force advanced toward Athens, taking other Greek cities on the way. Athens knew they couldn't stand up to this Persian force all by herself, sent a runner, the famous Pheidippides, to Sparta to ask for help. The Spartans claimed that they were willing—yes, certainly we'll help, but we can't make it just now. It's unlawful for us march now, before the full moon.

Now serving as guide for these Persians as they approached Athens was one from the family of Peisistratus, a man named Hippias. Hippias, who was a son of the former Athenian tyrant Peisistratus, and he hoped to be reinstated in to power by helping these Persians. As they approached Athens—and this is another one of the stories that Herodotus gives us—Hippias had a dream in which he slept with his mother. A good omen, he thought, suggesting that he would soon recover his mother city Athens. But, no. Before arriving in Athens, but while they're in Greece, Hippias had a sneezing attack, sneezed one of his teeth right out of his head—he's not so young anymore—and he couldn't find it on the ground. Oh no, he thought, this is what the dream meant. My tooth is now reunited with Athenian, with Greek ground at least, and that's the most we'll ever take: a bad omen.

The Persians set up at Marathon, outside of Athens, and the Athenians—knowing that they were not going to get the help from the Spartans, they were going to come too late—the Athenians went out to meet them with very little help from anyone else. Here is Herodotus's account of the attack, from Book 6:

> The dispositions made, and the preliminary sacrifice promising success, the word was given to move, and the Athenians advanced at a run towards the enemy, not less than a mile away. The Persians, seeing the attack developing at the double, prepared to meet it, thinking it suicidal madness for the Athenians to risk an assault with so small a force—rushing in with no support from either cavalry or archers. Well, that was what they imagined; nevertheless, the Athenians came on, closed with the enemy all along the line, and fought in a way not to be forgotten; they were the first Greeks, so far as we know, to charge at a run, and the first who dared to look without flinching at Persian dress and the men who wore it; for until that day, no Greek could hear even the word Persian without terror.

Now, we do hear a few details about this attack, about which part of the Athenian line was in advance, which part of the line held, which didn't; but we hear even more about the exploits of individuals. Herodotus gives us reports of certain marvelous happenings during the fighting. A certain Athenian who was struck blind in the midst of the fighting, claiming that some huge apparition had appeared nearby him. Although they were outnumbered two to one—probably something like 20,000 Persians to 10,000 Athenians—only 194 Athenians died according to Herodotus, and 6,400 Persians. Now as soon as the battle was over, the Persians withdrew from Marathon and they started making their way toward Athens. Here was the entire Athenian military force at Marathon, and it looked as though the Persian fleet would make it to Athens and be able to take the city. Rumors about treachery abounded at this point, some saying that there were certain in Athens, not just Hippias but others, who had suggested to the Persians that they make it to Athens then while they were bereft of their forces. But Herodotus says this wasn't the case, and in fact the Athenian army marched on the double back to Athens, made it there. The Persians saw them, and that was the end of the Persian invasion of 490.

We move on now to Book 7, and the second of the Persian invasions. Darius has died; his son Xerxes has taken over as king of the Persian

Empire and he plans a return to Greece on an even larger scale than his father had mounted. The Persian preparations were undertaken on a magnificent scale, and discussion of that takes up much of Book 7. Since 10 years earlier in 490 the Persian fleet had been caught in a storm rounding Mt. Athos on the way to Greece, Xerxes had a canal cut through the peninsula that connects the mountain to the shore. Also, Xerxes transported his land army across the Hellespont by means of a bridge of boats. Now, we heard about this in Aeschylus's *Persians*. When a first attempt at the bridge fell apart in the storm, Herodotus tells us, Xerxes actually cursed the sea, whipped it, and threw chains into it. Herodotus describes all of this with a sense of shock and outrage, quoting the barbarous and presumptuous words that Xerxes said to the sea: "I am your master, and I will cross you whether you want me to or not." Having thus subjugated both land by digging that canal and sea with his bridge of boats, Xerxes then led an army toward Greece so large that as it passed through certain areas they drained rivers dry.

Visions and omens were uniformly unfavorable for Xerxes, but he ignored them all. One of his advisors, as if referring in particular to Xerxes's cutting the canal and bridging the Hellespont, this advisor warned the king that his two greatest enemies were going to be the land and the sea. What he says is, no harbor would be big enough to protect the fleet from a storm, and the land could not possibly provide enough food to support such a huge army. Xerxes's has another advisor—a Greek, Demaratus, a former Spartan king who's now in exile—this advisor warns Xerxes that the Greeks, especially the Spartans, would not be overawed by the size of his army, and each one would be willing to take on any 10 Persians. Here's the way Demaratus describes these Spartans:

> So it is with the Spartans; fighting singly, they are as good as any, but fighting together they are the best soldiers in the world. They are free—yes—but not entirely free; for they have a master and that master is law, which they fear much more than your subjects fear you. Whatever this master commands they do, and his command never varies: it is never to retreat in battle however great the odds, but always to remain in formation and to conquer or die. If, my lord, you think that what I have said is nonsense, very well. I am willing henceforward to hold my tongue. This time I spoke

because you forced me to speak. In any case I pray that all may turn out as you desire.

We might be reminded in this speech of what we saw already between Solon and Croesus, the differences between the Greeks and the Persians, between the West and the East. Not ruled by a monarch these Spartans, but ruled by law, which is an even stronger force. In response to this advice from Demaratus, Xerxes just laughed and sent his advisor away.

Now on the Greek side there have been preparations as well. The Athenians had been building up their naval power. Some time before the Persian invasion, Athenian silver mines had been surprisingly productive, and it had been proposed that this unforeseen wealth should be split evenly among all Athenian citizens. But one Athenian, a man named Themistocles, persuaded the city to use that money instead to build a fleet of ships. This will become extremely important.

There are divine signs on the Greek side as well. As the Persians approached, an oracle said to the Athenians that they should trust in their wooden walls. Now, many Athenians thought that this referred to their Acropolis, sitting at the top of Athens, the Acropolis that was once surrounded by woody hedges. They proposed that the Athenians should make a stand against the Persians there inside the Acropolis, inside those wooden walls. But Themistocles—the same Themistocles—offered a different interpretation. The wooden walls were the ships. His interpretation carried the day, so Athenians left the city for safer places, took their possessions elsewhere, abandoned the city to the Persians and trusted in their navy, the wooden walls of their ships.

Now before we get to the decisive naval battle—that is, the Battle of Salamis—let's stop to look at a land battle. The Greeks first took a stand against the Persians at a narrow pass in northern Greece called Thermopylae, and there was a navy nearby at Artemisium. The Greek forces at Thermopylae were led by the Spartan king Leonidas and an advance guard of only 300 Spartan soldiers. They're waiting for reinforcements, but very few are there at the pass when the Persians arrive. A Persian spy, sent forward to assess the strength of the enemy, is absolutely astounded at the small number of Greeks and at their relaxed attitude. They're lounging around playing musical instruments, fixing their hair. Xerxes, hearing this, waited four days, expecting that this small group of Greeks will run away from the onset of this massive armament. They didn't run. Finally Xerxes threw his forces at the pass, and the small group of Spartans held it: once, twice, three times. Xerxes, Herodotus tells us, was watching from above, and three times he leaped up from his seat, jumped up from his throne in terror for his army. The Persians, Herodotus says, had many men but few soldiers.

Just then, with Xerxes at wits' end, a treacherous Greek, a native of the area, approached Xerxes with news of a secret pass over the mountain that would allow the Persians to surround the Spartans. Xerxes immediately sent a force along the path, and it's a path that Herodotus describes in great detail, as though he had walked it himself. So we have Persians surrounding this small Spartan force. The Spartans learned of this flanking maneuver, in plenty of time to retreat to safety and yield the pass to the Persians. Some few of the allies were actually sent away to safety, but the Spartans decided to remain, even though that meant certain death. Herodotus tells us here that an oracle had foretold that the Persians would either take the city of Sparta or kill one of her kings; and here is one of her kings to be killed. The slaughter was terrible, every Spartan died, including the king, Leonidas. Herodotus tells us that he made a point of learning the name of each of the 300 Spartans and then he goes on to quote from the several monuments that were subsequently erected there—erected at the pass to honor the dead, to preserve the memory of these great deeds.

Now on the naval front, an oracle from Delphi had instructed the Greeks to look to the winds for help, and indeed, a violent storm destroyed a large portion of the Persian fleet even as it was trying to arrive at Artemisium there off the coast of Thermopylae. The Greek fleet, still far outnumbered even though much of the Persian fleet had been destroyed, managed to hold its own and then made its way to Salamis, near Athens. There at Salamis—as we know from Aeschylus's *Persians*—the Greeks, led by Athenians, soundly defeated the Persian fleet. In Herodotus Book 8, we get the Greek side of the story. He matches up pretty well with what Aeschylus had said: Thanks to Athenian trickery, the Greek fleet defeated the Persians. Trusting in their wooden walls that is in their ships, the Athenians had abandoned their city; the Persians sacked it and they burned down the Acropolis, taking vengeance, as they said, for the burning of Sardis during the Ionian revolt.

But as these Persians were moving toward that area, the Greeks, the Greek fleet at Salamis, was wondering whether they should stop there to make a stand against these Persians. They were divided on where to make the next stand, since Thermopylae was now lost, Thermopylae which was a wonderful narrow pass to stop that approach. The next obvious place was at the Isthmus of Corinth, a narrow strip of land that could be defended by smaller Greek forces. By making a stand there, though, the Greeks would give up everything north of that point, not just the city of Athens. Furthermore, there was some concern that once the fleet which had gathered at Salamis, once it left there—even if they all said they were going to the Isthmus of Corinth—might simply dissipate, each contingent going to protect its own land, and all hope would be lost of a concerted Greek response to this Persian onslaught.

As other Greeks were deciding whether to take up a defensive position further south or to stay there at Salamis where they had gathered, the Athenian Themistocles—this man we've met before— sent a secret message to the Persians. We've heard about this message; now we learn this is the man who sent it. Pretending to offer the Persians help, he encouraged them to blockade the Greek fleet at Salamis, lest it slip away from Persian grasp. In fact, though, Themistocles's goal was to keep the entire Greek navy there at Salamis, where it could offer some assistance to the area around Athens, where the shallows and the narrow straits worked to the advantage of the smaller Greek ships. Also by having the Persians blockade the Greek ships in there, it would keep those Greeks from departing, leaving to some other part of Greece.

So the Persians moved in; the Greeks, still debating their departure, were told that they had to prepare to fight; all thanks to the clever deception of one Athenian, Themistocles. As we read in Aeschylus's *Persians*, the Greeks won a decisive naval victory there. Herodotus does describes individual confrontations and battles, as well as a variety of divine signs and portents, rather than giving us any overview of strategy. This is typical for Herodotus. After the destruction of his fleet at Salamis, Xerxes is ready to head home, leaving a force behind under his general, Mardonius; but he's concerned that the Greeks might sail directly to the Hellespont, destroy his bridge of boats, and thereby trap him in Europe. That, in fact, is what Themistocles proposed, the destruction of the bridge boats. Themistocles, though, was easily outvoted this time by those who wanted Xerxes to have an easy exit—we don't him stuck inside Greece—so Themistocles, ever thinking, made the best of that situation. He again sent a message to the Persians, telling them this time that he, Themistocles, had been the one to argue for preserving the bridge of boats, in order to help Xerxes, and to allow him to march home in safety. Themistocles thereby laid the foundation for friendship with the Persians, something that would come in handy soon, when he turned out to be a little too clever for the Athenians and had to leave his home city.

Xerxes sailed home; the Persian army retreated by land to Plataea, north of Athens, on their way back. There they were engaged in a battle Herodotus describes in Book 9. The Greek forces, led by the Spartans, soundly defeated the remnants of the Persian army at Plataea. Some additional naval operations were left, but the Persian threat, the massive invasion, had been turned away.

So, what do we make of Herodotus: father of history, father of lies, maybe both? It might help to recall the context of his work. While he did have some prose predecessors, he was looking back also to Homer, and even the tragedians, in setting about his work. His use of sources is often exemplary, even by modern historical standards, but he is clearly not limited by those standards. He has strong ideas about the shape of history, and those ideas guide his narrative, but at least he is explicit about what they are. One point that all concede is that Herodotus has indeed succeeded in saving these events from oblivion. He tells a compelling and a memorable story.

In the next lecture, we move on to the second great historian from the Classical Period, Herodotus's younger contemporary Thucydides and his masterpiece, the *History of the Peloponnesian War*.

Lecture Twenty-Seven
Thucydides I—The Peloponnesian War

Scope:

At the beginning of his *History of the Peloponnesian War*, Thucydides introduces himself as a different sort of historian. His war is the greatest ever, and his methods are superior to those used by earlier historians. In this lecture, we begin with the life of Thucydides and some background information on the war itself. Then, we consider in some detail Thucydides's style and his own statement of purpose and methods. He presents himself as accurate and scientific, careful about his sources, and dismissive of those features that make a history simply pleasant. Thucydides is indeed more modern in his historical methods than Herodotus, but questions about his objectivity and bias remain.

Outline

I. What we know about the life of Thucydides (c. 460–c. 400) comes largely from information he gives us.

    A. He was born into a wealthy family with ties to the north of Greece.

        1. He says that he began writing his history as soon as the Peloponnesian War started and that he was old enough throughout it to understand what was happening.

        2. When the plague struck Athens in 430, Thucydides himself caught it and survived.

    B. He was elected general in 424 but was held responsible for the Athenian defeat by Spartan general Brasidas at Amphipolis.

    C. He was exiled until the end of war and apparently spent some of that time in Sparta.

    D. He lived past the end of the war but did not finish his history of it. His younger contemporary Xenophon picked up the narrative where Thucydides ended.

II. We have touched already on the Peloponnesian War (431–404), the subject of Thucydides's history.

A. After the Persian Wars, Athens grew in wealth and stature.

    1. Claiming that they were protecting Greeks from further Persian invasion, Athenians organized an association of states called the *Delian League.*

    2. Through the 460s, Athens became increasingly democratic in its constitution.

    3. The Delian League became more obviously an Athenian empire when its treasury was moved to Athens in 454.

B. Sparta, meanwhile, remained a traditional oligarchy, allied with states throughout the Peloponnesus in the *Peloponnesian League.*

    1. The democratic tendencies of Athens worried the oligarchs of Sparta and her allies.

    2. The aggressive expansion of the Delian League (and then empire) brought Athens into direct conflict with allies of Sparta.

C. Hostilities between Athens and Sparta began in the 460s, with a pause for relative peace from 446–431.

    1. Thucydides cites two specific incidents involving allies of Athens and allies of Sparta as the immediate cause for the outbreak of war in 431.

    2. But the real cause, he says, is that the Spartans feared the growth of Athens.

D. The war itself falls into two parts, broken by the Peace of Nicias from 421–414.

    1. For the early part of the war, Athenians, under the direction of Pericles, and those living near Athens retreated within the walls of the city and avoided open conflict with the superior Spartan land forces, instead harassing them by sea.

    2. A terrible plague broke out in Athens in 430; Pericles was among the many who died from it.

E. After 10 years of indecisive fighting, with victories and losses on both sides, the two parties entered into a treaty, the Peace of Nicias, that was meant to last 50 years.

F. Even as hostilities continued during the peace, Athens set off on a major expedition against Sicily in 415. It ended in total defeat for Athens.

G. Hostilities resumed more openly in 414 and ended with the defeat of Athens in 404.

III. Thucydides starts by establishing this war as the greatest ever, then goes on to document the events, proceeding by summer and winter through each year of the war, until his account stops abruptly in the middle of the events of 411.

A. Book 1 gives a general introduction and the causes for the war.

B. Books 2–5 focus largely on the first 10 years of the war.

C. Books 6 and 7, deviating from the summer and winter organization, describe the Sicilian expedition.

D. Book 8 takes the second phase of the war down to 411.

IV. Thucydides was very much a man of his age, but there is a brilliant uniqueness in both his style and outlook.

A. The rationalism of the 5th century is evident in his search for human, rather than divine, causes for events.

B. The influence of rhetorical developments is clear in his frequent use of paired speeches, treating a subject pro and con.

C. We can also detect the influence of medical writers, whose general approach was to look for humanly intelligible rather than divine causes for things and to describe the world in precise detail in order to determine those causes.

D. Thucydides's prose is dense and, in places, famously difficult. Easy entertainment was not his goal.

E. His view of the world is complex, but we might begin by saying that he is interested here in power, especially how its exercise conflicts with or redefines morality.

1. In particular, he considers the Athenian attempts to manage the growing empire and what that entails.

2. His vision, and that of the characters in his *History*, is refreshingly unclouded by sentimentality: Those with power use it in their own interest; those without it appeal to morality or justice.

3. But in making these summaries, we are, in effect, extrapolating from Thucydides's works what we might call patterns, if not laws—a Thucydidean historical view or political philosophy, although he never states such views or philosophies explicitly.

4. Rather, Thucydides maintains an almost constant position of objectivity; however, we have to be constantly on the lookout for underlying strategies and hidden bias.

V. We start our look at the work itself by considering what Thucydides himself says about it.

A. After introducing himself, he continues, claiming that the Peloponnesian War is worth documenting because it far surpasses every other war.

1. To establish the greatness of the war, Thucydides goes into ancient history. In this section, referred to as the archaeology, we find no heroism and very little mention of individuals but an assessment of large forces and movements leading up to the power of Greece at the time of the Peloponnesian War.

2. He analyzes the Trojan War as a historical event and concludes that it went on so long simply because the Greeks were poorly provisioned at the start.

3. He then describes political changes in the Greek city-states and the slow growth of naval power and takes care of all of Herodotus in one line, mentioning Marathon and the defeat of Xerxes 10 years later.

4. The Peloponnesian War, by contrast, involved not only all Greeks, at the height of their wealth and power, but also the Persians and other non-Greeks, and it went on for a long time.

B. Other writers, he claims, believe all that they hear, without applying critical judgment. He does not mention Herodotus explicitly but gives an example of such credulity from Herodotus (1.20).

C. Thucydides claims he has firsthand knowledge of his subject.

1. In Book 5 (5.26), Thucydides reminds us that he lived through the whole war himself, being old enough at its start to understand it. Also, because of his exile, he had the opportunity to spend time with the Spartans.
2. He tells us in Book 2 (2.48) that he can describe the plague in detail because he suffered from it himself.

D. He claims to apply high standards to establishing the truth of what he says.
   1. He does not exaggerate or embellish in order to win an audience, as the poets and others do (1.21).
   2. The speeches he records he either heard himself or got from some other source; in all cases, he says, he records what was demanded by the occasion, staying as close as possible to what was actually said (1.22).
   3. He says he tests all information, whether from his own experience or from others, rigorously for accuracy. He checks his own memory against the accounts of others and double-checks what he hears from others.

E. Thucydides's goal is to create something useful for future readers. Because human nature and behavior remain unchanged through time, he says, knowledge of the past can help in understanding the future.

F. His comments seem to suggest that Thucydides was the first of all the authors we have encountered who intended his work for private study, rather than for public performance.

Essential Reading:
Thucydides, T*he Peloponnesian War*, Book 1.1–22.

Supplementary Reading:
Connor, *Thucydides*, Book 1.
Crane, *The Blinded Eye: Thucydides and the Written Word.*
Luce, *The Greek Historians*, chapters 4 and 5.
Pelling, *Literary Texts and the Greek Historian*, chapter 6.

Questions to Consider:
1. Thucydides makes considerable claims about his own accuracy

as a historian. Does he support those claims adequately?

2. Herodotus's methods seem well suited to his goal, namely, to preserve the memory of great deeds. How well do Thucydides's methods match his goal, to create an accurate record of what happened so others might learn from it?

Lecture Twenty-Seven
Thucydides I—The Peloponnesian War

Welcome back. In the last two lectures, we talked about Herodotus and his history of the Persian Wars. We move now to three lectures on the second of the great historians of the Classical Period, namely Thucydides, and his history of the Peloponnesian War—that war between Athens and Sparta that lasted from 431 to 404 B.C.E. In this lecture, we begin with the life of Thucydides and then some background information on the war itself. We move then to consider in some detail Thucydides's style and his own statements about his purpose and his methods.

At the beginning of his *History of the Peloponnesian War*, Thucydides introduces himself as a different sort of historian. His war, he says, is the greatest ever, and his methods are superior to those used by earlier historians. He presents himself as accurate, scientific, and careful about his sources. He's dismissive of those features that make a history simply pleasant or entertaining. Now, Thucydides is indeed more modern in these historical methods than Herodotus, but we'll see that questions about objectivity and bias still remain.

First, the life of Thucydides: Born in about 460, died about 400; we're uncertain about the particular dates. What we know about the life of Thucydides comes largely from information he gives us himself within the history. Thucydides was an Athenian, son of a man named Olorus. His family was wealthy with ties to the north of Greece, the area around Thrace. He says that he started writing his history as soon as the war started and was old enough throughout it to understand what was happening—that's one of the details that allows us to place his birth as we do.

When the plague struck Athens in 430, Thucydides himself caught it and survived. He was elected one of the 10 Athenian generals in 424 and had the misfortune of leading an Athenian army against the Spartan general Brasidas. When the Athenians lost to Brasidas at Amphipolis in 424, Thucydides was held responsible and was exiled from Athens for the next 20 years. This sort of fickleness was not at all uncommon in Athens, where prominent public figures often spent their lives between the extremes of public adulation and exile or even worse.

Exiled from Athens until the end of the war, Thucydides spent some of that time in Sparta, where he was able to study the war from the other side, and some of his time traveling elsewhere throughout Greece. Thucydides lived past the end of the war, we know that from references within the history to events later than 404, but Thucydides did not finish his history of the war. The work breaks off in mid-sentence during a description of the events of 411. Thucydides's younger contemporary, Xenophon, picked up the narrative where Thucydides left off.

Now before moving into the work itself, let's look briefly at its subject, the Peloponnesian War, which we've already touched on in several of our other lectures, especially the introduction to the 5th century, and also in our discussions of some of the plays of Euripides and the comedies of Aristophanes. After the Persian Wars, Athens, the great Greek naval power, grew considerably in wealth and stature. To offer protection from the continuing Persian threat, the Athenians organized an association of Greek city-states called the Delian League because it was based on the island of Delos. Most of the members were islands or those living along the coast, those that could be protected by the Athenian navy. Through the first half of the century—the 5th century—the Athenian constitution became increasingly democratic even as the Delian League gradually turned into an Athenian Empire—most obviously when the Delian League treasury moved from Delos to Athens, probably around 454.

Sparta, the great land power of Greece, had fought side by side with the Athenians against the Persians, but after the Persian War remained a traditional oligarchy with hereditary kings and allied with states throughout the Peloponnesus in what was called the Peloponnesian League. The increasingly democratic tendencies of Athens worried the oligarchs of Sparta and her allies; and the aggressive expansion of the Delian League and then what we might call the Athenian Empire, brought Athens into direct conflict with allies of Sparta.

Hostilities between Athens and Sparta began as early as the 460s—and remember, the Persian Wars ended only in 479. There was a pause for relative peace between 446 and 431, when the Peloponnesian War begins in earnest. In Book 1 of his history, Thucydides cites two specific incidents, involving allies of Athens and allies of Sparta, as the immediate cause for the outbreak of the war in 431. One involved a city far to the west, the city of Epidamnus. There was a difference of opinion about government within Epidamnus, certain inhabitants of the city were thrown out. There was a call for help. Corinth came in to help some of those in Epidamnus. Corinth was a Spartan ally, and so Athenians came to help those on the other side. That was one of the immediate causes.

The other involved a city far to the east, the city of Potidaea, where something similar happened. There was conflict within the city, there was an appeal to different sides, some going to the Spartan allies, some going to Athenian allies, Athens and Sparta being brought into conflict. Those were the immediate causes, but the real cause, Thucydides says, the underlying cause for the war was that Spartans feared the growth of Athens and her empire more generally.

The war itself falls into two parts, interrupted by the Peace of Nicias that lasted from 421 to 414. For the early part of the war, from 431 to 421, Athens pursued a strategy advocated by her leading statesman Pericles: Athenians and those living near Athens retreated within the walls of the city; this brought a lot of people in from the countryside. As it turned out there was room within these walls, because Athens had constructed not only walls immediately around her city, but also a set of long walls that went from the city of Athens right down to the coast, so that she would have direct access to the sea. People piled in from the countryside in between these long walls as well as into the city itself. Athens then refused to meet the superior Spartan forces in direct conflict on land. Spartans marched north, ravaged the countryside around Athens, even as Athenians watched from within the walls. This was the situation described in Aristophanes's *Acharnians*. Athenians, meanwhile, harassed Sparta and her allies as they could by sea, going around the coast.

In 430 a terrible plague broke out in Athens, and this was probably aggravated by all of the crowding of the people from the countryside inside the walls. Thucydides caught the plague and survived, but Pericles was among the many who died from it. After 10 years of indecisive fighting, with victories and losses on both sides, the two parties entered into a treaty in 421, the so-called Peace of Nicias, named for an Athenian general, and this peace was meant to last for 50 years. It didn't, of course. Even as hostilities continued during the peace, Athens set off on a major expedition against Sicily in 415, an expedition that ended in total defeat for Athens. Thucydides describes this in books 6 and 7 of his history. Hostilities between Athens and Sparta resumed more openly in 414, and ended with the defeat of Athens in 404.

Okay, let's turn to Thucydides's work itself. He starts by establishing this war as the greatest ever. Then he goes on to document the events of the war, proceeding in orderly and organized fashion by summer and winter through each year of the war, until his account stops abruptly in the middle of the events of 411. Book 1 gives us a general introduction and some of the background and the causes for the war; books 2 through 5 focus largely on the first ten years of the war, before the peace. Books 6 and 7, deviating somewhat from the summer and winter organization, describe the Sicilian expedition; and Book 8, unfinished, takes the second phase of the war down to 411, before it ends abruptly.

There are some ways we might characterize the work in general, some things to look out for as we read. Thucydides was very much a man of his age, living in late 5th century-Athens, and open therefore to all of the many innovations going on at the time. But there is a brilliant uniqueness in both his style and his outlook. The rationalism of the 5th century is evident in his search for human, rather than divine, causes for events. We'll see far less reliance on oracles, prophecies, and divine intervention than in Herodotus. The influence of rhetorical developments is clear in Thucydides's frequent use of paired speeches, often treating a subject first with a pro and then with a con as if in the assembly or a court of law; and there are many assembly speeches that are actually included in this history. We can also detect in Thucydides the influence of a group of writers we haven't mentioned yet in this course: the medical writers. The name Hippocrates is applied to much of the medical work from this period, and later periods, but there were many others who were active as well. The general approach of these medical writers was to look for humanly intelligible, rather than divine, causes for things—for diseases, for human problems—and to describe the world in precise detail in order to determine those causes. They look at climate. They look at diet. They look at the world around them rather than appealing to the gods to try to explain human problems. The influence of these medical writers is most obvious in the section on the plague in Book 2, but we can detect it throughout in

Thucydides's preference for human explanations and in his attention to detail.

Thucydides's prose style: It's very dense, and in places famously difficult to translate and to understand. He likes to express himself briefly; he's concise; he dislikes parallel expressions; he'll do anything he can to break up parallelism. Ask any student of the Greek language for corroboration of that. As Thucydides tells us, entertainment was not his goal, so he doesn't make it easy. At other places, though, and in a few sections, there is a fluidity and a vividness of description that moves the narrative right along, engagingly. He's not all so difficult.

Thucydides's view of the world is complex and not easily summarized, but we might begin by saying that he's interested throughout his work in power, and especially how the exercise of power conflicts with or redefines morality. These general sentiments, though, are always expressed in terms of the particulars of the war he's describing. Rather than discussing power or morality in the abstract, he considers the Athenian attempts to manage their growing empire and what that entails in terms of power and morality. The expression of those sentiments is strikingly direct. Thucydides's vision, and that of the characters in his history, is refreshingly unclouded by sentimentality. Those with power use it in their own interest, those without power appeal to morality or justice. In all cases, doing what is right is less important than doing what is expedient or helpful to one's own interests.

But in making these various summaries about Thucydides, we are, in effect, extrapolating from his works. We are drawing out of them these patterns, these historical views, or philosophies. Thucydides himself never states such views or philosophies explicitly, certainly not as explicitly as, for example, the statement in Herodotus about cyclical changes. Rather, Thucydides maintains an almost constant position, or we might say a pose, of objectivity: just the facts, as they happened. To a certain extent, he is indeed remarkably objective but we have to be constantly on the lookout for his underlying strategies, for hidden bias. Even if each event is accurately described, for example, we might ask about his selection of events. We might remember, more generally, that whenever an author claims objectivity, we should be careful to look for bias. In a way, we were on firmer ground with Herodotus; at least we had less expectation of finding there some sort of modern scientific history, and we entered the work more critically. With Thucydides, we have to be careful not to be lulled into believing all that he says.

Let's start our look at the work itself with the first paragraph and what Thucydides himself says about his work. He starts by introducing himself and his home, as Herodotus had done. He then claims that the Peloponnesian War is worth documenting since it far surpasses every other war. Here's his beginning:

> Thucydides, an Athenian, wrote the history of the war between the Peloponnesians and the Athenians, beginning at the moment that it broke out and believing that it would be a great war and more worthy of relation than any that had preceded it. This belief was not without its grounds. The preparations of both the combatants were in every department in the last state of perfection. And he could see the rest of the Hellenic race taking sides in the quarrel; those who delayed doing so at once, having it in contemplation. Indeed this was the greatest movement yet known in history. Not only of the Hellenes, but of a large part of the barbarian world; I had almost said, of mankind.

Notice if there is nothing here about preserving glory, as we saw in Herodotus, simply the claim that the war is worth recording since it is the greatest ever. To establish that greatness, Thucydides then goes into ancient history from his perspective. He reduces the significance of all that went before. This kind of negative beginning is not the most engaging start, but his aim is not to please. Now this section of the history is referred to as the archaeology, the early history of Greece. In this section we find no heroism; very little mention of individuals, but rather an assessment of large forces, movements, all of them beginning with the inconsequential nature of Greece and leading up to the great power of Greece at the time of the Peloponnesian War.

In the earliest days, says Thucydides, the Greeks had no sense of unity at all, not even a common name. Look at Homer, he argues, where the Greeks are not called the "Greeks" but rather Argives, Achaeans, Danaans: all particular geographical designations that are used in an attempt to refer to them all. There was no settled life in most places; on the sea, piracy was rampant and everybody carried arms for self-protection. Gradually, he says the cities on the coasts became wealthier than those inland, they built walls, and began to subjugate others. Only then was it possible for the Greeks to mount the expedition against Troy, the Trojan War; only when Agamemnon had distinguished himself as more powerful than others, politically and economically.

Thucydides then proceeds, as Herodotus had done before him, to discuss the Trojan War as a historical event and Homer as its historian. Thucydides applies his considerable reasoning powers to the catalogue of ships in Book 2 of the *Iliad*, calculating from it the number of men who went from Greece against Troy. Not such a large number after all, he concludes. But it was a number still sufficient to take Troy, and to take it quickly—no need for the 10 years if only the Greeks had been able to focus on the siege itself. But instead, the expedition was so poorly provisioned that some of the soldiers had to be foraging for supplies as others carried on the siege. In the course of this argument, Thucydides uses quotations from Homer to argue for the small scope of the Trojan War and, more generally, he applies a rational and economic critique to what we usually conceive of as a mythical and heroic war. Already, we have here an indication of Thucydides's tendency to question everything and to apply his own critical faculties to the assessment of events.

Still within this archeology, but moving on from the Trojan War, Thucydides describes political changes in the Greek city-states, the slow growth of naval power; then takes care of all of Herodotus in just a line or so, mentioning Marathon and the defeat of Xerxes 10 years later. Athens and Sparta, he says, were united in that effort; but not for long, as he describes in chapter 18 of Book 1. Now note in this passage that I'm going to read, that Thucydides often refers to the Spartans, and their Peloponnesian allies, as Lacedaemonians:

> For a short time the league held together, till the Lacedaemonians and Athenians quarreled and made war upon each other with their allies, a duel into which all the Hellenes sooner or later were drawn, though some might at first remain neutral. So the whole period from the Median War [that is, the Persian War] up to this, with some peaceful intervals, was spent by each power in war, either with its rival or with its own revolted allies, and consequently

afforded them constant practice in military matters. And that experience which is learnt in the school of danger.

Constant struggle from the end of the Persian War up to the beginning of the Peloponnesian War: the Peloponnesian War, an affair that contrasts with all earlier, in that it involved not only all Greeks, at the height of their wealth and power, but also the Persians and other non-Greeks; and it went on for a long time, with great suffering for all involved. There might be old stories, Thucydides says, about incredible natural events that marked previous wars: earthquakes, eclipses, and so on. That's all hard to believe. But those sorts of things really did happen in this war: famines, droughts, eclipses, and the greatest natural disaster of all, the plague in Athens.

In terms of methodology, Thucydides emphasizes at great length his precision and the laborious care of his research. He claims that other writers believe all that they hear, without applying any critical judgment at all. Here's one example of that:

> The way that most men deal with traditions, even traditions of their own country, is to receive them all alike as they are delivered without applying any critical test whatever. …

> So little pains do the vulgar take in the investigation of truth, accepting readily the first story that comes to hand.

Now he does not mention Herodotus explicitly in this context, but he does mention in this paragraph a misconception about the tyranny in Athens and one about the voting rights of kings in Sparta. Herodotus had written about both of these subjects. So as he dismisses these other historians, his eye is on Herodotus.

He now turns to his own methodology. He's gone through all of the past, of what went on in Greece before his war, not so great. Other historians were nothing like him. Thucydides, on the other hand, claims that he has firsthand knowledge of his subject. In Book 5 he reminds us that he lived through the whole war himself, old enough at the start to understand it. Also, because of his exile, he had the opportunity to spend time with the Spartans and others throughout Greece. In Book 2, the most chilling example of his firsthand approach to his material, he tells us that he can describe the plague in detail because he suffered from it himself. In every case, Thucydides tells us, he applies high standards to establishing the truth of what he includes in his history. He doesn't exaggerate or embellish in order to win an audience, as the poets and others do. Here's what he does:

> On the whole, however, the conclusions I have drawn from the proofs quoted may, I believe, safely be relied on. Assuredly they will not be disturbed either by the lays of a poet displaying the exaggeration of his craft, or by the compositions of the chroniclers that are attracted at truth's expense, the subjects they treat of being out of the reach of evidence, and time having robbed most of them of historical value by enthroning them in the region of legend. Turning from these, we can rest satisfied with having proceeded upon the clearest data, and having arrived at conclusions as exact as can be expected in matters of such antiquity. To come to this war: despite the known disposition of the actors in the struggle to overrate its importance, and when it's over to return to their admiration of earlier events, yet an examination of the facts will show that it was much greater than the wars which preceded it.

Such is his care in his methods. Now like his predecessors, Thucydides does include speeches in his history. But he records only those he either heard himself or got from some other source in particular, in all cases taking care. Here's what he says about his speeches:

> With reference to the speeches in this history, some were delivered before the war began others while it was going on.; some I heard myself, others I got from various quarters; it was in all cases difficult to carry them word for word in one's memory, so my habit has been to make the speakers say what was in my opinion demanded of them by the various occasions, of course adhering as closely as possible to the general sense of what they really said.

This is a hotly debated passage. Phrases like: "in my opinion," "demanded by the various occasions," "the general sense of what they really said," Thucydides leaves himself considerable latitude here, but he does at least raise the issue of the veracity or the accuracy of the speeches included. He's equally careful with his narrative sections; all information, whether from his own experience or from others, he says he tests rigorously for accuracy. He checks his own memory against the accounts of others and double checks. Here's where he describes that:

> [And] with reference to the narrative of events, far from permitting myself to derive it from the first source that came to hand, I did not even trust my own impressions. But it rests partly on what I saw myself, partly on what others saw for me, the accuracy of the report being always tried by the most severe and detailed tests possible.

This is the degree of accuracy that we're going to find, that we're going to expect to find in Thucydides. Now why, we might ask, is he going to such pains, if he's not interested in Homeric and Herodotean goals of preserving the glory of men and events? If he's not interested in entertaining, why is he doing this? His goal, he says, is to create something useful for future readers, since human nature and behavior remain unchanged through time. Here's where he says that:

> The absence of romance in my history, will, I fear, detract somewhat from its interest; but if it be judged useful by those inquirers who desire an exact knowledge of the past as an aid to the interpretation of the future, which in the course of human things must resemble if it does not reflect it, I shall be content. In fine, I have written my work, not as an essay which is to win the applause of the moment, but as a possession for all time.

This is an early statement, then, of the possibility of learning from the past, of understanding history so we don't repeat it. You might notice, too, the digs at Herodotus: There's no romance in this history, he says; It's not an essay to win immediate applause. This comment seems to refer to the public readings of Herodotus's work, and suggests that Thucydides is the first of all the authors we've encountered who intended his work for private study rather than for public performance. It's certainly true that it takes some time to study his prose.

So, we've seen that Thucydides's goals differ from those of Herodotus. That he considers himself far superior in terms of methodology, taking care to ensure the accuracy of everything in his history. He's even demonstrated that careful methodology in his dispassionate account of the early Greek history in that section we call the archaeology. In our next lecture, we continue with Thucydides, considering three particular passages from books 1 through 5.

Lecture Twenty-Eight
Thucydides II—Books 1–5

Scope:

In this lecture, we discuss three famous passages from Books 1–5 of Thucydides's *History of the Peloponnesian War*. Although we treat these passages in chronological order, the primary goal here is not to re-create the actual events of the war through Thucydides's account. Rather, our goal is to examine how Thucydides uses the Peloponnesian War as a stage for his larger considerations of human nature, particularly as it manifests itself in times of crisis. We start with a summary of the essential differences between Athens and Sparta, as expressed in speeches at Sparta before the war. Then, in Book 2, we turn a spotlight on Athens itself, at its peak in Pericles's funeral oration and at its lowest depths in the description of the plague. The Melian dialogue from Book 5 marks a particular event in the war but also raises larger questions about empire, power, and international relations.

Outline

I. In this lecture, we continue with Thucydides by discussing three famous passages from Books 1–5, examining how Thucydides uses the war as a stage for his larger considerations of human nature.

   A. We start with speeches at an assembly in Sparta before the war; we then move to Pericles's funeral oration, followed by the description of the plague. We conclude with the Melian dialogue.

   B. Taken together, these passages trace for us a change in Athens as the war progresses.

II. The speeches at Sparta in 432 (1.68–88) center on whether or not Sparta should declare war on Athens, but they also establish fundamental differences between the two combatants.

   A. The meeting has been called by Sparta's ally Corinth to try to persuade Sparta of the need to go to war, and the

Corinthians speak first.

    1. The Spartan nature is to be slow and inactive.

    2. The Athenians are famous for their speed and innovation.

    3. And so, conclude the Corinthians, Sparta must act now to stop Athenian expansion and aggression.

B. Athens has not been invited to the meeting, but an Athenian happens to be there on other business and responds to the Corinthian speech.

    1. He does not deny the Corinthian characterization of the Athenian nature.

    2. But he does defend Athenian behavior since the Persian Wars.

    3. He also cautions against being hasty in going to war and suggests talking first.

C. The Spartan king, Archidamus, responds to both speeches, warning the Spartans of the dangers of war with Athens and, indeed, of any war.

    1. He does not deny the Corinthian characterization of their dilatory nature.

    2. His long experience has taught him that arbitration is better than war.

    3. He suggests sending ambassadors to Athens and, in the meantime, preparing for war.

D. The otherwise unknown Spartan Sthenelaidas speaks briefly in favor of war and carries the day.

E. We do not know if this meeting actually happened, but it serves well (as the meeting between Solon and Croesus did for Herodotus) to introduce the essential nature of both Sparta and Athens.

III. In Book 2.35–46, Thucydides records the funeral oration of Pericles for Athenians who died in the first year of fighting. Immediately following that (2.47–54), he describes the physical and moral ravages of the plague in Athens.

A. In the funeral oration, instead of focusing only on the deeds of the dead, Pericles emphasizes the unique qualities of Athens, the city for which they died.

1. He praises the democracy both for serving the majority and for fostering an atmosphere of openness in the city.

2. Athenians have a high standard of living, with regular festivals that allow for relaxation and cultivation; yet even so, they are a formidable military force.

3. Everyone is encouraged to be engaged in public affairs, whether through action or deliberation.

4. In short, the city is an exemplar, the school of all Greece, and it produces men who are self-sufficient, versatile, and famous.

5. Pericles then encourages the crowd to love Athens and do all possible to preserve it.

6. Pericles then turns to the survivors, with comfort rather than condolence.

   a. He tells parents of childbearing age who have lost a son to have more children.

   b. He directs sons and brothers of the dead to try hard to match the standards of those who have won such glory.

   c. He cautions widows to keep a low profile, conveying a standard view of the public role of women at the time.

7. The speech has been praised since antiquity for so eloquently and persuasively extolling the excellence of Athens, but we should not take it out of context.

B. Part of that context is the description of the plague that struck Athens in 430.

   1. Thucydides refuses to look for causes, claiming instead that he will describe—which he can do well given that he had the plague—so that future generations might be better prepared for another outbreak.

   2. He gives vivid details about the course of the disease, in language that seems to owe much to the medical writers of his day.

   3. With so many dying, Athenians became careless about funerary rituals and the care of the dead. In other words, so soon after the highly ritualized and formal state burial celebrated by Pericles, we have a complete abandonment

of all proper burial practices.

4. Lawlessness became rampant, and all thought only of immediate pleasure because death was so randomly imminent.

5. In short, the plague narrative takes us from the height of Athenian civilization to its very depths.

IV. In 416, the Athenians were on the brink of attacking the island Melos, a colony of Sparta, and sent an embassy first to see if the Melians would yield. The dialogue between the Athenian ambassador and the Melians gives us a bald expression of Athenian power (5.84–116).

A. The Athenians disallow any talk of what is just or right, saying that such talk is appropriate only among equals and Athens is much more powerful than Melos.

B. Instead, the Melians must save themselves by yielding now to Athens. Athens cannot afford to let the Melians remain neutral; their choice is between war and survival.

C. Melos refuses to yield. The Athenians take the city, kill every adult male, and sell the rest of the population into slavery.

D. This passage is considered one of the clearest examples of Thucydides's unsentimental realism. It is cold, calculating, and detached.

E. We have come a long way from the Athens of Book 1 and Pericles's funeral oration. Whether moral abyss or effective pragmatism, the destruction of Melos prepares well for the Sicilian expedition that follows.

Essential Reading:

Thucydides, *The Peloponnesian War*, Book 1.68–Book 5.

Supplementary Reading:

Connor, *Thucydides*, Book 2–Book 5.

Hornblower, "Narratology and Narrative Techniques in Thucydides."

Questions to Consider:

1. The speeches at Sparta in Book 1 are all addressed to the growing conflict between Athens and Sparta, but it has been said that many of the arguments apply more broadly, to consideration of war at any time, in any place. How valid is that statement?

2. Why does Thucydides so abruptly juxtapose the funeral oration and the account of the plague? Can we read the plague description as a commentary, albeit inexplicit, on the glories of Athens that have just been described?

Lecture Twenty-Eight
Thucydides II—Books 1–5

Welcome back. In the last lecture, we introduced Thucydides, his work as a whole, his goals, and his methodology. In this lecture, we continue with Thucydides by discussing three famous passages from books 1 through 5 of his *History of the Peloponnesian War*. While we do treat these passages in chronological order, our primary goal here is not to try to recreate the actual events of the war through Thucydides's account. Our approach, in other words, is not primarily historical. Rather, our goal is to examine how Thucydides uses the Peloponnesian War as a stage for his larger considerations of human nature, particularly as that manifests itself in times of crisis.

We start in this lecture with a section of Book 1, with speeches at an assembly in Sparta before the war, speeches about the advisability of war; these speeches offer, in effect, a summary of the essential differences between Athens and Sparta. Then, we turn a spotlight on Athens herself in Book 2, at her peak in Pericles's funeral oration and, in a passage that follows that speech immediately, at her lowest depths in the description of the plague. Finally, the Melian Dialogue, from Book 5: that marks a particular event in the war, but also raises larger questions about empire, power, and international relations. Taken together, these passages trace for us a change in Athens as the war progresses.

We saw that Thucydides begins Book 1 by introducing himself and his methods. Thucydides then focuses on two particular incidents that brought Athens and her allies into conflict with Spartan allies, and in particular the city of Corinth: in the west, the city of Epidamnus, and in the east at Potidaea. These incidents led the Corinthians in 432 to call an assembly in Sparta of all the Spartan allies—that is, the Peloponnesian League—to consider taking action against Athens. Thucydides records from this assembly two pairs of speeches, a total of four speeches. While they center on whether or not Sparta should declare war on Athens, that's their particular point, they also do establish fundamental differences between the national characters of the two combatants and they serve thereby as an excellent introduction to the entire war narrative.

The meeting has been called by Sparta's ally, Corinth, to try to persuade Sparta of the need to go to war. Many Spartan allies air their grievances, and then—in the first speech Thucydides records from this assembly—the Corinthians themselves weigh in. Now note that Thucydides, and his characters, speak of the inhabitants of Sparta as Lacedaemonians. A little paraphrase and then we'll get to some sections from the speech itself. You, Lacedaemonians, says the unnamed Corinthian, you have been sitting idly by while the Athenians have been committing one act of aggression after another, ever since the Persian Wars. You, Lacedaemonians, allowed Athens to grow in power and you hesitate while they subjugate one city after another. You, Lacedaemonians, are the ones depriving all these Greeks of their freedom. For, they say, the true author of subjugation is not so much the ones who enslave a people as the ones who sit by and watch the enslavement when they have the power to stop it. You, Lacedaemonians, are to blame; and still you delay. That delay, says the Corinthian, is in the Spartan nature. Here's where he describes that:

> You, Lacedaemonians, of all the Hellenes are alone, inactive, and defend yourselves not by doing anything but by looking as if you would do something; you alone wait till the power of an enemy is becoming twice its original size, instead of crushing it in its infancy.

The Corinthians, in other words, are arguing for a pre-emptive strike, although it's almost too late for that against Athens. The Athenians, on the other hand, at least according to this Corinthian speaker, are famous for their speed and innovation. Here's that characterization:

> The Athenians are addicted to innovation, and their designs are characterized by swiftness alike in conception and execution; you have a genius for keeping what you have got, accompanied by a total want of invention. And when forced to act you never go far enough.

But back to the Athenians:

> Further there is promptitude on their side against procrastination on yours; they are never at home, you are never from it: for they hope by their absence to extend their acquisitions, you fear by your advance to endanger what you have left behind. They are swift to follow up a success, and slow to recoil from a reverse. Their bodies they spend

ungrudgingly in their country's cause; their intellect they jealously husband to be employed in her service. …

To describe their character in a word one might truly say that that they were born into the world to take no rest themselves and to give none to others.

Now coming from the Corinthians, the tone here is surprisingly neutral about the Athenians; coming from those who have suffered from Athenian aggression. Yes, Athenians are busybodies, always bothering others, but this description presents Athenians as enterprising, taking initiative, quick to act, and totally committed to Athens, body and soul. In fact, as we read this description of the two different forces, their two national characters, we have to wonder how in the world Athens eventually lost this war. So, concludes the Corinthian: You, Lacedaemonians, must act now to stop Athenian expansion and imperial aggression.

Athens has not been invited to this meeting, since of course Athens is not a member of the Peloponnesian League, but it just so happens that some Athenians are there on other business, and one of them responds to the Corinthian speech. The object of this speech is not to respond to any accusations about Athenian aggression, nothing in particular, nor to respond to these claims about the Athenian character, in fact, nowhere does this Athenian deny that Athenians are quick to act, expansionist, even imperialistic. He simply reminds the Spartans that war should not be hastily entered into. "We Athenians," he says, "have a right to all we have done and all we have obtained. We hate to dredge up ancient history, but of course it was only because of Athens at Marathon and again at Salamis, that the Persian threat was turned away. In short, we saved all of you, and we don't deserve these accusations of improper aggression." and continues the Athenian, "It was Athenian protection of Greeks that led to the creation of the Athenian Empire, and self-preservation that led Athenians to maintain it." Here's a brief section from the Athenian speech:

That empire we acquired by no violent means, but because you were unwilling to prosecute to its conclusion the war against the barbarian, and because the allies attached themselves to us and spontaneously asked us to assume the command. …

And at last, when almost all hated us, when some had already revolted and had been subdued, when you had ceased to be the friends that you once were, and had become objects of suspicion and dislike, it appeared no longer safe to give up our empire, especially as all who left us would fall to you. And no one can quarrel with a people for making, in matters of tremendous risk, the best provision that it can for its interest.

In that, says the Athenian, we've acted—in all of this we've acted—just like you Spartans. In assembling a group of allies, and holding on to them for our own safety as you've held on to yours for your own safety; that's just the way the world works: The weaker are always subject to the stronger. So, where are you coming from with all of these cries about justice, fair treatment of others? It's only the weak who talk about justice; the powerful simply use their power to get whatever they want. There's nothing new in that. In fact, the Athenian continues, we are famous for always talking about our problems with our allies, giving our allies access to courts: that's why they're restless. If we were as firm as you Spartans were with your allies then there would be no complaints. In any event, they say, let's not be hasty in going to war; let's not make the mistake of acting first and talking later. Let's talk, and see if we can settle our differences through arbitration. So ends the Athenian speech.

The Spartans are eager for war, but they go into a closed session of their own and, speaking now only to his fellow Spartans, the Spartan king Archidamus, a veteran of many wars, warns the Spartans of the dangers of war with Athens and indeed of any war. The Athenians, he says, have superior wealth and naval power to neutralize the Spartan advantage in land forces. Better, he says, to wait to talk, and build up reserves of cash and allies. He does not deny the Corinthian characterization of their dilatory nature. Here's Archidamus:

> And the slowness and procrastination, the parts of our character that are most assailed by their criticism, need not make you blush. If we undertake the war without preparation, we should by hastening its commencement only delay its conclusion: further, a free and a famous city has through all time been ours.

Right at the end of the speech, he says:

And we must not be hurried into deciding in a day's brief space a question which concerns many lives and fortunes in many cities, and of which honour is deeply involved—but we must decide calmly. This our strength peculiarly enables us to do. As for the Athenians, send to them on the matter of Potidaea, and send on the matter of the alleged wrongs of the allies—particularly as they are prepared with legal satisfaction, and to proceed against one who offers arbitration as against a wrongdoer, law forbids.

This comes from Archidamus's long experience: arbitration, better than outright war. So he says, and he proposes that the Spartans should send ambassadors to Athens, and in the meantime prepare for war.

Now, the final speech is from another Spartan, the otherwise unknown Sthenelaidas. He responds to Archidamus with a brief speech in favor of the war. I have no patience with these long speeches, he says, and I don't understand the Athenian arguments. If they once were good for Greece and now they're harming Greece, then they've done doubly wrong because they've ceased helping and started hurting. They have done wrong and it's up to us to stop them. This speech carries the day and the Spartans decide on war.

We don't know if this assembly, if this meeting of the Peloponnesian League, actually happened or if there were speeches anything like this. How would Thucydides know? What sources would he have? But the passage does serve well to introduce the essential nature of both Sparta and Athens. In that way, it works for Thucydides much like the meeting between Solon and Croesus did for Herodotus in setting up large global issues that will come into conflict.

Let's move on now to our second passage, in fact two juxtaposed passages from Book 2: the funeral oration of Pericles for Athenians who died in the first year of fighting, followed immediately by the physical and moral ravages of the plague in Athens. Let's start with the funeral oration.

It was the custom in Athens, we hear, for an orator to give a speech for all who died fighting for the city in the previous year. After the first year of the Peloponnesian War the speaker is Pericles, the Athenian general, statesman, strategist, and widely considered the greatest orator of his day. Certainly Thucydides was present for this speech; but are these the words of Pericles? We just don't know. In any event, this speech is one of the most highly praised, not only from antiquity, but of all time.

In this speech, instead of focusing only on the deeds of the dead, Pericles emphasizes the unique qualities of Athens, the city for which they died. He begins with comments about his own inadequacy to match the deeds of the fallen with appropriate words. It's a nice pose for an orator to take. But he says that since the custom was established by their ancestors, he'll go on with it. The greatness of those ancestors is where he begins: their role in adding to the strength of Athens, making it what it is now—a democracy, a pattern to all others rather than an imitator of anyone. Pericles praises the democracy both for serving the majority and also for fostering an atmosphere of openness throughout the city. The democracy favors the many over the few, gives equal access to justice to all, regardless of class or wealth.

Athenians, he goes on, have a high standard of living, with luxury items brought in from around the world and regular festivals that allow for relaxation and cultivation. Athenians need no painful discipline from the cradle—and here there's an implicit contrast with Spartan discipline, raised every male, to be a soldier—yet even so, Athenians are a formidable military force. One hallmark of the democracy, Pericles continues, is its reliance on so many of the citizens, all of whom were expected to be able to contribute, and the preparation for that contribution took many different forms. Here's a quotation from the speech:

> We cultivate refinement without extravagance and knowledge without effeminacy; wealth we employ more for use than for show, and place the real disgrace of poverty not in owning to the fact but in declining the struggle against it. Our public men have, besides politics, their private affairs to attend to, and our ordinary citizens, though occupied with the pursuits of industry, are still fair judges of public matters; for unlike any other nation, regarding him who takes no part in these duties not as unambitious but as useless, we Athenians are able to judge at all events if we cannot originate, and instead of looking on discussion as a stumbling-block in the way of action, we think it an indispensable preliminary to any wise action at all.

Everyone—in other words, not just the few—everyone is encouraged to be engaged in public affairs, whether through action or deliberation. He goes on to say that in short the city of Athens is an exemplar, the school of Greece; and it produces men who are self-sufficient, versatile, and famous throughout the world. Such is the Athens for which these men fought and died. No need, then, for particular praise of those who have died; by praising Athens he has praised what they created and what they suffered for.

The speech then becomes more obviously a rallying cry, an attempt to recruit even more support for the war. Pericles encourages those in the crowd to love Athens and do all possible to preserve Athens. He says:

> …you must yourselves realize the power of Athens, and feed your eyes upon her from day to day, till love of her fills your hearts; and then when all her greatness shall break upon you, you must reflect that it was by courage, sense of duty, and a keen feeling of honour in action that men were unable to win all this… For this offering of their lives made in common by them all they each of them individually received that renown which never grows old, and for a sepulchre, not so much that in which their bones have been deposited, but that noblest of shrines wherein their glory is laid up to be eternally remembered upon every occasion on which deed or story shall call for its commemoration. For heroes have the whole earth for their tomb; and in lands far from their own, where the column with its epitaph declares it, there is enshrined in every breast a record unwritten with no tablet to preserve it, except that of the heart.

Honor, yes, and lasting glory for all those who have fallen fighting for such a city as Athens. Homer rings pretty strong through this. Only now, at this point in the speech, does Pericles turn to the survivors, with comfort rather than condolence. They should be proud of those they lost. Parents of childbearing age, have more children. Sons and brothers of the dead: It's going to be difficult for you, but you should try hard to match the standards of those who have won such glory. Finally, widows: You win glory for yourselves in the only way women can, by keeping a low profile and attracting no attention for either good or bad. This comment on women is a sour note to our ears, but seems to convey a standard view of the public role of women at that time, and it certainly seems to have attracted no negative attention in antiquity. Instead, this speech has been celebrated since antiquity for so eloquently and persuasively praising the excellence of Athens and at the same time pressing the case for more support for the war: Athens deserves nothing less.

But we should be careful not to take the speech, and all the praise for Athens, out of its context within the history. Part of that context is the description of the plague that struck Athens in 430, a description that immediately follows the funeral oration. Now, the funeral oration was delivered during the winter, after the first fighting season, and the plague struck near the start of the second summer of the war. So, in juxtaposing the two events, we might argue that Thucydides is simply following his pattern of recording summers and winters in order. But there are clear connections between the two passages that suggest a more meaningful connection.

Thucydides mentions a few possible causes for this plague. He goes through a few of them—both what other people say about divine causes, and some possible human causes, but he gives up on that since none of these causes could be convincingly established. Instead he says that we will describe the plague in detail and he can do that very well, since he had it himself. He's going to describe it so that future generations might be better prepared for another outbreak: Another example of the value of history. Thucydides gives vivid details about the course of the disease, in language that seems to owe much to the medical writers of his day. The disease started in the head, with inflammation of the throat and bad breath. It then moved to the chest and the stomach, with coughing, vomiting, and retching. The skin broke out in ulcers, and the patient burned internally. After a week or so, if the patient was still alive, the disease caused a violent diarrhea, after which everyone died, almost. But even those who survived lost their eyesight or else some bodily extremities. Thucydides gives such a detailed description of the disease itself, and its contagious nature, that physicians and epidemiologists continue to make arguments about the identity of the disease. What could it have been?

But it is not only the physical toll that Thucydides describes. With so many dying, Athenians became careless about funeral rituals and the care of the dead. Some would leave the dead out in the street; others would take advantage of funeral pyres built by strangers, throwing their own corpse on first. In other words, so soon after the highly ritualized and formal state burial celebrated by Pericles, we have here a complete abandonment of all proper burial practices. The lawlessness extended far beyond burial practices as well. No one obeyed the laws anymore, those laws so celebrated by Pericles, as all thought only of immediate pleasure since death was so randomly imminent. Here he describes that:

> Nor was this the only form of lawless extravagance which owed its origin to the plague [referring to the burial customs]. Men now coolly ventured on what they had formerly done in a corner and not just as they pleased, seeing the rapid transitions produced by persons in prosperity suddenly dying and those who before had nothing succeeding to their property. So they resolved to spend quickly and enjoy themselves, regarding their lives and riches as alike things of a day. Perseverance in what men called honour was popular with none, it was so uncertain whether they would be spared to obtain the object; but it was settled that present enjoyment, and all that contributed to it was both honourable and useful. Fear of gods or law of man there was none to restrain them.

No sense of honor, no concern for the common good. In short, the plague narrative has taken us from the height of Athenian civilization to its very depths. Yes indeed, in fact the plague was a major catastrophe that killed a large percentage of the Athenian population. Even so, the effects described here by Thucydides reveal that the qualities Pericles so resoundingly celebrated were not so firmly based; they were not unshakable. The greatness of Athens does have its limits.

Finally, and more briefly, our third passage: Let's skip to Book 5, and the famous Melian dialogue. In 416, the Athenians were on the brink of attacking the island Melos, a colony of Sparta, and they sent an embassy first to see if the inhabitants would yield, would give up to Athens. Thucydides records a dialogue between the Athenian ambassadors and representatives of the Melians, a dialogue that gives us a bald expression of Athenian power. The Athenians begin by disallowing completely any talk of justice, morality, what's right. They say that such talk is appropriate only among equals: and Athens, of course, is much more powerful than Melos. Here's a brief statement of it; the Athenian says, "...for you know as well as we do that right, as the world goes, is in question only between equals in power; while the strong do what they can and the weak suffer what they must."

The Melians respond to this by arguing that the Athenians might regret that attitude, if ever they should fall from their position of power, and find the need themselves to appeal to justice. But the Athenians don't care about that. They're not persuaded. They're interested only here in what's best for the Athenian Empire now, its expansion and its preservation. It just so happens, as they would say, that it would help both Athens and Melos, according to the Athenians, if the Melians were to yield, rather than resist and suffer complete destruction. So, say the Athenians, the Melians must save themselves by yielding now to Athens. Athens cannot afford to let the Melians remain neutral. Their choice is between war and survival.

Melos and the Melians refuse to yield, holding out hope that the gods will help them, or else the Spartans. Hope, say the Athenians, is the indulgence of those with sufficient resources to back it up, and you have none. But still the Melians refuse to submit. We might recall a similar situation, some 80 years earlier, when an overwhelmingly powerful force asked Athens to submit and the Athenians refused. I'm thinking of the Persians here. Times have changed. Athens is now the imperial power, Melos the small city-state putting up resistance. But things turn out differently. Stated very briefly in Thucydides, the Athenians take the city, kill every adult male, and sell the rest of the population into slavery. This passage is considered one of the clearest examples of Thucydides's unsentimental realism, his clarity of vision in analyzing power: It's cold, calculating, detached. After the long debate, only a single sentence on the grisly results.

The Corinthian description of Athens from Book 1 has in some ways been fulfilled. The Athenians do take initiative and risks, they are aggressive and opportunistic. All of this now appears in an almost entirely negative light, and we might well look back differently at Pericles's funeral oration. Are these Athenians truly the model for all of Greece? Whether this passage, the Melian dialogue, shows us a moral abyss or simply effective pragmatism, the destruction of Melos prepares well for the Sicilian expedition that follows, when the Athenians attack an island that won't prove such an easy mark.

In the next lecture, our third and final lecture on Thucydides, we look at his description of that expedition to Sicily, in books 6 and 7.

Lecture Twenty-Nine
Thucydides III—Books 6–7

Scope:

Books 6 and 7 of Thucydides's *History* are something of a departure from the rest of the work, a self-contained unit on the Athenians' ill-fated expedition against Syracuse in Sicily. What begins with optimism and unparalleled wealth ends in complete and utter defeat for the Athenians. This movement from the heights of power to such unexpected depths parallels what we often find in tragedy. Also, in the depiction of the Athenians as the imperial aggressors against the democratic Syracuse, Thucydides recalls the earlier Persian Wars, with implicit comparisons between the Persian aggressors and the Athens that has developed in recent decades.

Outline

I. Book 6 of Thucydides's *History* begins with the bald declaration that Athens has decided to subjugate Sicily.

    A. Only gradually does Thucydides explain the context of that decision.

        1. In 421, open hostilities between Sparta and Athens temporarily came to an end with the Peace of Nicias, meant to last for 50 years.

        2. In 416, an Athenian ally in Sicily sent a request for aid, thereby giving Athens an excuse to attack the Spartan ally Syracuse in Sicily.

    B. The Athenian generals Nicias and Alcibiades debate the pros and cons of the expedition.

    C. Nicias is an older man, noted as much for his piety as for his wealth.

        1. He argues that Sicily is too far away and that Athens has plenty of enemies and rebelling allies closer to home.

        2. The Athenians should beware, he warns, of young generals who hope to win personal fame and fortune from the expedition.

D. Alcibiades, the young general obliquely slandered by Nicias, argues that the Sicilian expedition is in the best interest of Athens (6.16–18).

    1. Thucydides characterizes Alcibiades as a spendthrift eager for personal glory. His personal behavior was wildly licentious, but his conduct of public affairs was good.

    2. Later events prove Alcibiades a brilliant general, and Thucydides blames the Athenians for distrusting him; they made the mistake of confusing his public and private behavior.

    3. The Sicilians, Alcibiades says, are ruled by mobs and frequently change their laws.

    4. We have to help an ally in need and, at the same time, show how we despise the Spartan threat.

    5. He concludes by reminding the Athenians that it is in their national character to be active, to take risks, and to set off on adventures.

E. Nicias, in his first misjudgment of this narrative, argues that the Athenians must send a massive force if they hope to succeed. He was trying to dissuade the Athenians but instead inspired them to make the expedition larger and richer than before (6.19–24).

    1. In the enthusiasm for war, dissenters feared to speak openly against it (6.24).

    2. Thucydides emphasizes the size, splendor, and cost of the expedition in terms that might recall Xerxes's campaign (6.30–31).

II. We then cut to an assembly in Syracuse— a democracy much like Athens herself—where two speakers debate the need to prepare for an Athenian invasion.

A. The first speaker insists that Athens is on the way.

    1. He compares the Sicilians to the Greeks faced with the approaching Persians. Those defending their country must pull together in the face of a foreign aggressor.

    2. He suggests that they go meet the Athenian fleet in southern Italy. The plan is not pursued, but it reveals a mentality not unlike the Athenians'.

B. The second speaker urges a moderate response to the rumor of invasion.

    1. In the process, he pointedly praises the democratic features of Syracuse (6.39).

    2. Thucydides reminds us that Athens has not previously fought against a democracy; in this case, the Athenians are unable to win over the foe by promising a change in government (6.20 and 7.55).

III. As preparations are underway, someone smashes the statues of Hermes that guard doorways throughout Athens (6.27–29, 53, 60–61).

A. In response to the offer of rewards, informers accuse Alcibiades of the crime, saying it is a prelude to overthrowing the democracy and seizing power for himself.

B. Alcibiades demands a quick trial to face the charges before the expedition, but his enemies fear the influence of the army, all of them behind Alcibiades, and they delay until after the expedition has left.

    1. He is found guilty in absentia at the trial, and a ship is sent to retrieve him from Sicily.

    2. Alcibiades slips free of his captors and finds his way to Sparta, where he gives the Spartans valuable information (6.89–92).

    3. He advises the Spartans to establish a year-round fortification near Athens and to send a Spartan general to help in the defense of Syracuse. The Spartans eventually act on both, with devastating results for Athens.

C. The Athenians, meanwhile, are left in Sicily with Nicias, an unimaginative and unwilling general.

IV. The Athenians win several key victories over Syracuse and are on the verge of taking the city when the Spartan general Gylippus arrives, and the tide turns against Athens.

A. Nicias, now in a defensive mode, asks that the Athenians be withdrawn or reinforced (7.11–15); hoping for the former, he gets the latter, under the Athenian general Demosthenes (different from the great orator in Lecture Thirty-Three).

B. Even with reinforcements and the initial Athenian success of a daring night raid on the heights above Syracuse, the Athenians suffer another defeat.

C. Demosthenes advises leaving Sicily, but Nicias delays, fearing the wrath of the Athenians back home.

D. When Nicias has seen the considerable reinforcements the Syracusans have received from an ally in Sicily, and he is finally ready to retreat, there is an eclipse of the moon. Those who read the signs forbid troop movement for 27 days, and the pious Nicias obeys (7.50). Thus, the besiegers are condemned to stay in Sicily.

V. After a Syracusan victory in a naval battle in the harbor of Syracuse, the Athenians try to retreat but lose their entire force.

A. The Athenians modify their ships by adding grappling hooks, but the Syracusans, out-innovating the innovators, stretch hide across their prows so the hooks do not catch.

B. The battle is fiercely fought, with Athenians watching from the shore of the harbor as their fleet is destroyed.

C. The defeated Athenians regroup on land but fail to escape the environs of Syracuse, held in check by a false message that the passes are heavily guarded.

D. When the Athenians finally do retreat by land, the Syracusans are well prepared, but the Athenians are demoralized, ill-provisioned, poorly led, and disgraced.

E. Many Athenians are killed on the march, including Nicias and Demosthenes. The Athenians not killed on the march are imprisoned in a quarry in Syracuse, where they die slowly of exposure, disease, and starvation.

VI. This was the greatest achievement in Greek history, says Thucydides—at once the most glorious victory for the winners and the most calamitous defeat for the losers.

A. The earlier emphasis on Athenian wealth and numbers now becomes a negative; so much was lost.

B. As in the Persian Wars, we see the result of an imperial war of aggression.

C. Athens does recover from this blow but loses the war to Sparta in 404.

VII. Looking back from the end of the Sicilian expedition, we can see that many of the same qualities that were admirable in the description of Athens earlier have led to the disaster now.

    A. Thus, there is a degree of predictability in the path that Athens has followed, from a democracy aggressively protecting its own people to an empire that lives by subjugation and dies by overreaching.

    B. Perhaps it was inevitable that Athens became what it did, given who she was.

    C. If we think of Athens as the hero of Thucydides's work, then we see her as a hero unwilling to change her nature, whose own greatest strengths lead eventually to her fall. In that, we can see that Thucydides's history owes much to tragedy.

    D. But we cannot forget the extraordinary care and accuracy of his account of the war. Thucydides was rarely copied—he was too much of a genius in his style, too singular in his outlook—but his influence cannot be overestimated.

Essential Reading:
Thucydides, *The Peloponnesian War*, Books 6 and 7.

Supplementary Reading:
Connor, *Thucydides*, Book 6–Book 8 and conclusion.

Questions to Consider:
1. What led to the Athenian disaster in Sicily? Was it an inevitable result of the natural Athenian tendency toward action and innovation? Was it human error, because Nicias instead of Alcibiades was in charge? Some combination of the two?

2. Thucydides gives us an account of specific events during the war, but some critics have extracted from the changing fortunes of Athens a statement of political philosophy about the dangers of democracy and imperialism. What lesson, if any, do these events teach later generations?

Lecture Twenty-Nine
Thucydides III—Books 6–7

Welcome back. In our last lecture, we talked about three passages from books 1 through 5 of Thucydides's *History of the Peloponnesian War*, all of them describing the city of Athens in one way or another. Books 6 and 7, the subject of this lecture, our final lecture on Thucydides, are something of a departure from the rest of the history, a self-contained unit on the Athenians' ill-fated expedition against Syracuse on the island of Sicily. The Athenians set out on the expedition during a lull in the fighting—the Peace of Nicias that was engineered by the Athenian general of that name.

The expedition that began with optimism and unparalleled wealth ended in complete and utter defeat for the Athenians. This movement from the heights of power to such unexpected depths parallels what we often find in Greek tragedy. Also, in the depiction of the Athenians as the imperial invaders against the democratic Syracuse, Thucydides recalls the earlier Persian Wars, with implicit comparisons between the Persian aggressors and the Athens that has developed in recent decades.

Book 5, you recall ended with the Melian Dialogue, with Athens ruthlessly—or we might say practically—destroying a weak and previously neutral state. Book 6 begins with the simple and unexplained declaration that Athens has decided to subjugate Sicily. Only gradually does Thucydides back up and explain the context of that decision. In 421, open hostilities between Sparta and Athens temporarily came to an end with the Peace of Nicias, a peace that was meant to last 50 years. Five years into that peace, in 416, an Athenian ally in Sicily sent a request to Athens for aid against Syracuse, who was a Spartan ally. That gave Athens an excuse to move into Sicily and to attack Syracuse.

But the placement of this expedition within the history immediately after the Athenian ruthlessness at Melos creates certain expectations in those of us who are familiar with the patterns of Greek tragedy, and with the fall of the mighty that we so often saw there. Even more concrete expectations come from the example of the Persians referred to implicitly throughout, explicitly a few times: the Persians and their earlier failure in Greece. Three Athenian generals are chosen to lead the expedition; we're going to be focusing on only two of those. Early in Book 6, before the expedition departs, two of those generals, Nicias and Alcibiades, debate the pros and cons of the entire expedition. It's already been voted in, but Nicias in particular wants to reconsider that idea, that decision.

Now Nicias—central in establishing the peace with Sparta that was named after him—is an older man, noted both for his piety and for his extreme wealth. Nicias argues against the expedition, saying that Sicily is too far away, that Athens has plenty of enemies back at home and even allies that are rebelling and need to be kept in check. We have no business going across the sea to win for ourselves new enemies. In addition, he says, the Athenians should beware of young generals who support the expedition largely in the hopes of winning from it personal fame and fortune. Here's where he says that:

> [And] if there be any man here, overjoyed at being chosen to command, who urges you to make the expedition, merely for ends of his own—especially if he be still too young to command—who seeks to be admired for his stud of horses, but on account of its heavy expenses hopes for some profit from his appointment, do not allow such a one to maintain his private splendour at his country's risk, but remember that such persons injure the public fortune while they squander their own, and that this is a matter of importance, and not for a young man to decide or hastily to take in hand.

This is not an entirely veiled jab at the other general, Alcibiades—a brilliant young man, famous for his spendthrift ways, and for his unparalleled victories in chariot races—that's the comment about the stud of horses. Alcibiades responds to Nicias, arguing for the expedition. Thucydides introduces Alcibiades with a brief character summary, one of several that appear throughout the history, passages that stand out against the background of our usual fact and objectivity as Thucydides claims. Alcibiades, he says, was the warmest advocate for the expedition and he was indeed, as Nicias has said, eager for personal wealth and glory. Alcibades personal behavior was wildly licentious, Thucydides agrees to that, but even so, he says, his conduct of public affairs was good. Later events prove this true, that Alcibiades is indeed a brilliant general. Thucydides blames the Athenians for distrusting Alcibiades. They're making a mistake, he says, of confusing Alcibiades's exemplary public behavior for his less admirable private behavior.

Alcibiades responds and in his speech, he first answers the personal charges, then says that these Sicilians, they'll be easily defeated, not a worthy enemy for us at all. These are a people ruled by mobs and they frequently change their laws. In fact, as we'll find out, Syracuse is a democracy, with a political system similar to the Athenian democracy. What Alcibiades is describing—with this reference to mob rule and so forth, he's describing it in its worst light—is the functioning of a democracy. Alcibiades continues by saying we have an ally in need; and an opportunity, with this expedition, to show the Spartans how much we despise their continuing threat back home at Greece. He concludes by reminding the Athenians of their national character, much as the Corinthians had described it way back in Book 1. It's our nature to be active, to take risks, to set off on adventures, and we'll surely fail if we adopt a do-nothing policy now, as Nicias advises. Near the end of his speech he says:

> In short, my conviction is that a city not inactive by nature could not choose a quicker way to ruin itself than by suddenly adopting such a policy, and that the safest rule of life is to take one's character and institutions for better and for worse, and to live up to them as closely as one can.

In effect, he's saying that Athens must attack Sicily if Athens is to remain Athens—and in a sense, he's right. This should be the end of the assembly, but Nicias can't save himself, he responds, he gives another speech, a second speech. In this first misjudgment of his in this narrative, he tries to dissuade the Athenians from the expedition by saying that they'll have to send a truly massive force to Sicily if they hope for any sort of success. But instead of dissuading the Athenians, this speech just inspires them to make the expedition far larger and richer than before. It completely backfires on him, and so the speeches end.

There is such general enthusiasm for the expedition, Thucydides tells us, that dissenters—and yes, there were some dissenters—they feared to speak openly against it, lest they be considered unpatriotic. So the armament is prepared, with unparalleled size, splendor, and cost. Thucydides so emphasizes the magnitude of this undertaking that we might recall another massive invasion force, the Persians under Xerxes. I'll read part of the description of that, "Indeed this armament that first sailed out was by far the most costly and splendid Hellenic force that had ever been sent out by a single city up to that time." In the course of this, each ship tries to outdo the others in preparation—here I'll continue:

> From this resulted not only a rivalry among themselves in their different departments, but an idea among the rest of the Hellenes that it was more a display of power and resources than an armament against an enemy. ... Indeed, the expedition became not less famous for its wonderful boldness and for the splendour of its appearance, than for its overwhelming strength as compared with the peoples against whom it was directed, and for the fact that this was the longest passage from home hitherto attempted, and the most ambitious in its objects, considering the resources of those who undertook it.

Such is the fleet prepared by the Athenians for the attack on Sicily.

We then cut, we shift our view, to an assembly in Syracuse, a mirror in some ways of what we're used to seeing in Athens. We realize that for the first time in this war, Athens is going up against a state that's constituted much like herself, a democracy. After all, we have just witnessed the debate between Nicias and Alcibiades in Athens, and now we turn to a debate in Syracuse that's similar in format, if not in content. The debate is about rumors that Athens is preparing to attack. The first speaker insists that Athens is indeed on the way and that Syracuse must make preparations now.

He explicitly draws a parallel to the Persian Wars, saying that the Sicilians now are in a similar situation as the Greeks were when they faced the approaching Persians. Those defending their country, he says, have to pull together in the face of a foreign aggressor. Athens, in this view, has clearly shifted from the position of self-defense against the imperial aggressor to being that aggressor herself. This Syracusan even suggests that the people of Syracuse, the army should go meet the Athenian fleet in southern Italy as they make their way across to Sicily. That plan is not pursued, but it reveals a mentality, a taking of initiative, that's not unlike what we've seen in the Athenians.

The second speaker in this Syracusan assembly denies the rumors; Athens is way too smart to set out against Sicily in the midst of their own war. He urges Syracuse, the people of Syracuse, just to wait and see. In the process, this speaker pointedly praises the democratic features of Syracuse, features that have made the city sufficiently strong to withstand any attack up to this point. Thucydides reminds us that Athens has not previously fought against a democracy. When fighting Spartan-backed oligarchies, Athens has often been able to win over the foe not by force of arms, but by promising a change in government. But that's not possible here; Syracuse is already a democracy.

Meanwhile, back in Athens, as preparations for the expedition are underway, there is a civic and religious scandal. Someone has gone through the city at night smashing or defacing the statues of Hermes that typically guard doorways throughout the city. Now, these are more or less pillars that are marking boundaries between one house and another. Simply pillars, oftentimes with a small head of Hermes at the top, and the only other decoration on it would be an erect phallus. In some accounts we can imagine what's being chopped off here on these statues is the phallus. Thucydides doesn't give us that detail, but it's an outrage whatever happens. Now in response to the offer of rewards, informers come forward to say who did this terrible deed. They blame Alcibiades; and they say that the crime is simply a prelude to his attempts to overthrow the democracy entirely and seize power for himself. After all, they say, we all know about Alcibiades's loose lifestyle.

Alcibiades demands a quick trial, to face these charges that are in the air. He wants to face the charges before he goes off on the expedition, but his enemies fear the influence of the army; the navy, now amassed, ready to go under the leadership of Alcibiades to Sicily. They delay until after the expedition has actually left. After they're gone, the trial is held; Alcibiades is found guilty in *absentia*. A ship is sent from Athens to retrieve Alcibiades from Sicily. Here begins the eventful and romantic wanderings of Alcibiades, at different moments he is Athens's savior and her greatest enemy. Alcibiades is able to slip free of his captors. He gets away from this ship that's come to bring him back to Athens. He makes his way through Italy and finally ends up, of all places, in Sparta, where he talks his way into the good graces of these enemies of Athens. He does that in part by offering to the Spartans valuable strategic advice for getting the better of Athens. After all, the Athenians are now his enemies—they're out to arrest him—so he's doing all he can to help the enemies of his enemy.

The advice that Alcibiades gives in particular: He advises the Spartans to establish a year-round fortification near Athens, not simply coming up every year and then leaving. The second piece of advice: to send a Spartan general to help in the defense of Syracuse. The Spartans eventually act on both of these pieces of advice, with devastating results for Athens. Now, Alcibiades soon wears out his welcome in Sparta, at least in part because of his not-so-secret affair with the wife of one of the kings of Sparta. Years later he ends up back in the good graces of the Athenians, remarkably, after all he's done against them. But that's another story.

Back now to Sicily: With the departure of Alcibiades, the Athenians in Sicily are left under the leadership of Nicias, an unimaginative, even unwilling, general. Nevertheless, the Athenians win several key victories over Syracuse, taking a strategic position on a height just outside the city, defeating Syracuse in a cavalry engagement and they even start constructing walls around Syracuse in attempt to isolate her from the rest of Sicily and to cut her off from any possible aid. Syracuse responds to that strategically by trying to block the Athenian walls with counter walls. But things look bad for Syracuse, and if Syracuse falls, all of Sicily falls to Athens.

Then, at the start of Book 7, everything changes. Sparta, in response to Alcibiades's advice, sends the general Gylippus with a small number of ships, and the tide begins to turn against Athens. Already, in the second chapter of Book 7, Thucydides speaks of Syracuse having escaped all danger. His view has now shifted toward the end of the conflict and the defeat of Athens. We now follow with him, throughout Book 7, the gradual and painful disintegration of Athenian power. Gylippus, soon after he arrives, retakes the heights above Syracuse, he cuts off the Athenian walls with the counter walls, and he throws Nicias and the Athenians into a defensive posture.

Nicias, ever fearing the worst, sends a letter home to Athens, detailing the severity of the situation. He asks that the Athenians be withdrawn from Sicily; entirely or else supported with a force equal to the one first sent out. He also asks to be replaced himself, relieved of his command—he's suffering from some sort of kidney ailment. Not well. He hopes of course, does Nicias, that the whole force will be recalled to Athens, the whole expedition called off now that its difficulty has become evident. But no, his rhetoric backfires again:

The Athenians back home vote to stay the course. They send more forces, more troops after that first huge expedition, and they refuse to relieve Nicias of his command. So reinforcements arrive, under the Athenian general Demosthenes—not to be confused with the orator Demosthenes, another man we'll talk about in a later lecture.

Now this Demosthenes has been successful previously in the war, particularly in swift and decisive attacks, so he seems to be a good foil to Nicias's uncertainty and caution. Soon after he arrives, Demosthenes orchestrates a daring night raid on the heights above Syracuse. The element of surprise leads to some initial Athenian success, but that strategy—fighting at night—then backfires. The Athenians get lost in the dark, they start fighting with each other, falling off the cliffs, and they retreat in mass confusion. This was Demosthenes's one great attempt. After it's failed, Demosthenes advises that the Athenians should leave Sicily immediately.

Nicias, though, all of a sudden is torn, he's uncertain. He's thinking that they might still take Syracuse. He in fact, as Thucydides tells us, has some friends inside Syracuse, and he's heard from them that perhaps Syracusans are ready to give themselves up to Athens. He delays. He waits. Also Nicias fears the wrath of the Athenians back home if they were to retreat. We've seen before the way that Athenians can respond to failed generals. The command is divided, Nicias and Demosthenes not agreeing, and nothing is done. The Athenians stay where they are, just as the Syracusans receive considerable reinforcements from allies throughout Sicily.

Now, seeing those reinforcements come, Nicias is finally convinced that they have to retreat immediately. But just then, on August 27, 413 B.C.E., there is an eclipse of the Moon—we have that information from our astronomer friends. Those who read the signs forbid troop movement for 27 days. After you see an eclipse, you have to wait, and the pious Nicias obeys. Nicias, says Thucydides, was over-addicted to divination, and the besiegers, the Athenians, are condemned to stay in Sicily for another month. The Syracusans now recognize their advantage, and they make the bold move of attacking the previously invincible Athenian navy. Nobody had dared to do that; and they have considerable success. Athenian morale in response falls to an all-time low, and Syracuse decides to follow up that victory with another, more decisive, naval engagement. They do that by entrapping the Athenian navy within the harbor of Syracuse, cutting off their escape route.

A battle is brewing now as the Athenian ships have to fight their way out of the harbor. The buildup to this battle underlines its importance. We have a catalogue, in Thucydides, of the allies fighting on each side; not as long as the Homeric catalogs, but telling nonetheless. Never was a larger group assembled outside a single city, says Thucydides. Athenians have prepared for this battle by modifying their ships. They've added grappling hooks—this is the good old Athenian innovation—grappling hooks so they can attach themselves to the Syracusan ships, jump on board and fight that way. But the Syracusans, out-innovating the innovators as it were, stretch hides, animal skins, across their prows so that the Athenian grappling hooks won't be able to catch and take hold. Before the battle, Nicias addresses the Athenians; on the other side, Gylippus addresses the Sicilians; both speeches included in full by Thucydides. It should end there, but Nicias goes on. He's still appalled at the situation, he recognizes the gravity and the danger, and he gives another speech. This one is not recorded in Thucydides. Thucydides simply says in this speech Nicias said all the sorts of things that a desperate man before a huge battle would say, all the sorts of things said by those at the time of crisis.

The description of the battle itself is famously vivid, as we hear now about the fighting itself between the ships, now about the reactions of Athenians watching from the shore, and finally about the devastating loss suffered by the Athenian navy in the harbor of Syracuse. We recall, of course, the battle of Salamis, but now it's the Athenian navy penned in near a foreign enemy's city. It's the Athenian navy that's completely destroyed.

The defeated Athenians regroup on land, and prepare to march away immediately from Syracuse, to salvage some sort of safety for themselves now that they know they can't sail home. But a message reaches them that very night before they take off. A message that Syracusans are guarding all the passes that lead away from the city of Syracuse, guarding the passes waiting to wipe them out if they should try to get away quickly. This turns out to be a false message; there are no Syracusans at the passes; they're all back in the city celebrating their naval victory over Athens. It would have been the perfect time to escape. This was a false message intended to delay the Athenian retreat, and it works. It reminds us, too, of the Athenian use of a false message before the battle of Salamis, the message sent by Themistocles that tricked the Persians into blocking the exits from Salamis.

So the Athenians wait. They formally do retreat by land, the second day after their defeat at sea, and the Syracusans really are, by now, well prepared to destroy them. As the Athenians leave their camp, they are demoralized by the dead left unburied, they're ill-provisioned, poorly led by generals who can't agree on the best course, and beyond all, this is a troop, this is a force that's been disgraced. After all, as Thucydides tells us, this was the greatest reversal that ever befell a Greek army: after such fanfare at their departure from Athens, to suffer such extreme defeat. We might recall in that statement the ending of some of our tragedies; *Oedipus the King*, where the chorus comments on the uncertainty of fortune, how one so great could fall so far.

As they march away from Syracuse, many Athenians are killed on the march, with the greatest slaughter coming at a river where the Syracusans guarded the crossing. Here's an account of that:

> Once there [at the river] they rushed in, and all order was at an end, each man wanting to cross first, and the attacks of the enemy making it difficult to cross at all; forced to huddle together, they fell against and trod down one another, some dying immediately upon the javelins, others getting entangled together and stumbling over the articles of baggage, without being able to rise again. Meanwhile, the opposite bank, which was steep, was lined by the Syracusans, who showered missiles down upon the Athenians, most of them drinking greedily and heaped together in disorder in the hollow bed of the river. The Peloponnesians also came down and butchered them, especially those in the water, which was thus immediately spoiled, but which they went on drinking just the same, mud and all, bloody as it was, most even fighting to have it.

This is an ignoble end to these Athenians, and both Nicias and Demosthenes are killed. The few survivors are imprisoned in a quarry in Syracuse, where they die slowly of exposure, disease, and starvation—you can visit this quarry, it's still there in Syracuse, a chilling place. This, says Thucydides, was the greatest achievement in Greek history. I'll quote him:

> This was the greatest Hellenic achievement of any in this war, or, in my opinion, in Hellenic history; it was at once most glorious to the victors, and most calamitous to the conquered. They were beaten at all points and altogether; all that they suffered was great; they were destroyed, as the saying is, with a total destruction, their fleet, their army— everything was destroyed, and few out of the many returned home. Such were the events in Sicily.

The earlier emphasis on Athenian wealth and numbers has now becomes a negative; so much was ventured and so much was lost. As in the Persian Wars, we see here in the Sicilian expedition the result of an imperial war of aggression. Athens, once the savior of Greece for repelling the aggressors, has become the aggressor herself against a Syracuse that survives by acting in many ways like the Athens of old. Thucydides's history goes on for one more book, carrying the events of the war down to 411. Athens does, somewhat amazingly, recover from the tremendous loss in Sicily but, after the events Thucydides describes, Athens loses the war to Sparta in 404. Looking back from the end of the Sicilian expedition, we can see that many of the same qualities that were admirable in the description of Athens earlier led to her fall.

Back in Book 1, Thucydides had introduced us to an Athens that was always active, taking initiative, looking for new opportunities. We can say that it was this addiction to innovation that led Athens to expand her empire and to attack Sicily. Thus, there is a degree of predictability, even inevitability, in the path that Athens has followed, from a democracy protecting her own people to becoming an empire living by subjugation and dying by overreaching; an inevitability in what Athens has become.

Now, if we think of Athens as the hero of Thucydides's work, then we see her as a hero unwilling to change her nature, whose own greatest strengths lead eventually to her fall; in that, we can see that Thucydides's history does owe much to tragedy.

But we shouldn't forget, as we leave Thucydides, the extraordinary care and accuracy of his account of the war. I've been emphasizing some of the ways that his bias shows through, in part because that bias is less evident. Thucydides was rarely copied—too much of a genius in his style, too singular in his outlook—but his influence cannot be overestimated.

We leave Thucydides now and we turn in our next lecture to another author of great influence, Plato.

Lecture Thirty
Plato I—The Philosopher as Literary Author

Scope:

In this lecture, we examine some of the literary qualities that appear throughout Plato's philosophical dialogues. Rather than discussing the philosophical ideas or systems that might be extracted from the dialogues, we look in some detail at the way Plato has chosen to present those ideas. He never speaks in his own voice, and ideas are not stated categorically but emerge from discussion, modified by the particular nature of each dialogue and by the strengths and weaknesses of the cast of characters in each. Despite arguments within certain dialogues against Homer and other poets, Plato himself borrows much from them in his own style. The *Republic*, for example, includes arguments against the poets as distant imitators of reality, yet it concludes with a poetic description of life after death. Other examples of similar practice appear throughout the corpus. What, then, is Plato's attitude toward literature?

Outline

I.   We now turn to Plato and his philosophical dialogues.

   A.   Our purpose in these lectures is to examine some of the literary qualities that appear throughout those dialogues rather than to discuss the philosophical ideas or systems that might be extracted from them

   B.   Plato never speaks in his own voice; rather, ideas and arguments emerge from conversations between Plato's characters.

   C.   What, then, is the attitude within the dialogues toward literature? Several dialogues contain strong arguments against poetry, yet Plato himself borrows much from the poets in his own style. Plato, in other words, contradicts in the form of his dialogues what his characters say within them.

II. Plato (c. 429–347) is careful to reveal nothing of himself in his dialogues, and we have little information about his life.

A. A group of letters attributed to Plato gives some detail (especially the seventh), but we should treat that information with care.

B. Having come from a wealthy and aristocratic background, Plato devoted himself to philosophy after listening to Socrates.

C. Unlike Socrates, he established a formal school, the Academy, for the study and teaching of philosophy.

D. Also unlike Socrates, who wrote nothing, Plato wrote numerous philosophical dialogues, almost all of them including Socrates as a central character but never including himself as a speaker.

III. The dialogue format allows Plato to act as midwife or gardener of ideas, helping others formulate their own views rather than telling his own.

A. There is, thus, an elusive quality to the dialogues that has prompted discussion since antiquity.

  1. Some sift the dialogues for Platonic dogma, looking for what Plato thinks and even a complete philosophical system in the words he gives his characters.

  2. Others see Plato as testing, questioning, and by his very reticence, inviting his readers and students to come to their own conclusions.

  3. It has been said by the English philosopher Whitehead that all of Western philosophy is "a series of footnotes to Plato," so great is his influence on all that followed. But it has also been said that Plato cannot be blamed for all that has been done in his name.

B. Certain ideas do recur in his dialogues, and it will be helpful to introduce one here: his theory of forms or ideas.

  1. The dialogues present themselves as records of conversations between Socrates and others.

  a. The early or Socratic dialogues seem to give us a relatively unadulterated view of the historical Socrates as he carried on conversations.

  b. The middle-period dialogues seem to come from the days of Plato's Academy; Socrates is still a prominent character, but now, Plato shows him espousing new ideas and theories—that's where we find the theory of forms.

    c. In the late dialogues, Socrates plays a less central role, and the discussion turns to such subjects as logic and political philosophy.

  2. According to the theory of forms, all that we see and know in this physical world is partial, changeable, and only a reflection of its eternal and unchanging form or idea, which can be comprehended only through philosophical study.

  3. In this view, there exist outside of the sensible world ideal forms of justice, beauty, truth, goodness, and so on.

  4. The most important human pursuit is the attempt, by means of philosophy, to apprehend these forms.

IV. Our emphasis here is on the literary quality of Plato's corpus. We begin with the views expressed within the dialogues themselves about various types of literature.

  A. Three dialogues in particular, the *Apology*, the *Ion*, and the *Republic*, comment on poetry.

  B. The *Apology* is Socrates's defense speech against charges of impiety.

    1. In explaining why he always went around questioning people, Socrates states that an oracle of Apollo at Delphi declared that he, Socrates, was the wisest man. Socrates, who always claimed he knew nothing, set out to find a wiser man than he.

    2. He talked to all sorts of people and had no luck finding someone wiser than he.

    3. When he spoke to poets, he found that they could recite beautiful poetry, but when he asked if they could explain the poetry, they could not. He concluded that the poetry came to them simply through inspiration, not through wisdom or understanding.

  C. The *Ion* is a conversation between Socrates and Ion, a performer of the Homeric poems.

    1. Socrates suggests that poets, such as Homer, and the

performers of their poems, such as Ion, have no real knowledge of what they are doing; they are possessed by divine inspiration, conduits of a divine voice.

2. Poetic inspiration is, thus, something passed from the gods to a poet, to the performer, and to the audience, like magnetism through a set of iron rings.

3. While poetry in this view is closely connected to the divine, the emphasis here is on the essentially irrational nature of poets, unable to give an explanation of themselves or their work.

D. The *Republic*, a wide-ranging work on political and moral philosophy, contains several statements about art and literature, particularly their place in society.

1. In Books 2 and 3, Socrates discusses the qualities of an ideal state and suggests that only true and beneficial poetry be allowed in the state.

2. Homer and Hesiod and their like tell stories that make the gods appear less than perfect, and they include examples of humans acting ignobly; they must be severely edited.

3. The danger, he continues, is greater when the poetry is mimetic, that is, when the poet adopts the voice of his characters (as often in Homer) instead of narrating about the characters.

4. The poet, or the reader of the poetry, runs the risk of becoming like the characters in these mimetic scenes, and not all of the characters are good models.

5. Finally, in Book 10, Socrates generalizes further: The world as we see it is simply a pale imitation of true and eternal reality, and art of all kinds is simply an imitation of this world. It is, thus, an imitation of an imitation.

6. Hence, poetry stands at three removes from reality and should be entirely banished from the ideal state.

V. Plato complicates things, though, by resorting often and effectively to poetry itself and the techniques of poetry in his dialogues.

A. In the first place, the dialogues are entirely mimetic rather than narrative; every word is presented in the voice of one or another character. And not all of the characters are admirable or noble.

B. Throughout the dialogues, Plato's characters reveal a close acquaintance with poetry, especially the poetry of Homer, referring often to famous scenes or passages to bolster their points.

C. Plato's characters, especially Socrates, often resort to a form of discourse that shares much with poetry. Instead of arguing a point logically, he tells an imaginative story that illustrates his point. We have three examples.

1. Just after the banishment of poets in the *Republic*, Socrates describes the system of reward and punishment in the afterlife in the so-called Myth of Er, the story of a man who had a near-death experience, saw what waits on the other side, and came back to tell the tale.

2. In the *Phaedo*, the dialogue that describes the last hours of Socrates's life, Socrates says just before his death that he has insufficient time to discuss and prove the nature of the world, but he can tell a descriptive story about it.

3. Finally, Plato introduces in two different dialogues, the *Timaeus* and the *Critias*, a story that has endured through the centuries about an island kingdom called Atlantis.

a. In the distant past, the story goes, Athens brought an end to an imperialistic attack by Atlantis, then both were utterly destroyed by earthquake, wiping out memory of the event.

b. Thus, Plato has his character concocting a story and attesting to its truth—a myth that serves as a foundation of his argument.

VI. These dialogues, then, say one thing about poetry and do another. Plato has given us plenty to ponder and to figure out for ourselves. It is no wonder that articles and books appear regularly and consistently addressing Plato's views on art, poetry, and literature.

Essential Reading:

Plato, *Ion* and *Republic*, Books 2, 3, 10.

Supplementary Reading:

Asmis, "Plato on Poetic Creativity."

Clay, D., *Platonic Questions: Dialogues with the Silent Philosopher*, chapter 2.

Nightingale, "Sages, Sophists and Philosophers: Greek Wisdom Literature."

Questions to Consider:

1. What are the advantages and the disadvantages to writing philosophy in the dialogue form?

2. Plato's Socrates does not think highly of poetry, yet Plato himself resorts to poetic devices in his dialogues. How might we resolve or explain this apparent contradiction?

Lecture Thirty
Plato I—The Philosopher as Literary Author

Welcome back. Our last three lectures were on Thucydides's *History of the Peloponnesian War*, a work that ends abruptly—in the middle of a sentence, in fact. Thucydides gives us no summation, no concluding words, nothing to help us come to easy conclusions about him or his work. Thucydides does speak in his own voice in his work, if only rarely, but even there his statements have led to a variety of interpretations.

We turn now, for the next three lectures, to an author who never speaks in his own voice, but whose own personal views are regularly cited and even quoted. Our author is Plato and his works are philosophical dialogues. Our purpose in these three lectures is to examine some of the literary qualities that appear throughout those dialogues. Rather than discussing the philosophical ideas or systems that might be extracted from the dialogues, and often are, we will be looking in some detail at the way Plato has chosen to present those ideas. I repeat: Plato never speaks in his own voice and he states no ideas of his own categorically or even explicitly; rather, ideas and arguments emerge from conversations between and among Plato's characters. Those ideas and arguments are modified by the particular nature of each dialogue and by the particular strengths and weaknesses of the cast of characters in each dialogue. We have to be careful, in other words, that we distinguish between the views of Plato the author—if we can establish those views at all—and the views of the characters that he creates. Distinguishing between those two is in many ways a literary question.

So, what is the attitude within the dialogues toward literature? Several dialogues contain strong arguments against poetry, often against Homer in particular. Yet Plato himself borrows much from the poets in his own style. His great dialogue the *Republic*, for example, includes arguments against the poets as distant imitators of reality, as we'll soon see, yet it concludes with a memorably poetic description of life after death. Other examples of similar contradictions appear throughout the dialogues of Plato. Plato, in other words, contradicts in the form of his dialogues what his characters say within them.

In this lecture, we start with brief comments on the life of Plato and his genre—the philosophical dialogue. We then summarize the various views toward poetry and literature that appear throughout the dialogues with a few particular examples; and we conclude by looking at some of the passages that seem to contradict in practice those views as stated.

Who was Plato? Born around 429 and died in 347, Plato is careful to reveal nothing of himself in his dialogues, and we have little information about his life. A group of letters is attributed to Plato and they give us considerable biographical detail, especially the seventh letter, but we should treat that information with care. We're not sure who actually wrote those letters. We can safely say that Plato came from a wealthy and aristocratic Athenian background and that he devoted himself to philosophy after listening to Socrates—Socrates, whom we've already met earlier in this course in Aristophanes's comedy, *The Clouds*. Plato was one of the young men who were captivated by Socrates's constant and public questioning; and he seems to have been particularly affected by the trial and execution of Socrates in 399.

Socrates had been charged with corrupting the youth and certain types of religious impropriety, and one of Plato's earliest works is a version of Socrates's speech of defense against those charges—the document we call the *Apology*, from the Greek *apologia* that means defense speech. Socrates is not saying he's sorry for anything in that speech. After Socrates's death, Plato in many ways became the heir to his mentor's interests and methods, but unlike Socrates, Plato established a formal school, the Academy, for the study and teaching of philosophy. Also unlike Socrates who wrote nothing, Plato wrote numerous philosophical dialogues, almost all of them including Socrates as a central character but never including Plato himself as a speaker. Let's turn now to look at that genre.

The dialogue format allows Plato to stay in the background making no authorial statements or judgments. The dialogues present themselves, on one level, as simply the record of conversations between Socrates and various others—and Socrates doesn't appear in all of them. To borrow two of the images within the dialogues, this format, with the absence of authorial direction, allows Plato to act as a midwife of ideas, helping others formulate their own views; or as a gardener, nurturing ideas in others rather than expressing his own.

We might contrast the position of say Hesiod in the *Theogony*, where the poet, you might recall, explicitly establishes his own authority and voice through his close connection to the Muses. In fact, the early philosophical tradition from which Socrates and then Plato emerged tended to value highly the insight and expertise of the individual philosopher. The Sophists in particular tried to establish for themselves personal reputations, traveling throughout the Greek world on the strength of those reputations. But Socrates denied that he had any such expertise; he stayed in Athens, barefoot, wearing shabby clothes, asking questions and claiming that he knew nothing. Plato, in his own way, adopted a similar sort of personal anonymity, refusing to include himself as a character within his dialogues.

Since we have no authorial voice in the dialogues, no one to settle questions for us once and for all, these dialogues have an elusive quality, and that quality has led to discussion about them ever since antiquity. Some interpreters insist on sifting the dialogues for Platonic dogma, looking in the interaction of characters for indications of what Plato thinks or, as one book is titled, *What Plato Said.* They even build complete philosophical systems from the words he gives his characters. Since Socrates is such a central character within the dialogues and usually so dominant in the conversations, it is tempting to take Socrates as a spokesman for Plato, and simply to say that Plato expresses his views through the mouth, the person, the character of Socrates.

But the relationship between the author and his main character—between Plato and the Socrates of his dialogues—is more complex than that. Those who try to reconstruct the views of the historical Socrates have labored to distinguish his views from those of the character Socrates within the dialogues. Those who try to establish a particularly Platonic philosophy have to sort out the sometimes shifting, sometimes contradictory statements of the Socrates within the dialogues. One collection of essays, a recent collection that addresses the problem, has the apt title: *Who Speaks for Plato?* Who, indeed.

There's another view about these dialogues, and that is to say that there is no dogma in them at all. To deny the presence of dogma or any sort of systematic philosophy within the dialogues and to see Plato rather as testing, questioning, and by his very silence inviting his readers and students—that is, us—inviting us to come to our own conclusions. In that view, Plato is carrying on the tradition of Socrates, emphasizing not his own wisdom, but throwing the weight of responsibility onto each listener or reader. He raises questions, gives us a method, a means for approaching difficult questions, and then leaves us to the hard work of finding our own solutions.

The influence of these dialogues has been immense, and we could go on indefinitely assessing various responses to them. There's one school of thought that in fact Plato did write down a systematic philosophy or a dogma, but we've lost all of that. We could go on indefinitely looking at possibilities, but instead, let's recall what the English philosopher Whitehead said, that all of Western philosophy is "a series of footnotes to Plato," so great is his influence on all that followed. But let's remember, too, that Plato cannot be blamed for all that has been said and done in his name. Our interest here is not in the many traditions of Platonism—fantastically interesting traditions—not in the various directions they have taken, but in some aspects of the dialogues themselves.

Now, before turning to our discussion of Plato as literature and Plato on literature, it will help us to summarize one argument that does recur in several dialogues: the so-called theory of forms or ideas. As I've mentioned, these dialogues present themselves as records of conversations between Socrates and others. Some of the dialogues more obviously than others do just that, and we typically refer to these as the early dialogues—or Socratic dialogues—since they seem to give us a relatively unadulterated view of the historical Socrates as he carried on conversations. A second group—the middle period dialogues—seem to come from the days of Plato's Academy; Socrates is still a prominent character, but now Plato shows him espousing new ideas and theories. That's where we find the theory of forms or ideas. Finally, in the so-called late dialogues, Socrates plays a less central role and the discussion turns to such subjects as logic and political philosophy.

What is this theory of forms from the middle period dialogues? Something like this: All that we see and know in this physical world is partial, changeable, and only reflection of its eternal and unchanging form or idea; a form that cannot be comprehended by the senses, but only through philosophical study. In this view there exists outside of the sensible world an ideal form of justice, beauty, truth, goodness, and so on. The most important human pursuit, then, is the attempt, by means of philosophy, to apprehend these forms or the ideas. There's one way that Plato conveys this idea or this theory in a memorable way at one passage in the *Republic*, with the so-called "Allegory of the Cave."

The theory of forms is something like this: All of us humans are like people who have been imprisoned inside a cave, chained so that we can look only forward where we see images dancing across the wall in front of us. We take those images for reality; all they are, though, is the shadow. They're shadows of shapes that are being moved behind us, with a fire behind them to reflect them onto the wall in front of us. That's all that we can see. If we were able to break free of those chains and go outside of the cave, we would see the real world. We would come closer to an apprehension of these forms or ideas. The person who does that—who breaks free and gains some insight into these forms—then goes back into the cave, back into the state of most humanity, he can't see too clearly because of the darkness. That's the state of the philosopher who tries to explain to all of us in our blindness the way reality really works. Now, we'll come back to this idea of forms or ideas several times in our discussion of Plato, so let's leave it there.

Since our emphasis here is on the literary quality of Plato's corpus, we begin with the views expressed within the dialogues themselves about various types of literature and art more generally. Three dialogues in particular, the *Apology*, *Ion*, and the *Republic*, contain explicit comments about poetry with implications for literature more generally. Let's look at parts of each of these.

I mentioned that the *Apology* is the defense speech, Socrates's defense speech, against charges of corrupting the youth and impiety. In it, he has to explain why is it that he's always going around the city questioning people, annoying people, leading them to bring these charges against him. Well, he explains. Socrates says that there was an oracle of Apollo at Delphi that said that, he, Socrates, was the wisest man. Socrates was appalled at this, since he was always claiming that he knew nothing. So he set out to find the truth of that oracle, and he did it by questioning people throughout Athens, trying to find somebody who actually was wiser than he. He talked to politicians; he talked to craftsmen; and he had no luck finding someone wiser than he. But he did also talk to poets, thinking these are certainly people that will know something more than I do. He talked to the poets and he found that, yes, indeed, they could recite beautiful poetry. But when he asked them what it meant, could they explain it. They absolutely were at a loss. They couldn't do that. They couldn't give an account of what they had written. Their poetry, he concludes, is coming to them simply through inspiration, not through any sort of wisdom or understanding. So he's frustrated even in that attempt to find somebody wiser than himself.

Let's move on now to the *Ion,* another example of commentary on art and literature. That's a short dialogue, a conversation between Socrates and a man named Ion, who is a professional performer of the Homeric poems. Ion claims that he knows not only how to perform Homer's poems, but also how to explain them. But he is unable, he says, to say much that's worthwhile about any other poet. How can that be, wonders Socrates, if there's so much overlap between the poetry of Homer and the poetry of others? They talk about similar themes; they have similar sorts of ideas. How is it that you can speak only about Homer? The explanation, Socrates concludes, is that Ion has no real knowledge or understanding of what he's doing in reciting and explicating Homer, but he is possessed by divine inspiration. The same goes for Homer himself, and all other poets—this is much like what we saw in the *Apology*. The poets have no intellectual grasp of what they're doing and in fact intellect would just get in the way of good poetry. These poets and Ion, the performer of poetry, they're all conduits of a divine voice. Socrates explains that poetic inspiration is something passed from the gods to a poet, then to the performer of the poetry, like Ion, and finally to the audience. He uses an image to describe this: It's like magnetism, going through a series of iron rings. Now while poetry in this view is closely connected to the divine, the emphasis here is on the essentially irrational nature of poets: poets who are unable to give an account of themselves or their work.

Now let's turn now to the *Republic* and its commentary on poetry. The *Republic* is a wide-ranging work on political and moral philosophy, and it's one that contains several statements about art and literature and particularly their place in society. In books 2 and 3, Socrates discusses the qualities of an ideal state and suggests that only true and beneficial poetry should be allowed a place in that state. Homer and Hesiod, he says, and all like them, they tell stories that make the gods appear less than perfect, and they include examples of humans acting in ignoble fashion. They must be severely edited. Here's where he says that:

> And, as for saying that a god, who is himself good, is the cause of bad things, we'll fight that in every way, and we won't allow anyone to say it in his own city, if it's to be well governed, or anyone to hear it either—whether young or old, whether in verse or prose. These stories are not pious, not advantageous to us, and not consistent with one other.

Terrible censorship, we might be saying. But he goes on. The danger, Socrates continues, is greater when the poetry is mimetic, that is, when the poet adopts the voice of his characters—as often in Homer, as throughout tragedy and all drama—adopting the voice of a character instead of simply narrating about the characters. The poet, or the reader of the poetry, runs the risk of becoming like the characters in these mimetic scenes, and not all of the characters are good models. Here's his comment on that:

> It seems, then, that if a man, who through clever training can become anything and imitate anything, should arrive in our city, wanting to give a performance of his poems, we should bow down before him as someone holy, wonderful, and pleasing, but we should tell him that there is no one like him in our city, and that it isn't lawful for there to be. We should pour myrrh on his head, crown him with wreaths, and send him away to another city.

The dangers of imitating a less than admirable character are great. But Socrates does leave open the possibility here of the imitation of noble and admirable characters. He allows, in other words, for the presence in his ideal city of mimetic poetry if the stories and characters are in accord with the principals of the city.

Finally, another passage in the *Republic*, in Book 10: Socrates generalizes further about poetry, and indeed about all art. Referring to the theory of forms we mentioned earlier, Socrates says that the world as we see it is simply a pale imitation of true and eternal reality. Art of all kinds is then simply an imitation of this physical world. It is thus an imitation of an imitation. Hence, poetry stands at three removes from reality, and something so far removed from the truth has no place in this ideal state. No longer are we distinguishing between types of poetry and literature; all of it is worthless.

These are strong, and strongly negative, views about art; but Plato complicates things by including in his dialogues frequent and effective references to poetry itself, and by incorporating into the dialogues literary techniques. In the first place, the dialogues themselves are entirely mimetic, rather than narrative; every word in them is presented in the voice of one or another character, not in the voice of the Plato, our author. Not all of the characters are admirable or noble; we need think no further back than Ion—very pleasant, very engaging, but certainly a shallow individual. Also, throughout the dialogues, Plato's characters reveal a close acquaintance with poetry—especially the poetry of Homer—referring often to famous scenes or passages to support their points. Maybe even more telling are the regular offhand references to the poets, quotations from them. Poetry is clearly ingrained in the fabric of these characters, a natural part of their speech, their conversation, their lives.

Perhaps most puzzling, though, in light of those negative statements and arguments about poetry, is that Plato's characters—and especially Socrates—often resort to a form of discourse that shares much with poetry. Instead of arguing a point logically or systematically, Socrates and others will resort to an imaginative story to illustrate a point: the "Allegory of the Cave," for example, an allegory to get across the idea of the theory of forms. Let's look now at three examples of this use of poetic techniques.

First: We've heard about the banishment of poets in the dialogue the *Republic*. But after that, late in the dialogue, Socrates describes the system of reward and punishment in the afterlife, and he does it in the so-called Myth of Er, the story of a man who had a near-death experience; he saw what waits on the other side; and he came back to tell the tale. It's a long and beautiful myth.

We hear that Er was thought to have been killed on the battlefield but in fact he wasn't. When the bodies were collected, all the others had started to putrefy, but his was still fresh. He was awakened from the battlefield and he told the story of what he had seen. He saw where the bodies go, where the souls go after their death. It's a huge meadow with four doors, two going up, two going down. Those who had lived a good life get to go straight upward; those who had some crimes on the conscience had to go down into the lower door and be cleansed before they could come back. After this process, all the souls again gathered in this huge meadow and each one got to select a life, the next life as they went back into the world. We hear that Ajax was there. He chose for himself the life of a lion, not a human being at all. Odysseus was there; after all of the suffering of his life, he chose the most private, quiet, unknown life of all.

We hear many details about this afterlife and the things that go on there, absolutely imaginative. Here we are, at the end of 10 closely argued books, with many claims in them against the use of poetry, art, stories, as we've seen, and Socrates tells this story. Or, we might say, Plato concludes this massive dialogue with a story. This story about Er, Socrates says, is unlike the ones Odysseus told about his adventures; but even that reference reminds us that with this story we're in the world of Homeric storytelling.

Now, the Myth of Er is a beautiful story. It illustrates in compelling ways the need to live properly, even philosophically; but it offers a resoundingly literary conclusion to a work that has little good to say about literature. Now we find another, similar example of this kind of contradiction in the *Phaedo*, the dialogue that describes the last hours of Socrates's life, and the discussions he had then with his followers. As Socrates is awaiting the hemlock that will carry out his death sentence, he's asked by one of his friends for a description of the world as it really is, not as it appears to us. Socrates responds that he has insufficient time to discuss and prove the things of the world, but says that he can tell a descriptive story about them. Here's what he says:

> …I do not think it requires the skill of Glaucus [in other words, it wouldn't be such a hard thing] to tell you what they are, but to prove them true requires more than that skill, and I should perhaps not be able to do so. Also, even if I had the knowledge, my remaining time would not be long enough to tell the tale. However, nothing prevents my telling you what I am convinced is the shape of the earth and what its region are.

He goes on then with an imaginative description of the world. We humans living as if at the bottom of the sea, we look up we think we see the sky; we don't see real truth, we don't see absolute reality—a story, then, to get across one of his philosophical points.

Finally, and perhaps most famously, in two different dialogues, the *Timaeus* and the *Critias*, Plato introduces a story that has endured through the centuries, about an island kingdom called Atlantis. In the distant past, the story goes, the city of Athens brought an end to an imperialistic attack by Atlantis, and then both were utterly destroyed by earthquake, wiping out memory of the event. Plato's motives for introducing this story are much debated, but what is clear is that Plato has his character concocting a story—yes, I don't think there really was an Atlantis. This is a myth that serves as a foundation of his argument. The very insistence here on the truth of that story should make us suspicious. This is another example, in other words, of the use of what we might call a *literary device*, a story or myth, within a philosophical dialogue.

To sum up, these dialogues then say one thing about poetry and literature and they do another. Since Plato never speaks in his dialogues, he offers no solution to that apparent contradiction, but he leaves us with plenty to ponder, to figure out for ourselves. It's no wonder that articles and books appear regularly and consistently addressing Plato's views on art, poetry, and literature.

In the next two lectures, we discuss two of the most brilliant of Plato's dialogues, at least from a literary perspective: the *Symposium* and the *Phaedrus*.

Lecture Thirty-One
Plato II—*Symposium*

Scope:

The next two lectures take us through two of Plato's most polished literary masterpieces, the *Symposium* in this lecture and *Phaedrus* in the next. The *Symposium* is the story, told many years after the fact, of a party at which each attendee delivers a speech on Eros, the personification of love. Philosophers who are uninterested in the literary aspects of Plato's dialogues often look only at one speech, delivered by Socrates, for the dialogue's kernel of philosophical truth. We, on the other hand, take into consideration not only the other speeches but also the introductory framing of the party and the riotous interruption near the end. We will see that distinctions between philosophical and literary parts of the dialogue are impossible to draw and that the dialogue is best read as the seamless whole that Plato gave us.

Outline

I. In this lecture, we study the *Symposium*, the story of a celebratory party at which each member of the party agrees to deliver a speech in honor of love.

II. The dialogue begins with Apollodorus, one of Socrates's followers, in mid-conversation with an unnamed character who has asked him to tell what happened at the famous party at the house of Agathon, a tragic playwright.

   A. Someone else had recently asked Apollodorus the same question, chasing after him in his eagerness to know, and Apollodorus now recounts the details of that meeting.

      1. Apollodorus was not at the party but heard about it from Aristodemus, another member of Socrates's circle, who was there.

      2. A man named Phoenix has also been talking about the party, also having heard details from Aristodemus.

   B. Thus, even before the account of that party begins, we have the sense that it is important, interesting to many, and worth attending to.

C. At the same time, we learn that the party took place long ago and that the version of it we will hear has been filtered through several tellings.

III. It will help to pause here for a brief introduction to two aspects of Athenian culture that underlie this dialogue: the nature of the symposium and Athenian sexual customs.

A. The symposium was a social gathering for aristocratic males.

1. The events included food, drink, and entertainment of various sorts provided by the so-called flute girls.

2. Typically, the men reclined at these parties, two to a couch.

3. Strict protocols were followed, as the host, or one appointed in his place, would decide how much and how quickly the guests would drink.

4. These symposia seem to have been important venues not only for relaxation and entertainment but also for passing along aristocratic values in an increasingly democratic Athens.

B. Aristocratic Athenian males of the 5th century often formed erotic attachments with boys.

1. It was viewed as natural and traditional for an Athenian male to seek sexual gratification from a younger male, and for the younger male to yield in return for the attention, admiration, and social standing given him by the older male.

2. However, it's somewhat misleading to refer to these relationships, or these men, as homosexual, because these same men also married women and raised children.

3. The Greek terms for those involved in these relationships are usually translated as "lover" for the older male and "beloved" for the younger.

IV. This gathering is in celebration of a dramatic victory by Agathon. Socrates was supposed to arrive with Aristodemus, but Socrates fell into a deep reverie on the way and stopped, only to arrive later. Because all the guests are still queasy from the previous night's drinking, they decide that instead of drinking, they will give speeches on Eros, the personification of love.

A. Phaedrus, a young follower of Socrates, starts with a traditional speech of praise that focuses on the lineage and the good consequences of love, with mythological examples.

B. The next man to speak, Pausanias, is more analytical, identifying two types of love: Earthly love desires only physical satisfaction, while heavenly love is long-lasting and interested in the moral well-being and improvement of all involved.

C. Aristophanes is to speak next, but he has the hiccups. Eryximachus, a doctor, first offers Aristophanes several cures for hiccups; he then expands Pausanias's analysis to a general, even global, duality between good and bad desires and, further, to general scientific laws.

D. Aristophanes, now cured, offers a very different view of love, one that accounts for the various types of human desire.

    1. Once upon a time, there were three sexes: male, female, and a mixture of the two.

    2. Each being was spherical in shape, with four arms, four legs, two faces, two sets of genitalia, and so on.

    3. Because these mortals behaved arrogantly toward the gods, Zeus cut them in half, right down the middle, then sewed skin and shifted parts to result in mortals as we now know them.

    4. Each half now yearns for its other half: Some desire the other sex for completion, some desire the same sex, depending on how each was configured before the split.

E. Agathon, the poet, delivers a beautiful and almost poetic speech of praise.

F. The philosophical core of the dialogue comes in Socrates's speech, which he attributes to a woman named Diotima, invented for this speech.

    1. Socrates starts by saying that he had misunderstood the assignment—he thought the idea was to tell the truth about love, not just make pretty statements.

    2. He goes on to say that Diotima had instructed him in the ways of love, telling him how love of a single example of physical beauty on Earth can lead to the philosophical love of the eternal forms of beauty, truth, and goodness.

3. There is a progression of love toward those forms, moving upward, as on the steps of a ladder. The progression goes as follows: Love of a single body leads to recognition of the beauty of all bodies, then to an appreciation of the greater beauty of the soul, and from there, to an apprehension of true, unchanging beauty.

4. Thus, love of beauty in this world is a necessary stepping stone toward understanding the eternal form of beauty.

V. At this philosophical climax, there is a commotion at the door and a very drunk Alcibiades crashes the party.

A. Invited to join in, he offers a eulogy, not of love, but of Socrates.

B. Alcibiades, one of the most sought-after youths in Athens, had been so taken by Socrates's wisdom that he had taken on the role of lover, rather than beloved, with the older (and physically unattractive) Socrates.

C. Socrates, though, was not interested in Alcibiades's advances, suggesting that Alcibiades was too much interested in the physical world.

D. After Alcibiades's eulogy, the speechmaking gives way to uproarious drinking.

VI. We can understand the dialogue as a whole as demonstrating in a variety of ways the procession toward ideal beauty that Socrates describes in his speech.

A. First, in order to get at the truth of what happened at the symposium, we have to work through layers of opinion, hearsay, and retelling.

B. And there is a similar progression in each of the earlier speeches. There is something of value in each one, but each is just an imperfect approximation of what love really is or how love can be so centrally important in a philosophical life.

C. The speech of Socrates, from Diotima, then outlines that progression toward beauty explicitly.

D. Alcibiades's speech, describing the behavior of Socrates, gives us a concrete example of what we've been discussing in the abstract.

E. Plato gives us no clear answers, but he does give us plenty of hints and leaves the answers sufficiently unclear to make us continue reading the dialogue, talking about it, and asking about what happened at that famous dinner party at Agathon's.

Essential Reading:

Plato, *Symposium*.

Supplementary Reading:

Corrigan and Glazov-Corrigan, *Plato's Dialectic at Play: Argument, Structure, and Myth in the Symposium*.

Rutherford, *The Art of Plato: Ten Essays in Platonic Interpretation*, chapter 7.

Stokes, *Plato's Socratic Conversations: Drama and Dialectic in Three Dialogues*, chapter 3.

Questions to Consider:

1. Plato takes great care to characterize the participants in this dialogue, giving each an individual personality. Does that make any difference in the interpretation of what they say?

2. The dramatic date of the *Symposium* is in 416, days after Agathon's first victory and just before the Sicilian expedition and Alcibiades's troubles. Athenian readers of this dialogue would have known all that. Should this historical information make a difference in our interpretation of the dialogue?

Lecture Thirty-One
Plato II—*Symposium*

Welcome back. In the last lecture: We introduced Plato; the genre of the philosophical dialogue; and we discussed what the dialogues say about poetry and how they use poetry. The next two lectures take us through two of Plato's most polished literary masterpieces, two of those philosophical dialogues in particular: the *Symposium* in this lecture and *Phaedrus* in the next.

The *Symposium* is the story, told many years after the fact, of a celebratory party at which each member of the party agrees to deliver a speech in honor of love. Now philosophers who are not so interested in the literary aspects of Plato's dialogues often look only at one speech in the *Symposium*, namely, the one delivered by Socrates. They look there for some sort of kernel of philosophical truth within the dialogue. We, on the other hand, are going to take into consideration not only all the other speeches, but also the introductory framing of the party, and also the riotous and drunken interruption near the end of the dialogue by Alcibiades—our friend from Thucydides. We'll see that distinctions that are sometimes drawn between philosophical and literary parts of the dialogue are really difficult to draw, and that the dialogue, in fact, is best read as a seamless whole—the seamless whole that Plato has, in fact, given us.

The dialogue begins with a man named Apollodorus—this is one of Socrates's followers—in mid-conversation with an unnamed character. He's asked Apollodorus a question; the dialogue begins with Apollodorus answering that. This unnamed character has asked Apollodorus to describe to him what happened at the famous party, the symposium at the house of the tragic playwright Agathon. Apollodorus answers and says well, someone else had recently asked him the same question; somebody who had actually chased him down the street in his eagerness to know, and Apollodorus now recounts the details of that retelling, when he had told it to that earlier person. Apollodorus himself was not at the party, but he did hear about the party from Aristodemus, another of Socrates's circle, and this is a person who was in fact there. A man named Phoenix has also been talking about this party, also having heard details from Aristodemus. Apollodorus says that he—after hearing from Phoenix, after hearing from Aristodemus—he himself checked details of the story with Socrates himself.

So Apollodorus proceeds to tell the story of the symposium, as he heard it from Aristodemus. Most of the dialogue, then, is filled with reminders of its second-hand nature: He said that, he said that, indirect discourse and so on. Now why, we might ask, is there so much of this in the way of introduction? So much emphasis on the telling, the retelling, all this confusing discussion of what happened at the party itself, and who was there, and who can tell us about it? We might well sympathize at this point with those who just skip this part and get right into what they call the philosophical meat of the dialogue. But that's not what Plato does; he gives us this introduction. We do him an injustice if we don't try to understand the dialogue as he presents it to us. All indications suggest that Plato was a man in command of his prose style—in fact, there are lots of people who will learn Greek simply so that they can have direct access to Plato's Greek prose. He also seems to be well in command of the construction of his dialogues. So it seems only reasonable that we trust Plato not to have made parts of his dialogues disposable.

Let's look back at that introduction. One result of this introductory material is that even before the account of the party itself begins, we have the sense that it is important, interesting to many people, and well worth attending to. Everyone is talking about this symposium and wants to know about it. To go back for a moment to that unnamed character outside of the dialogue who first starts asking the questions. Why does Plato put him in there? Well, who are we but unnamed characters outside of the dialogue? We, too, are asking questions, wanting to learn what happened at that party.

But at the same time—another possible explanation for this long and involved introduction—at the same time we do learn from Apollodorus that the party took place long ago, when he was still a child, and that the version of it we will hear has been filtered through several tellings and retellings. We might recall, at this point, the discussion of art, literature, poetry in the *Republic*, that discussion where all of that type of art was seen as an imitation of an imitation. Well, this introduction takes us even further from the actuality of the dinner party, and it should arouse our critical sensibilities, warn us that we have to approach this dialogue carefully, thoughtfully.

Now before we move further into the dialogue, it will help to pause here for a brief introduction to two aspects of Athenian culture that are taken for granted in the dialogue: those two are the symposium as a social event and some aspects of Athenian sexual practice. First the symposium: We talked briefly about this in our discussion of lyric poetry, as a venue for the performance of some of those poems. In short, the symposium was a social gathering for aristocratic males, elite males, we might say. The events at the symposium included food, drink, and entertainment of various sorts, sometimes provided by the so-called flute girls. Typically, the men at these parties reclined on couches, two to a couch. We'll see in the *Symposium* of Plato that it's important who is lying where. Strict protocols were followed, as the host, or someone appointed in his place, would decide how much and how quickly the guests would drink and also what other sorts of events would take place at the symposium. We'll see some discussion of that protocol in Plato's *Symposium*. These symposia seem to have been important venues, though, not only for relaxation and entertainment, but also for solidifying and passing along aristocratic values in an increasingly democratic Athens. After all, in Athens everyone could go to the assembly, but the symposium was a decidedly upper-class affair with a relatively closed group of people attending.

Now among the shared values of this Athenian elite were certain sexual practices, attitudes towards sexual practices. For example, it was not uncommon for aristocratic Athenian males of the 5th century to form erotic attachments with boys. It was viewed as natural and traditional for an Athenian male to seek sexual gratification from a younger male; and in turn for the younger male to yield to those approaches, in return for the attention, the admiration, and social standing given him by the older male. Now it's somewhat misleading to refer to these relationships—or to these men—as homosexual, for at least two reasons. One is the fact that the same men, the ones involved in these relationships, also married women and raised children. Maybe you're thinking, well, it's just for the social standing, for the outside appearance. But also, distinct from these relationships, there are references to certain few men and certain few relationships that seem homosexual in a modern sense; only in those few do we see a clear preference, over an extended period, for same-sex relations.

But for the more widespread male relationships, there is some terminology that might prove useful. The Greek terms for those involved in these relationships are usually translated as "lover" for the older male, the *erastes* in Greek; and "beloved" for the younger, the *eromenos*. Now you'll note the presence in both of those terms of the root word *eros*, for love. Most of the love discussed in the speeches here in the *Symposium*—and then again in the *Phaedrus*—in the next lecture, most of those discussions of love refer to this sort of relationship.

Back now to our symposium: This gathering took place in celebration of a dramatic victory by Agathon. We hear even before the symposium itself starts that Aristodemus arrived at the party supposedly planning to arrive with Socrates, but along the way Socrates fell into some sort of deep reverie. He simply stopped under a portico somewhere, sent Aristodemus on to the party, and Socrates was deep in thought. Well, the party started, people said, "Should we go get Socrates?" "No, no, no, this is common practice. He's thinking about something. When he finishes, he'll arrive." And sure enough, after some time Socrates did show up at this party. Remember that, we'll get back to it later.

Now all of the guests at the party agree that they're still queasy from the previous night's drinking, when they had actually started the celebration with Agathon. All of them are queasy except for Socrates, who can take any amount of liquor, any amount of alcohol, and not be bothered the least. But all of the others decide that instead of drinking at this party, they'll go around the room, each of them in turn giving a speech on the god Eros, the personification of love. That's the protocol for this symposium. That's what they decide to do instead of drinking. A great supporter of that idea is one of the guests at this party, Eryximachus, a medical man, who agrees, yes, this is by far the best thing we could do. Too much drink is not good for a person. We'll see his speech in a few minutes. In fact I'll summarize the speeches of all of these participants at various lengths; each of them is at least worth mention.

Now the first speech is by a man named Phaedrus; he's a young follower of Socrates and the star of the dialogue the *Phaedrus* that we'll discuss in our next lecture. He delivers a traditional speech of praise that focuses on the lineage of Eros and the good consequences of love. He supplies many mythological examples. In light of all these examples, Phaedrus concludes, love is the most ancient of all gods, the most honored, and the most powerful in helping men gain virtue. There's nothing terribly deep here, but this speech does present us, right away, with almost all of the typical commonplaces about love.

We move on then. The report says that there were several more speeches that Aristodemus couldn't remember exactly. So we move next to a man named Pausanias. The next speech—the speech by Pausanias—is more analytical, focusing on two types of love, not just one. There is earthly love that desires only physical satisfaction, while heavenly love is long-lasting and interested in the moral well being and the improvement of all involved. Things, in other words, are more complex, more involved when we start talking about love, than Phaedrus had been suggesting in the first speech.

Next it's Aristophanes's turn to speak, but he has the hiccups. This would only happen to Aristophanes; and so he has to pass on to the next person, Eryximachus. This is our doctor. Eryximachus, this medical man who's very proud of being a medical man: first he offers Aristophanes a cure for his hiccups. What you need to do is hold your breath; and if that doesn't work trying gargling; and if that doesn't work what you need to do is take a feather and tickle your nose, because certainly if you sneeze that will take of your hiccups. So there you have it, cures for the hiccups from Plato. Eryximachus then launches into his speech and what he does is to expand Pausanias's analysis. He extends it to a general, or an even global, duality between good and bad desires. He applies this argument even further, to general scientific laws: Love plays a part in every aspect of the world, he argues, even the universe—the movement of the stars, the changing of the seasons.

By the time he's done, Aristophanes is cured. He thanks Eryximachus for the cure and now offers a very different view of love: one that brings us back down to Earth and grapples directly with the various types of human desire. Aristophanes begins: Once upon a time, there were three kinds of human beings: male, female, and a mixture of the two. Each of those beings was spherical in shape, with four arms, four legs, two faces, two sets of genitalia, and so on. But here's his description—or rather Plato's explanation, or Plato's version of Aristophanes's description:

> …the shape of each human being was completely round, with back and sides in a circle; they had four hands each, as many as legs as hands, and two faces, exactly alike, on a rounded neck. Between the two faces, which were on

opposite sides, was one head with four ears. There were two sets of sexual organs, and everything else was the way you'd imagine it from what I've told you. They walked upright, as we do now, whatever direction they wanted. And whenever they set out to run fast, they thrust out all their eight limbs, the ones they had then, and spun rapidly the way gymnasts do cartwheels, by bringing their legs around straight.

A brilliant description, but the brilliance here really is that Plato has so thoroughly captured Aristophanic style in the way he's told this. These mortals, Aristophanes goes on, behaved arrogantly toward the gods and the gods actually thought about wiping them out. But then who would offer sacrifice to the gods? Zeus came up with a great idea: Let's just cut them in half. That way it will cut them down to size a little bit, and there will also be twice as many of them to offer us sacrifices; so that's what they did, "like splitting a boiled egg with a hair," says Aristophanes. Zeus cut them right in half, right down the middle, then sewed their skin together, shifted parts around, to result in mortals as we now know them. Ever since that cutting, the story goes on, each half yearns for its other half: Some desire the other sex for completion—if there were two males in that original, they desire each other. Some look for the other sex, depending on how each was configured before the split. Here's where he describes that:

> And so, when a person meets the half that is his very own, whatever his orientation, whether it's to young men or not, then something wonderful happens: the two are struck from their senses by love, by a sense of belonging to one another, and by desire, and they don't want to be separated from one another, not even for a moment. These are the people who finish out their lives together and still cannot say what it is they want from one another. No one would think it is the intimacy of sex—that mere sex is the reason each lover takes so great and deep a joy in being with the other. It's obvious that the soul of every lover longs for something else; his soul cannot say what it is.

What each one of us really wants, he goes on, is to be welded back together with our other half. Now all of this is very silly, very typical of the fantastic plots that we encountered in Aristophanes, but at another level it's really a moving evocation of the powers of love in this world. Another thing that it does is it reduces the importance in that location of the physical sexual intimacy and talks about the yearning of a soul to be complete by connection with another person.

Next up is Agathon, the tragic poet hosting the symposium whose victory is being celebrated here. He gives us a beautifully polished, it's an almost poetic speech of praise—he demonstrates some of the rhetorical flourish that's so popular at the time. In this speech we're back at the level more or less where we began, that first speech of praise by Phaedrus. The difference is that the form of expression in this speech is so much more lofty or elevated, so much more suited to its speaker, the tragic poet.

We come now, after the speech of Agathon, to the so-called philosophical core or kernel of the dialogue in Socrates's speech. A speech that he refuses to take credit for himself, after all, Socrates claims to know nothing himself. Instead, he attributes his speech to—or his knowledge about love to—a woman named Diotima; this is apparently someone who was invented just for this purpose. Now this is a long speech, many ideas, many twists and turns, actually a dialogue between Socrates and Diotima, and I'll summarize here only parts of it.

Socrates starts, as soon as Agathon is finished, by saying that he clearly misunderstood the assignment. He, Socrates, thought the idea was to tell the truth about love, not just make pretty statements. "If you want the truth," he says, "I can do that; but I can't do what Agathon's been doing, or some of you others." He then proceeds to question Agathon, exposing some of the illogicalities, the untruths in the speech of Agathon. It's all done in a very friendly way, of course. Here we get, in this dialogue, something of the way that we can imagine Socrates would have been questioning people out on the streets of Athens: in quick, rapid-fire exchanges where he brings them to a realization of their own errors. By the time Socrates is done with this little exchange with Agathon, Agathon is just saying, "Clearly I didn't know what I was talking about." Now in an earlier dialogue, Socrates might have stopped there, with a simple demonstration that his interlocutor didn't know what he was talking about; a destruction of everyone else's argument with nothing to replace it. But here Socrates does offer something true in his view about love.

Diotima, Socrates says, had instructed him in the ways of love, telling him how love of a single example of physical beauty here on Earth can lead gradually to the philosophical love of the eternal and unchanging forms of beauty, truth, and goodness. The way she explains it, a human being will catch sight of some beautiful object, some beautiful individual here in this world. From recognition of that beauty there will than be a wider sort of understanding of beauty in all physical forms. The next step is a recognition of internal beauty— the beauty of a soul. From there, the next step is the recognition of the beauty that is eternal and everlasting. There is a progression, in other words, a progression of love toward those forms, those ideas that we've heard about. It moves upward, from the physical to this eternal and unchanging, as if on the steps of a ladder or stairs. Here's a summary of it:

> This is what it is to go aright, or be led by another, into the mystery of Love: one goes always upwards for the sake of this Beauty, starting out from beautiful things and using them like rising stairs: from one body to two and from two to all beautiful bodies, then from beautiful bodies to beautiful customs, and from customs to learning beautiful things, and from these lessons he arrives in the end at this lesson, which is learning of this very Beauty, [with a capital B in this translation] so that in the end he comes to know just what it is to be beautiful.

Thus love of beauty in this world is a necessary stepping stone, a starting point toward that highest goal: a comprehension of the eternal form of beauty.

Included in this speech is an eloquent evocation of that eternal beauty. It never changes, it never began, it never ends. It's not one thing to one person, another thing to another person. It's not in some ways ugly and in some ways beautiful. It's perfect, complete, always there, always existing. That is the goal of a philosophical life, that ideal form of beauty. And love on this earth is one of the impulses that moves us toward it.

This is a great philosophical climax, a climax of all the speeches. We expect, we might expect, the dialogue to end here. But no, there's a commotion at the door and a very drunk Alcibiades crashes the party. Now we've met Alcibiades before, this the ambitious young general who was then recalled from Sicily for his alleged involvement in smashing those statues of Hermes. The dramatic date of this dialogue, that is, the date when we imagine it took place, was before the incident with the statues, when Alcibiades was still the toast of the town, the richest, most handsome, and most promising young man in Athens, although some were suspicious of his behavior. Alcibiades is invited to join the group at Agathon's, and at first he says, what's the matter with you all? You obviously haven't been drinking enough. Here we are, deep into the night, and you're not drunk yet. Here, pour me some wine; and he drains off at one swig a huge cupful of wine and then he says here, Socrates, you do the same. Socrates of course goes along with it.

Alcibiades though is then invited to take part in the activity of the evening, namely giving a speech in praise of love. It's Eryximachus, the doctor, who reminds Alcibiades that he really shouldn't be behaving as he is. Alcibiades, though, claims that he cannot offer a eulogy on love, but what he can do is give a speech of praise of Socrates. And so that's exactly what he does, to the great embarrassment of Socrates. As Alcibiades describes him, Socrates is like one of the little statues of the god Silenus: ugly on the outside—and in fact this was a god that did look something like Socrates in most of the statuettes we've seen, bald, pug-nosed, overweight—ugly on the outside, but opening up to reveal something truly godlike within. Alcibiades has been absolutely possessed by this inner beauty of Socrates, and he proceeds to describe the effect of that love for Socrates that he has felt.

He describes, in fact, his attempts to seduce Socrates. Alcibiades first invited Socrates to the gymnasium with him, this is his response to this philosophical attraction to Socrates. First to the gymnasium, then to dinner, finally to bed: yes, here we have the most sought-after youth in Athens, who was so taken in by Socrates's wisdom that Alcibiades now plays the role of lover rather than beloved, and he's in pursuit of the older and physically unattractive Socrates. And here's how he explains that. Alcibiades is trying to get across why it is that he, the beautiful young Alcibiades, is going after Socrates.

> Well [he says] something much more painful than a snake
> has bitten me in my most sensitive part—I mean my heart, or
> my soul, or whatever you want to call it, which has been
> struck and bitten by philosophy, whose grip on young and

eager souls is much more vicious than a viper's and makes them do the most amazing things.

That's his explanation for his attraction to Socrates. Socrates, though, was not at all interested in Alcibiades's sexual advances. He declined them by suggesting that Alcibiades was too much interested in the physical world. This is all in Alcibiades's speech. He goes on then, Alcibiades does, with a memorable description of a campaign that he was on with Socrates. A description of Socrates the soldier, fighting for Athens. Socrates had an amazing resistance to the cold, wearing only his old thin cloak as around Athens, even on the coldest nights. Never wearing shoes even as they marched over ice, never bothered by hunger, able to drink them all under the table when necessary, absolutely fearless in battle, standing up to any sort of foe; and Alcibiades tells a story of one time that Socrates stood for 24 hours outside out of a tent, lost in thought—as he was for that brief time before this dinner party. In short, Alcibiades has described the many ways in which the physical world, the one we grasp with our senses, has little meaning or significance for Socrates.

After Alcibiades's eulogy, the speechmaking gives way to uproarious drinking that lasts through the night. Everyone finally passes out except Socrates, who got up and went about his business as the morning came, followed by the faithful Aristodemus.

Let's look back now, over the entire dialogue, and view it through the lens of that central, and centrally important, speech by Socrates. We can understand it as a whole as demonstrating in a variety of ways the procession toward ideal beauty that Socrates describes in that speech. That puzzling introduction to the dialogue, those layers of opinion, hearsay, and retelling. We've seen how that creates a sense of excitement and also arouses our critical sensibility. Now, we might say also that these various layers are the steps we move through in order to arrive at the kernel or the dialogue itself. In other words, the dialogue mirrors in its structure the idea that's at its center. We have to work through those layers in order to get to the meaning of the dialogue; Plato is certainly not going to spell it out for us. And there is a similar progression in each one of the earlier speeches, each one providing something valuable, all of them an imperfect approximation of what love really is. The speech of Socrates then gives us that progression, that progression toward beauty.

Finally, Alcibiades's speech, describing the behavior of Socrates, gives us a concrete example of what we've been discussing in the abstract. Alcibiades, it seems, has gotten things a little backwards. He begins with a love of the internal, the intangible, the philosophical. He falls in love with Socrates's ideas rather than with his physical body; and then tries to move from that philosophical love down the ladder, as it were, to a physical love. And it just doesn't work. Now if, as I have been suggesting, Plato is simply trying to describe in this dialogue the ways that our senses, our physical comprehension, can lead to philosophical insight, why doesn't he just say that, instead of constructing an entire dialogue that illustrates it in a variety of ways? Well, that's the same as asking why he writes philosophical dialogues at all, rather than treatises that simply set forth his ideas clearly. And the answer seems to be that he wants us to work at it. He's not going to give us simple answers. Rather he provides them within this framework, this framework of the entire dialogue, making us, too, want to read the dialogue, think about it, and find out what went on that famous dinner party at Agathon's.

In the next lecture, we move on to another dialogue on the subject of love, and other things: the *Phaedrus*.

Lecture Thirty-Two
Plato III—*Phaedrus*

Scope:

Phaedrus is another dialogue about love and rhetoric, another of Plato's acclaimed masterpieces, but this one takes place outside the walls of Athens and has only two participants, Socrates and his young admirer Phaedrus. Again, there is a clearly philosophical core within one of Socrates's two speeches about love, but the dialogue contains much besides that: an introduction to the setting and the speakers, a speech attributed to the orator Lysias and Socrates's speech in response to that, and a large section of the dialogue devoted to an analysis of rhetoric. Since antiquity, readers who look for philosophical precision have been puzzled by the apparent lack of unity in the dialogue. Here, we examine the dialogue with an eye toward the characters involved. The twists and turns reveal Socrates's subtle and careful attempts to engage his interlocutor—and, by extension, Plato's readers—in a more serious study of philosophy.

Outline

I. *Phaedrus*, a dialogue between Socrates and his young admirer Phaedrus, takes place outside the walls of Athens in a pastoral setting. Like the *Symposium*, it begins with a seemingly non-philosophical conversation that nonetheless adds to the argument.

   A. In the first sentence, Socrates asks Phaedrus where he is coming from and where he is going.

      1. These simple questions become meaningful in light of the rest of dialogue. In fact, an old story suggests that Plato did indeed take great care with the opening words of his dialogues.

      2. We might interpret Socrates's greeting as a question about Phaedrus's educational progress: He is coming from the study of rhetoric with the orator Lysias and, in the course of this dialogue, moving toward the study of

philosophy with Socrates.

    B. It is also significant that the two leave the city, moving away from the setting of the morning's rhetoric and toward a pastoral setting filled with the inspiration of rural deities. This setting is odd, however, for two reasons.

        1. Socrates famously never liked to leave Athens, except on military service for the city.

        2. Socrates gladly joins Phaedrus in his rhetorical exercises, but Socrates is almost consistently hostile toward the orators of his day and to the study of rhetoric.

II. The first half of the dialogue consists of three speeches on the subject of love.

    A. Phaedrus reads the first one, written by Lysias, from a manuscript he has brought with him in order to practice and memorize the speech.

        1. Lysias's speech, spoken by one who claims he is not in love, argues that it is better for a beloved to yield to a non-lover than to a lover.

        2. In a list of examples, Lysias points out the dangerous emotions that drive a lover; better by far to become involved with one who is rational and in control of himself.

    B. Socrates responds to this argument for calm rationality by saying that watching Phaedrus deliver it has driven him into an ecstatic frenzy.

    C. Socrates then claims that voices of past authors are welling up within him, encouraging him to deliver a better speech on the same subject.

        1. He begins by breaking the deceit: The speaker is not really a non-lover but a lover trying to get a jump on the competition by posing as a non-lover.

        2. His speech gets at the same point as Lysias's: It is dangerous for a beloved to become involved with a lover.

        3. But the presentation is far better organized and systematic, beginning with a definition of love and moving through a series of clear points.

D. As they prepare to go back to Athens, Socrates's familiar divine sign prevents him from returning to the city.

    1. This divine sign never compels Socrates toward any sort of activity but often checks or stops him when he's heading in the wrong direction.

    2. The sign sits oddly with his usually rational behavior but seems at home in this setting.

E. Socrates feels compelled to deliver another speech, to make up for the impiety in what he has just said. He must make amends to love, a divine force, for presenting it in such a negative light.

    1. This speech is often seen as the philosophical core of the dialogue, in the midst of much that can be ignored.

    2. Madness, he begins, can be a blessing when it comes from the gods; the task is to prove that love is one form of that divine madness.

    3. He then describes the soul, comparing it to a charioteer controlling two horses, one good and one bad. This is another famous use of story or analogy, rather than argument.

    4. The goal of the chariot-soul is to fly upward (fighting the earthbound tendencies of the bad horse) to the regions beyond the heavens, where the soul can gaze upon and contemplate the eternal forms.

    5. As in the *Symposium*, when the soul sees beauty in this world, that sight stirs recollection of the true and eternal beauty beyond the heavens and brings the soul closer to that true beauty.

    6. To summarize, as in the *Symposium*, love is an important part of the philosophical life, providing the first impulse for a journey toward the eternal truths.

F. Thus, in his first speech, Socrates beat Lysias at his own game and, in his second, pointed out the shortcomings of Lysias's views and offered in their place the more fulfilling pursuit of truth in its ideal form. In short, he has offered philosophy in the place of rhetoric.

    1. The dialogue could end here, with Socrates's prayer that Phaedrus become a student of philosophy rather than rhetoric.

    2. But Phaedrus does not get it and predicts that Lysias will now have to compose a speech on the new theme that Socrates has developed.

III. Thus, the conversation continues, with the talk turning to rhetoric and the mechanics of a good speech as taught by the Sophists and the handbooks.

    A. It is at this point that many commentators think the dialogue falls apart, losing its focus, but in fact, Socrates is following in the pedagogical direction required by Phaedrus's limitations.

    B. Socrates knows all the technical treatises and rules of rhetoric, as he knew how to compose a speech in Lysianic style. The two look back over the speeches they have delivered, analyzing them according to these various rules, and the Platonic speech in Lysias's style really takes a beating.

    C. But Socrates also knows a better method of communication and persuasion.

        1. The speaker must first know the truth about the subject.

        2. It is also essential to understand thoroughly the audience and the type of speech that will most effectively reach that audience.

        3. In fact, all through this dialogue, we have been watching Socrates apply these methods in his conversation with Phaedrus: First, he corrected what Lysias (and he himself) had been saying about love; then, he altered his presentation, from speeches to discussion of speeches, in order to reach Phaedrus.

IV. The last subject raised in this conversation is the value of writing. This comes in a story Socrates tells about the invention of writing in Egypt.

    A. When the Egyptian god Theuth presented to the king Thamus the art of writing, the king pointed out its faults.

    B. Socrates is once again reverting to a story, rather than argument, to make his point. The section on writing thus serves as a summation of Socrates's attempts to bring

Phaedrus to the study of philosophy.

1. Lysias, represented in this dialogue by his written speech, cannot address the particular needs of Phaedrus. At best, Phaedrus will memorize the speech, thereby internalizing someone else's ideas—and not very good ones at that.

2. Socrates, on the other hand, has revealed a flexibility of both thought and presentation, changing his conversational methods to suit the needs and limitations of Phaedrus.

3. We might say that as the spoken word is superior to the written, so is Socrates's philosophy superior to the rhetoric of Lysias.

4. We don't know how things will turn out, but the two men leave together, with Phaedrus emphasizing their friendship.

Essential Reading:

Plato, *Phaedrus*.

Supplementary Reading:

Dodds, *The Greeks and the Irrational*, chapter 3.

Rutherford, *The Art of Plato: Ten Essays in Platonic Interpretation*, chapter 9.

Schenker, "The Strangeness of the *Phaedrus*."

Questions to Consider:

1. Since antiquity, commentators have argued about whether this is a dialogue about love, about rhetoric, or about something else. How would you summarize what it is about? On what basis?

2. Socrates's long second speech deserves careful scrutiny. In what way does the rest of the dialogue act out the themes and ideas raised in it?

Lecture Thirty-Two
Plato III—*Phaedrus*

Welcome back. In our last lecture, we discussed Plato's *Symposium* and saw how his construction of the various parts of the dialogue contributed to what we might call a philosophical meaning within it. In this lecture, we turn to another dialogue, the *Phaedrus*—which like the *Symposium* is a Middle Period dialogue, and like the *Symposium* deals with love and rhetoric. It's another of Plato's acclaimed masterpieces. This one, though, the *Phaedrus,* takes place outside the walls of Athens, in a pastoral setting, and it has only two participants—Socrates and his young admirer friend, Phaedrus.

As in the *Symposium*, here in this dialogue there is a clearly philosophical core within one of Socrates's two speeches about love. But the dialogue also contains much more. There is an important introduction to the setting and the speakers. There's a speech attributed to the orator Lysias, and Socrates's speech in response to that one; and there's a large section of the dialogue devoted to an analysis of rhetoric, a more technical analysis. Finally there's a discussion of the shortcomings of the written word.

Since antiquity, readers of this dialogue have been puzzled by its apparent lack of unity, especially since within this dialogue itself there's one of Plato's clearest discussions of the need for unity within a work of literature. All recognize this dialogue as a pleasant conversation, but some think it's not much more than that. What is the dialogue about? Here we examine this dialogue with an eye toward the characters involved. We'll see that the twists and turns reveal Socrates's subtle and careful attempts to engage his interlocutor—that is, Phaedrus, and by extension all of us—in a more serious study of philosophy.

Phaedrus, like the *Symposium*, begins with a seemingly non-philosophical conversation that nonetheless adds to the argument, adds to the whole. The dialogue begins with Socrates greeting his young friend Phaedrus, and asking him two brief questions: Where have you been, and where are you going? Now these are simple questions, nothing to attract particular attention, but they do or can become meaningful in light of the rest of the dialogue. We do, in fact, have o old story that suggests that Plato took particular care in writing the opening of his dialogues. It was said that Plato went through multiple drafts of the opening of his dialogue the *Republic*, writing and rewriting just the first few words of that dialogue until he had them exactly as he wanted them. In this case, we might interpret Socrates's greeting as questions about Phaedrus's educational progress: As we learn in the course of the dialogue, Phaedrus is coming from the study of rhetoric with the orator Lysias and, if only gradually and imperfectly, moving toward the study of philosophy with Socrates.

But Phaedrus gives a more concrete answer to those questions. He's spent the morning in the city listening to a speech by Lysias, and he's now going outside the city walls to walk and practice the speech. He's hoping to learn it by heart. Now this man Lysias, as we'll see in the next lecture, was one of the leading orators of the day. Socrates gladly joins Phaedrus in his walk in the country, and in his rhetorical exercises—claiming that he, too, just like Phaedrus, is passionate about rhetoric.

Now this is odd, in at least two ways: first of all, Socrates famously never liked to leave the city of Athens except when on military service for Athens; after all, his business was with people, questioning, conversing, trying to come up with answers to these problems that he was always posing. His business was not with trees, pastures, cool springs; they couldn't answer him. But here Socrates goes on at some length about the particular beauties of the walk that they take outside the walls. He mentions details about the rustic spot where they decide to stop and talk. They're under a plane tree, with a spring running under it; the air is fresh, and it echoes with the sounds of the cicada's song. Also, it turns out that this shady pastoral setting is dedicated to a river god, and it has a shrine set up there to this river god and to the nymphs who inhabit this area. A setting filled with the inspiration of rural deities. Why, we might ask, this emphasis on the setting, and its difference from the city, where all the other dialogues take place? Hold on to that thought. Second, the second oddity about Socrates here: In other dialogues by Plato, Socrates is almost consistently hostile toward the orators of the day and indeed to the study of rhetoric. Why does he express such a passion for speeches and the speech of Lysias here? Well, keep those questions in mind. We'll return to them.

Socrates and Phaedrus find their shady spot in the country and they start in on the speeches. There's going to be a total of three: three speeches in this dialogue. The first delivered by Phaedrus from Lysias's text, and the next two by Socrates. In order to practice Lysias's speech, Phaedrus has brought with him into the country, a written copy of that speech. He hoped to practice it, in an attempt to memorize it without looking at the text, but, since the text is present and Socrates catches a glimpse of it, Socrates asks him to read it out, word for word.

This speech, Lysias's speech, is a rhetorical exercise not intended for the courtroom, not for the assembly, but simply a showcase for his rhetorical talents. It's a speech of seduction, directed to a boy, and spoken by a man who claims that he's not in love with the boy but still wants to seduce him. The argument, and here's the cleverness of it all, Phaedrus says, the argument is that it's better for the boy to yield his favors to a non-lover rather than to a lover. In a list of disjointed examples, Lysias's speech, as read by Phaedrus, points out the dangerous emotions that drive a lover, all these emotions that are to be avoided if this boy would only yield to one who doesn't love him.

Is this really a speech written by Lysias that Plato has incorporated into this dialogue? Or is it a parody of Lysias written by Plato? We just don't know; opinions differ. The style is so close to what we see in other speeches by Lysias; and as we've seen, though, from Aristophanes's speech in the *Symposium*, Plato is able to mimic the style of other authors within his dialogues. In any event, the speech argues that it's far better to become involved with a man who is completely rational and in control of himself, rather than one who has given way to the emotions of love.

When Phaedrus finishes the speech, he turns to Socrates and asks what he thinks of it. "How does the speech strike you, Socrates? Don't you think it's simply superb—especially in its choice of words?" And Socrates answers:

> It's a miracle, my friend; I'm in ecstasy. And it's all your doing, Phaedrus. I was looking at you while you were reading and it seemed to me the speech had made you radiant with delight; and since I believe you understand these matters better than I do, I followed your lead. And following you I shared your Bacchic frenzy.

Socrates, in other words, responds to this argument for calm rationality by saying that watching Phaedrus deliver it has driven him into an ecstatic frenzy. Even Phaedrus is aware of the irony in that comment. But, of course, Socrates continues, the speech hardly does justice to its subject. In fact, Socrates says, he himself knows that he can do better on the same subject. Not because he has any rhetorical skill, no, he claims no knowledge: but because he feels voices of past authors welling up within him, voices encouraging him to deliver a better speech on the same subject. Later, he'll say that he was also inspired by the local deities of this rustic spot and even by the presence of Phaedrus. No, Socrates takes no credit for this speech, and he even emphasizes that fact by covering his head, as if in shame, as he delivers the speech. He's going to disown the speech even further very soon.

In the speech itself, Socrates begins by breaking through the fundamental deceit in Lysias's speech. The speaker who is trying to seduce the boy is not really a non-lover at all. Rather, he is a lover trying to get a jump on the competition by posing as a non-lover. That's what Socrates says about his speech, and by implication that's what we're to understand about Lysias as well, that all of Lysias's speech was based on a lie; at least Socrates admits that up front in his version. Socrates's speech gets at the same point as Lysias's: It is dangerous for a beloved to become involved with a lover, given all of the irrationality and problems brought on by love. The difference, though, is that in this speech the presentation is far better: far better organized, far more systematic. It begins with a definition of love and then moves through a series of clear points that build on each other toward the conclusion. Phaedrus likes this speech, but he seems unaware that it is so superior in form to Lysias's, and he wants Socrates to add more to it. "Okay, Socrates, you've talked about the dangers of yielding to a lover, but now tell me why the boy should yield to a non-lover?" No, Socrates says, he's finished, he's said his piece—on that subject at least. So it's over and they prepare to return to the city. But Socrates just then pauses, and says that he can't yet leave. Here's what he says:

> My friend, just as I was about to cross the river, the familiar divine sign came to me which, whenever it occurs, holds me back from something I'm about to do. I thought I heard a

voice coming from this very spot, forbidding me to leave until I made atonement for some offense against the gods.

This divine sign Socrates mentions is indeed familiar, showing up in several of the other dialogues. It never compels Socrates toward any sort of activity, but it often appears to check or stop him when he's heading in the wrong direction. In the *Apology*, for example, Socrates says, "You might wonder why I didn't enter into public life; well, it was because my divine sign prevented me from doing that, and I always listen to that." Now this divine sign seems an odd feature of a man who's so completely rational in most cases, completely rational and logical. In this case, though, in this setting filled with rural inspiration, and in a Socrates who seems so unusually full of passion, this sign seems right at home. So, the sign has prevented Socrates from leaving; prevented him from leaving, and he realizes that what he has to do is deliver another speech, to make up for what he's done, the impiety in what he has just said about love. He must make amends to love, a divine force, for presenting it in such a negative light.

So Socrates delivers a second speech, and this speech is the one that's usually seen as the philosophical core of the dialogue; in the midst of much that's ignored by some readers. The speech begins with madness. "Madness," Socrates says, "can be a blessing when it comes from the gods." For instance in poetry, what is poetic inspiration but a form of madness; and it's only with that inspiration that poetry is any good. What about prophecy? Those who are in touch with the gods have a sort of a madness and that enables them to see the future. The task here is to prove that love is a form of that divine madness. Now the next step in the argument, maybe somewhat surprisingly, is a brief logical argument—after this praise of madness—a logical argument for the immortality of the soul. This is one of the driest and most prosaic sections of the entire dialogue; but what it does is present a foil, a contrast with what follows, Socrates's description of the soul. Here's where he starts:

> That, then, is enough about the soul's immortality. Now here is what we must say about its structure. To describe what the soul actually is would require a very long account, altogether a task for a god in every way; but to say what it is like is humanly possible and takes less time. So let us do the second in our speech. Let us then liken the soul to the natural union

of a team of winged horses and their charioteer. The gods have horses and charioteers that are themselves all good and come from good stock besides, while everyone else has a mixture.

Yes, human beings, Socrates goes on, have a mixture in their soul. There's a charioteer, but instead of having two good and noble horses, one is good and noble and the other is just the opposite. Now this is another famous use of story or analogy within a philosophical dialogue. We might recall the similar moves in the Myth of Er in the *Republic*, or else the description of the world in the *Phaedo*. In any event, what we have here is a soul that's likened to a chariot. A charioteer with these two different horses, the goal of the chariot-soul is always to fly upward to the regions beyond the heavens, where the soul can then gaze upon and contemplate the eternal forms. This is easy for the gods: They're always flying around up there in view of these forms. For humans, with this mixed bag of horses, it's harder. The charioteer and the good horse move in that direction, upwards, but they're always held back by the earthbound tendencies of the bad horse. As in the *Symposium*, when the soul sees beauty in this world, that stirs a desire within this chariot-soul to comprehend a more lasting and eternal beauty. Here's a description of that, a couple brief sections on it:

> Now when the charioteer looks in the eye of love, his entire soul is suffused with a sense of warmth and starts to fill with tingles and the goading of desire. [Skip down a little bit.] When the charioteer sees that face, [that is, a face of physical beauty] his memory is carried back to the real nature of Beauty, and he sees it again where it stands on the sacred pedestal.

Now, since the soul is immortal, as we had argued earlier, it already knows that form of eternal, everlasting beauty. The soul has viewed that. That's why the language here is about recollection or remembering or recalling. The sight of particular and physical beauty in this world reminds the charioteer—the soul—of that real and eternal beauty.

Socrates describes in some poetic detail how this process takes place. When the soul catches sight of something beautiful in this world, it starts sweating, feeling feverish, the soul becomes warm and starts melting off a hard outer shell, allowing wings to sprout—yes, these are the wings on this chariot or the horses—these wings that will carry the soul up to see the eternal beauty. The soul aches as these wings start growing, it tingles and throbs like the gums of a teething child. It's an intense description of the feeling and we haven't heard anything like this, nothing quite like this, since we left Sappho and her description of the feelings of love. Here we find it in an author who elsewhere bans poetry from his city.

But to summarize, as in the *Symposium*, here love is an important part of the philosophical life, providing the first impulse for a journey toward eternal truths. Now let's pause before we go on with this dialogue, to look for a moment at what Socrates has done so far. In his first speech, he beat Lysias at his own game, offering a better speech—better-constructed speech—on the same subject. In his second speech—Socrates's second speech—he has effectively pointed out the shortcomings not only of Lysias's rhetorical technique but also of his fundamental argument. In the place of Lysias's sterile rationality, he has offered the more fulfilling pursuit of truth in its ideal form. In short, Socrates has offered philosophy in the place of rhetoric.

Now the dialogue could end right here, with the prayer at the end of Socrates's second speech. In that prayer, Socrates first asks the gods' forgiveness for his earlier blasphemy of love, saying that it was better for a boy to yield to a non-lover. He also prays that Phaedrus might now give up his pursuit of rhetoric and become a student of philosophy. It would be a wonderful conclusion if Phaedrus were only to agree to that: recognize the beauty of Socrates's second speech, recognize the superiority of what Socrates is explaining, describing. But even at this point it becomes evident that the subject of these first two speeches was not randomly chosen. There is a seduction of a sort going on within the dialogue itself, as Socrates is trying to seduce Phaedrus away from his fascination with Lysias and his rhetoric.

In that seduction we hope—well, with the pedagogical seduction we might call it—we think it might have worked here, and it could end here. But no, Phaedrus just does not get it. He doesn't see the superiority in what Socrates has said, and he predicts, instead, that Lysias will now have to compose a speech on the new theme that Socrates has developed. He's not ready yet—Phaedrus is not ready yet—for real understanding. All he wants is more speeches, he doesn't care what they're about. The conversation continues, with the talk turning to rhetoric, and to the mechanics of a good speech as taught by the Sophists and handbooks.

It's at this point that many commentators—ancient and modern—think that the dialogue falls apart, losing its focus; but in fact, Socrates is following in the pedagogical direction that seems to be required by Phaedrus's own limitations. He didn't get it from the speeches, so now if Phaedrus wants to talk about rhetoric, so be it. Socrates will follow that angle in trying to win Phaedrus over to philosophy. Now the talk turns to technical treatises and the rules and handbooks of rhetoric. It becomes clear that Socrates is an expert in that area as well—this is hardly surprising, since Socrates knew so well how to compose a speech in Lysianic style in response to Lysias. At this point, Socrates and Phaedrus start looking back over the speeches they've delivered, all three speeches: not talking about the subject matter, but analyzing them according to these various rules from the rulebooks. And here is where Lysias's speech—or the Platonic speech in Lysias's style—really takes a beating.

Socrates says, "Well, that speech of Lysias: so many different ideas, but just thrown out there. It's like a famous epigram, an epigram in four lines that can be organized however you want. It doesn't matter which line comes first." That was Lysias's speech. No sort of organization. No sort of unity. Now, Socrates does indeed know all these rules of rhetoric, as he demonstrates in talking about these speeches, but he also knows, as he tells Phaedrus, a better method of communication and persuasion, a true form rhetoric. He describes that to Phaedrus: The speaker—the true rhetorician—must first know the truth about his subject, and understand it thoroughly. Even if his goal is to deceive his audience, he better know his subject in and out, so that he can take his audience where he wants them to go: the subject matter first of all. Second, it's also essential that the speaker thoroughly understand his audience: the soul of his audience; the nature of his audience; what it is about his audience that will be moved, that will respond. And finally, the effective speaker has to know what sort of speech will most effectively reach that particular type of audience.

This is a lot to do. This is a difficult form of rhetoric, this true rhetoric. It's far more difficult to achieve these goals than following rules from a guidebook. It in fact begins to sound more like the study of philosophy than of rhetoric. But Socrates does lead Phaedrus to agree that this description of rhetoric is in fact better, that this is the only way to practice rhetoric appropriately. "Yes," Phaedrus says, "I agree, I see what you're talking about." In fact, all through this dialogue we've already been watching Socrates apply these very methods in his conversation with Phaedrus. First the subject matter: He corrected what Lysias and he himself had been saying about love, that's the part about knowing the truth of the subject. Then Socrates altered his presentation, moving from speeches to this discussion of speeches, in order to reach the audience that he knows so well—Phaedrus—at a level that he can understand. And he provides him with a type of speech, finally, a type of discussion, that seems to be working a little better in drawing Phaedrus along to where he wants him to be.

The last subject raised in this dialogue is about writing: the value of writing. This comes in a story that Socrates tells about the invention of writing in Egypt. The story goes that the Egyptian god Theuth presented to the Egyptian king, Thamus, a variety of his inventions, including the art of writing. He said that writing would be a great help in improving memory. King Thamus, however, disagreed, and pointed out the problems with writing. Here's one passage from this story that Socrates is telling, the response to this invention of writing:

> You have not discovered a potion for remembering, but for reminding; you provide your students with the appearance of wisdom, but not with its reality. Your invention will enable them to hear many things without being properly taught, and they will imagine that they've come to know much while for the most part they will know nothing. And they will be difficult to get along with, since they will merely appear to be wise instead of really being so.

That will be the effect of writing. In addition, something written—another problem with writing—something written always says the same thing, no matter who the audience might be. It can't change to suit the needs of the audience as, we saw, that true rhetoric should, and as Socrates has been doing in his conversation with Phaedrus. Now, we should note here that Socrates is once again reverting to a story, rather than an argument, to make his point. Phaedrus even questions that, "Where'd you get that story, Socrates?" Socrates says, "What does it matter if it makes a good point?" And it does; the point serves as an excellent summary, in a somewhat roundabout way, of Socrates's attempts throughout the dialogue to bring Phaedrus to the study of philosophy.

The references to writing here make us think immediately of Lysias, who is present in this dialogue only in the form of his written speech. That speech, in the view of this story, is seen as static, unable to change in order to address the particular needs of its audience, the needs of Phaedrus. At best, Phaedrus will memorize the speech, thereby internalizing someone else's ideas, not very good ideas at that. There will be little, if any, real communication going on, little learning. Socrates, on the other hand, has revealed a flexibility of both thought and presentation, changing his ideas as the situation demanded, and changing his conversational methods to suit the needs and the limitations of Phaedrus. Now, some are puzzled by the dismissal of writing within this dialogue that's so beautifully written. Why would Plato include something that seems to turn on itself, to turn on the beauty of the written dialogue itself? Well that's an interesting problem, but the primary reference of it seems to be to Lysias and his speech, and a commentary on the writing in that speech.

So we might say: that as the spoken word is superior to the written, so is Socrates's philosophy superior to the rhetoric of Lysias. Plato hasn't said that in so many words, but he's demonstrated it throughout the dialogue, going back as far as the introduction. I've been suggesting a duality in the dialogue, a choice that Phaedrus has between two options: between Socrates and Lysias, between philosophy and rhetoric. One way that Plato develops that duality is through a contrast between Lysias's sterile, rational, urban setting; and the vivid and lively world, the surprisingly irrational world, with Socrates out in the country. In fact, Plato seems to be overemphasizing the irrationality of Socrates throughout this dialogue as a foil to the rationality or what passes for rationality with Lysias. We don't know how things are going to turn out with Phaedrus, but the two men leave together emphasizing their friendship.

We leave Plato now, after only a brief taste of the ways that he uses literary devices, stories in his dialogues. We've said little about many of his dialogues, and I encourage you to read those. In fact, much better to read Plato than to read the things said about Plato; they're much more accessible, the dialogues themselves. In our next lecture, we will turn now to the other side of the argument, as we leave philosophy and turn to rhetoric to discuss a speech that Lysias really did write, and one by the greatest of the Greek orators, Demosthenes.

Lecture Thirty-Three
Rhetoric and Oratory

Scope:

This lecture builds, in one sense, on much that we have already discussed. From Homer onward, Greek literature reveals a deep interest in the role and power of speeches, and we begin the lecture by considering some examples from other literary genres. By the late 5th century, that interest develops into a formal rhetoric, with teachers, professional practitioners, and its own complex set of rules. We discuss that development here and look at examples from two of the leading orators from the 5th and 4th centuries: Lysias, whose courtroom speeches are not only windows into Athenian life but also models of stylistic clarity and character portrayal, and Demosthenes, the greatest of the orators, whose masterful compositions document both personal travails and political intrigue of the highest order.

Outline

I. Rhetoric and oratory are areas that we might not think of as literary, but they are essential features of all the Greek literature we have been reading.

   A. Rhetoric now carries the connotation of being contrived, artificial, or highly formalized speech, often aiming toward some unpleasant goal or intending to deceive.

   B. But in the *polis* (especially one as democratic and argumentative as Athens), verbal persuasion was essential to all political activity and, hence, became the foundation of education and a force in almost all literature.

II. Rhetoric became a subject of intense study in its own right during the 5th century, especially in democratic Athens, although origins of the study of rhetoric have been traced back to Sicily.

   A. The activity of the Sophists often centered on the teaching of rhetoric, as we have seen in Aristophanes's parody of the Sophists (*Clouds*) and in Plato's response to them (*Phaedrus*).

B. These speakers and teachers produced a great quantity of formal rulebooks about rhetoric. Plato's pupil Aristotle wrote the most influential of those handbooks. His *Rhetoric* treats such topics as the form of rhetorical argument, the psychology of the audience, and aspects of rhetorical style.

III. In his handbook, Aristotle divided all oratory into three groups based on the use or venue of the speech, and all three types are evident not only in public life but also in the literature we have already read.

    A. *Epideictic oratory*, or oratory for show, is a large category of speeches that includes those delivered at funerals, festivals, or other public occasions—outside of the courtroom and the assembly.

        1. One of the earliest examples of epideictic oratory comes from a man named Gorgias, a Sicilian who came to Athens in the late 5th century.

        2. We have already seen one of the most famous examples of epideictic speech, Pericles's funeral oration in Thucydides.

        3. The speeches in Plato's *Symposium* and *Phaedrus* all fall into the epideictic category.

    B. *Forensic oratory* is the category of courtroom speeches, for both prosecution and defense.

        1. One famous example of forensic oratory that we have mentioned in this course is Plato's version of Socrates's defense speech, the *Apology*.

        2. The forensic speeches of Lysias, working in the hyperactive Athenian legal system, are also among the best we have. Lysias wrote both for himself and for others who could afford his services.

        3. It was effective forensic oratory that Strepsiades in *The Clouds* hoped his son would learn in Socrates's Thinkery so that he could evade the claims of his creditors.

        4. We also saw forensic style in Jason's response to Medea in Euripides's play. To her accusations, he set up an elaborate and carefully organized response, as though he were in a court of law.

5. Another tragic example of forensic oratory is seen in Aeschylus's *Eumenides*, which ends in a courtroom scene.

C. The *polis* gave rise to *political* or *deliberative oratory*. In public assemblies, the success of a given agenda depended on its persuasive presentation.

   1. The 4th-century orator Demosthenes was considered in antiquity as the greatest of all orators; his political speeches warning of the dangers of King Philip of Macedon (the *Philippics*) are among his most powerful.

   2. We have seen this type of speech as far back as the assemblies in the Homeric epics.

   3. Sophocles's *Oedipus the King* begins with a deliberative speech, as the old priest seeks help in the midst of the plague.

   4. We might also recall the assembly scene reported in Euripides's *Orestes*, when we heard about several different deliberative speeches that shaded into the forensic.

   5. Thucydides's history is filled with deliberative speeches, for example, in the debates at Sparta in Book 1.

   6. For a particularly unsuccessful deliberative speech, we might turn to the attempts by Dikaiopolis in the assembly at the beginning of Aristophanes's *Acharnians*.

IV. Lysias (c. 445–c. 380) was not an Athenian but a resident alien in Athens, with somewhat reduced legal rights. Many examples survive of forensic speeches he wrote for others.

A. His prose is remarkably clear and lucid, and his narrative skill was much admired.

B. He was celebrated for his *ethopoeia*, his ability to create with his language a distinct and sympathetic persona for each of his clients.

C. His speech *On the Killing of Eratosthenes*, written between c. 400 and 380, displays these qualities well.

   1. The defendant, Euphiletus, had killed Eratosthenes for having an affair with his wife. Euphiletus argues here that the killing was not premeditated (which would be a

crime) but was a natural result of catching the adulterer in the act.

2. Euphiletus describes in vivid detail his pre-adultery domestic arrangements, leading us step-by-step toward the realization of the truth.

3. He portrays his wife as far more clever than he but saves the worst for Eratosthenes, a professional adulterer who is exposed by a former lover.

4. Finally, Euphiletus presents himself, not as a defendant, but as a righteous agent of the state, with little choice but to kill Eratosthenes, as the law demands.

5. As with almost all of these speeches, we do not know how the case turned out.

V. Demosthenes (384–322) is considered the greatest of Greek orators. Both forensic and political speeches survive from his period of intense activity, c. 355–322.

A. He was born into a wealthy family, and his earliest speeches were forensic, as he went to court to protect his inheritance from unscrupulous guardians.

B. His intense work ethic probably inspired the famous story that he practiced delivering speeches on the beach with pebbles in his mouth to build strength.

C. His style owes much to Thucydides: He gets his point across with conciseness, even as the syntax is sometimes involved, and he avoids the ease and comfort of parallel syntactical constructions.

D. In the 350s, Demosthenes became alarmed at the growing power of Philip of Macedon, the father of Alexander; starting with the *First Philippic* in 351, he delivered several speeches encouraging Greeks to unite against this threat.

1. The central theme of this and many of Demosthenes's speeches is that the Athenians must overcome their inaction and apathy, make concrete plans, and put them into action. He makes that point bluntly and forcefully early in the speech.

2. Even as he points out the dangers in Philip's approach, he emphasizes that Athenians can indeed stop him if they take immediate action.

3. He offers concrete suggestions for the deployment of forces, both mercenary and Athenian, to meet the threat.

4. In one memorable passage, he compares the previous Athenian actions to the boxing of an untrained foreigner, responding to each blow with no larger plan in mind.

5. The Athenians did not follow Demosthenes's advice, but the speech is generally recognized as a rhetorical (if not a tactical) masterpiece, and it seems to have launched Demosthenes's public career.

Essential Reading:

Lysias, *Against Eratosthenes*, and Demosthenes, *Philippic 1*.

Supplementary Reading:

Carey, "Observers of Speeches and Hearers of Action: The Athenian Orators."

Worthington, *Persuasion: Greek Rhetoric in Action*.

Questions to Consider:

1. How do you think the jury voted after hearing Lysias's speech against Eratosthenes? How would you vote?

2. Even if, as historians often argue, the advice in *Philippic 1* is patently impracticable, how could this speech have helped launch Demosthenes's public career?

Lecture Thirty-Three
Rhetoric and Oratory

Welcome back. In the previous lecture, on Plato's *Phaedrus*, we saw a less than flattering view of traditional rhetoric, at least as Socrates contrasted that rhetoric with philosophy. It's only fair, then, that we spend one lecture on rhetoric itself. This lecture builds, in one sense, on much that we have already discussed in this course. From Homer onward, the Greeks and Greek literature reveal a deep interest in the role and power of speeches of all sorts. By the late 5th century, that interest in speeches develops into a formal rhetoric, with teachers, professional practitioners, and its own complex set of rules. Aristotle, in his influential handbook on rhetoric, divides speeches into three categories, depending on the venue of their performance, and we'll look at some examples from all three categories—many of them speeches we've already encountered. Finally, we discuss examples from two of the leading orators from the 5th and 4th centuries: First, Lysias, whom we met, or at least heard about, in Plato's *Phaedrus*. His courtroom speeches are windows into Athenian life, but also models of stylistic clarity and character portrayal. Then Demosthenes, the greatest of the Greek orators, whose masterful compositions document both personal travails and hardships, and political intrigue of the highest order; we'll look at one of his *Philippics*.

Now, rhetoric and oratory is an area that we might not think of as being particularly literary, but it is indeed an essential feature of all the Greek literature we've been reading, and came to hold a place of its own, as a literary genre in its own right. In the modern world, rhetoric often carries the connotation of being contrived, artificial, highly formalized speech, often aiming toward some unpleasant goal, or intending to deceive. It's not uncommon to draw a distinction between a person's real meaning and what can be considered only rhetoric—as if the rhetoric were some form of packaging or spin. If we were to apply an adjective to the word rhetoric, we might come up with something like empty or flowery; such is the general disdain for rhetoric. Plato would probably be pleased with that.

But from the earliest times, among the Greeks public speaking was an essential part of a man's identity. Achilles, we hear in *Iliad* 9, was taught to be a speaker of words and a doer of deeds, and he does both of those in the *Iliad*. He speaks at length and we know about his deeds. The Homeric Odysseus is often judged favorably for his skill in speaking, even when he looks a little shabby from all of his travels. Later, in the world of the Greek *polis*, and especially in a *polis* as democratic and argumentative as Athens—verbal persuasion was essential to all political activity, and hence became the foundation of a man's education. Given this importance of rhetoric in everyday life, it's hardly surprising that we find so many examples of rhetoric within literature, and that rhetoric developed into a highly sophisticated genre of its own.

It was only in the 5th century, and especially in democratic Athens, that rhetoric became a subject of intense study in its own right. But the study of rhetoric, as far as we can tell, did not originate there in Athens, and was certainly not limited to Athens. Origins have been traced back to Sicily, to Syracuse in particular, in the mid-5th century; and it's not hard to see why. As we saw in Thucydides, books 6 and 7, Syracuse was a democracy, dependent, as was Athens, on public speaking. And we even had some examples of those public speeches from Syracusans in Thucydides. It seems that the practice of public speaking and the study of public speaking flourished there in Syracuse, and teachers as well as practitioners then spread from there throughout the Greek world.

These teachers of rhetoric formed the core of the group that we've talked about as Sophists. That's the group we've seen parodied in Aristophanes's *Clouds* and, at least in a subtle way, argued against in Plato's *Phaedrus*. These speakers and teachers produced a great quantity of formal rulebooks about rhetoric, each Sophist creating his own distinct manual. They're the ones that Socrates and Phaedrus talked about in the *Phaedrus*, those rulebooks or manuals. In the 4th century, one of Plato's own pupils, the philosopher Aristotle, wrote the most influential of those rhetorical handbooks. His *Rhetoric* treats such topics as: the form of rhetorical argument, the psychology of the audience, and particular aspects of rhetorical style. Not so far, in some ways, from that true rhetoric that Plato had Socrates describe in the *Phaedrus*.

In that rhetoric handbook, Aristotle divides all oratory into three groups, based on the use of the speech or its performance venue. The distinctions that he draws are somewhat arbitrary; there's going to be, or there is, some overlap among the different groups that he distinguishes, but we will use his categories here in order to give some order to our discussion. Note that all three types of speech, as they are divided up by Aristotle, appear not only in public life but also in the literature that we have already read.

Aristotle's first category is *epideictic oratory*, or oratory for show; although that seems to belittle it, it shouldn't. This is a large category of speeches that includes all those delivered at funerals, festivals, or other public occasions; as well as those delivered by an orator to showcase his abilities. This group includes pretty much any speech delivered outside of the courtroom and the assembly or some sort of situation that's meant to recreate the courtroom or assembly.

One of the earliest examples of epideictic oratory comes from a man named Gorgias. He was one of the Sicilians who came to Athens in the late 5th century, bringing with him his art of speaking and rhetoric. He appears as one of Socrates's verbal opponents on the subject of rhetoric in Plato's dialogue called *The Gorgias*. Not much of his work survives, but we know that he was highly influential. We get a taste of his highly ornate, almost poetic prose in his epideictic speech in defense of Helen. Yes, this is the Helen who went to Troy and launched the Trojan War. It wasn't her fault, argues Gorgias in this speech. Central to his argument is his emphasis on the power of persuasive speech. One way that his own speech persuades us of Helen's innocence is by arguing that she herself fell under the spell of persuasive speech, and who could blame her for that? The speech is full of rhymes, repetitions, and plays on words—a real *tour de force*.

On a more serious note, we've already seen and discussed one of the most famous examples of epideictic speeches that survive from antiquity, and the 5th century in particular: namely Pericles's Funeral Oration in Book 2 of Thucydides's *History of the Peloponnesian War*. That funeral oration is a public speech, intended, as we have seen, not only to honor the dead, but also to emphasize the cohesion of all Athenians, to reinforce their support for the ongoing war with the Spartans, and to motivate them toward even greater sacrifice. As we learn at the beginning of the speech, in Thucydides, it was a tradition for a speaker to offer such an oration, such an epideictic speech every year. This is indeed a serious use of epideictic oratory.

Also falling into this epideictic category are the speeches in praise of love from Plato's *Symposium*; all those speeches that were offered as entertainment at the party that then took on some sort of more philosophical meaning. Also those speeches from the *Phaedrus*: the one attributed to Lysias and the two responses by Socrates, all epideictic. For an author who had little good to say about rhetoric, Plato turns out to be not so bad at writing speeches himself.

Aristotle's second category of oratory is *forensic*, that is, the category of courtroom speeches, for both prosecution and defense. Now, we should remember as we talk about forensic oratory that the jury in Athens consisted of a minimum of 200 people, and could include a cast of thousands. Sources suggest that this large audience was not always polite or attentive. One famous example of forensic oratory that we've already mentioned in this course—although we haven't read it together—is Plato's version of Socrates's defense speech, the *Apology*. After delivering the speech, Plato says—and we know from other sources as well—that Socrates received the death penalty. But not because of any weakness in this speech; it's beautifully constructed from start to finish. Its technical excellence might come as something of a surprise, since Socrates starts out by saying that he's completely ignorant about public speaking. "I'm old man," he says, "and I come before you jurors for the first time in my life. I don't know how to present a speech in my defense, so please bear with me if I speak to you simply as I speak to others out in the marketplace in Athens." Well that's just a pose, then as now, it's a ploy to win audience support: Unaccustomed as I am to public speaking … and it's a pose that reveals something about audience feeling—or expectations of audience feeling—toward professional speakers. It suggests that the audience, the jurors in this case, are not going to want to hear from somebody who is polished and professional.

The forensic speeches of Lysias, working in that hyperactive Athenian legal system, are among the best we have, and we'll look closely at one example of those in a few minutes. Lysias wrote these speeches both for himself but more often for others who could afford to pay for his services. Other forensic oratory: It was in Aristophanes's *Clouds* that we saw the teaching of forensic oratory, that's what Strepsiades hoped his son would learn in Socrates's Thinkery, so that in a courtroom he could talk his way out of the claims of all of his creditors. We also saw forensic style in Jason's response to Medea in Euripides's play. To her livid and highly emotional accusations, Jason set up an elaborate and carefully organized response, as though he were in a court of law. One other tragic example of forensic oratory, Aeschylus's *Eumenides*; that ends with that courtroom scene, not long speeches, but there is Apollo arguing for the innocence of Orestes. What does he do? Special pleading, particular arguments—and they work.

Aristotle's third category is *political* or *deliberative oratory*: speeches for the assembly. This was a type of rhetoric particularly well suited to the *polis* and to the public assemblies, where the success of a given agenda depended on its persuasive presentation. Demosthenes, an Athenian from the 4ᵗʰ century, was considered in antiquity as the greatest of all orators. I've already said that a few times; everybody else says it, too. His *Philippics*, political speeches warning of the dangers of King Philip II of Macedon, are among his most powerful, and we'll look at one of those in a few minutes. Within literary contexts, we have seen examples of this type of speech as far back as the assemblies in the Homeric epics. We might think of Agamemnon addressing the troops, a sort of an assembly there, in *Iliad* 2; or Telemachus, coming of age early in the *Odyssey*, addressing the people of Ithaca. Sophocles's play *Oedipus the King* begins with a deliberative speech, as the old priest makes a public plea for help in the midst of the plague. We might also recall the assembly scene that was reported in Euripides's play *Orestes*. We heard there about several different deliberative speeches that really shaded into the forensic, as the city tried to decide how to deal with Orestes. There we see a good example of the overlap—the possible overlap—between categories.

Thucydides's history is filled with deliberative speeches, as, for example, in the debates at Sparta in Book 1, where we hear the many arguments for and against war with Athens. In the Melian dialogue from Thucydides's Book 5, we don't have speeches. We don't have these deliberative speeches, we have a dialogue, and it was particularly because the Melians recognized the persuasive ability of the Athenians. Once let them into the assembly giving a speech and everybody is going to yield to them; no, let's just meet their ambassadors and have a dialogue. For a particularly unsuccessful deliberative speech, we might turn to the attempts by Dikaiopolis in the assembly at the beginning of Aristophanes's *Acharnians*.

Now, all of these are just a few examples of each of Aristotle's types of oratory, examples that I hope give some sense of the prevalence and the widespread use of rhetoric in its many manifestations. Let's move on now to a slightly closer look at two orators and their works, Lysias and Demosthenes.

Lysias, who was born around 445, died around 380, was not an Athenian citizen but a resident alien in Athens with somewhat reduced legal rights. Many examples survive of his forensic speeches most of which he wrote for others. The hallmark of Lysias's style is clarity and lucidity; a style that was evident in his epideictic speech in the *Phaedrus*. In his forensic speeches, his narrative skill also was much admired. Another of his strengths, an important one for a forensic orator, was his ability to create convincing character portraits in his speeches. The Greeks called this creation of character *ethopoèia*, and Lysias was a master, able to create with his language a distinct and sympathetic persona—if he wanted to—for each one of his clients.

His speech, the one we're going to look at here, is *On the Killing of Eratosthenes*. This was written sometime between 400 and 380, and it displays these various qualities well. Here's the background to the case: The defendant is named Euphiletus, and he has hired Lysias to write a speech in his defense. Euphiletus, we learn from the speech, had killed a man named Eratosthenes for having an affair with his wife. It was not illegal in Athens to kill an adulterer caught in the act, but it seems that Eratosthenes's family has brought charges against Euphiletus, claiming that the killing was premeditated, maybe just using this charge of adultery as pretext. That it was not in fact an act of passion. To get off, Euphiletus has to convince the jury that the killing of Eratosthenes was not premeditated.

So the speech begins with a beautiful narrative section. Euphiletus describes in vivid detail his pre-adultery domestic arrangements, leading us step by step toward his realization of the truth, the truth of what was really going on. In a passage that's valuable for reconstructing domestic life, Euphiletus tells us that when he first married, yes, he took proper care of his wife. He was suspicious of her, as any good husband should be, but once their child was born and she proved herself a good wife, he started allowing her more freedom. Trouble really began, though, at a funeral of a family member. This is one of the few occasions when an Athenian woman of certain rank was allowed to be out in public. His wife was out in public and she was seen by Eratosthenes, and that's when the seduction began—this he finds out later. He tells us in this narrative at the beginning of the speech that he and his wife live in a small house, with the women living upstairs and the men living downstairs. Of course, wherever the husband is, that's where the wife will be, but that's the general organization of the household. Here is how he describes a change in that household:

> After the birth of my child, his mother nursed him; but I did not want her to run the risk of going downstairs every time she had to give him a bath, so I myself took over the upper storey, and let the women have the ground floor. And so it came about that by this time it was quite customary for my wife often to go downstairs and sleep with the child, so that she could give him the breast and stop him from crying. This went on for a long while, and I had not the slightest suspicion. On the contrary, I was in such a fool's paradise that I believed my wife to be the chastest woman in all the city.

This is a middle-class life of domestic bliss that Euphiletus is describing here. We don't know what his life was really like, but that's the persona, the character, that Lysias is creating here. Euphiletus, poor Euphiletus, just a regular guy; a person who trusts his wife. It could be any one of us. One night, his wife went downstairs to take care of the baby, responding to the baby's cries. Euphiletus tells us in this narrative that later he found out what was going on. The nurse would actually pinch the baby to make it cry whenever this adulterer Eratosthenes was on the scene. So the baby starts crying, the wife goes downstairs, but as she's leaving this one time, Euphiletus tells us, she started teasing her husband Euphiletus, saying, "Now I'm going to go downstairs, but I know what you're going to do, start fooling around with the maid like the last time." As she laughs going out the door, she locks that door, making sure that her husband won't get out to fool around with the help. But she has other plans really. That night, Euphiletus tells us, he heard an unusual amount of activity coming from downstairs. His wife had an explanation for it, but Euphiletus is beginning to have his doubts. As he says:

> But it did seem to me, members of the jury, that she had done up her face with cosmetics, in spite of the fact that her

brother had died only a month before. Still, even so, I said nothing about it.

After some time, as the narrative goes on, Euphiletus tells us that an old woman, sent by Eratosthenes's previous mistress, came to him and told him everything about what was going on with his wife. It turns out, as we hear from this, that Euphiletus's wife is far more clever than her husband; such is Lysias's character portrayal of her. But the real villain in this story is Eratosthenes, a professional adulterer, who is exposed in this case by a former lover. Euphiletus now, finally, put together all the pieces. He forced one of his serving women to admit her role in the affair, and she then agreed to tell him when Eratosthenes was next in the house.

He came back, and when Eratosthenes arrived, the servant told Euphiletus. He went out, rounded up friends, and they burst into the bedroom to find the naked Eratosthenes with the wife of Euphiletus. On the spot, Euphiletus accused Eratosthenes of his crime, presenting himself in this speech not as a defendant, on trial for murder, but rather as a righteous agent of the state: Eratosthenes is the guilty one and Euphiletus has little choice but to kill Eratosthenes, as the law demands. Here's what he says—he accused Eratosthenes, and here is what happens next:

> He answered that he admitted his guilt; but he begged and besought me not to kill him—to accept a money-payment instead. But I replied, "It is not I who shall be killing you, but the law of the State, which you, in transgressing, have valued less highly than your own pleasures. You have preferred to commit this great crime against my wife and my children, rather than to obey the law and be of decent behavior." Thus, members of the jury, this man met the fate which the laws prescribe for wrong-doers of his kind.

The speech continues with a reading out of the pertinent laws, particularly about the right to kill an adulterer, and with Euphiletus's argument that he was simply obeying that law. Now, we don't have the speech of prosecution, the speech against this, and, as with almost all of these speeches, we don't know how the case turned out. We can imagine what Eratosthenes's family might have argued, it's hinted at in some of the speech: that Euphiletus had a grudge against Eratosthenes and tried to set him up in some way, bringing him to the house to kill him, making it look like an act of passion. But we just don't know. On Euphiletus's side is Lysias's vivid and sympathetic portrayal of him as a loyal and loving husband, betrayed by his conniving wife and this serial adulterer.

Let's turn now to Demosthenes, who lived from 384 to 322. Widely considered, as I've said, the greatest of Greek orators, and both forensic and political speeches survive from his period of intense activity from about 355–322. Demosthenes was born into a wealthy family, and his earliest speeches were forensic, as he went to court to protect his inheritance from unscrupulous guardians. Demosthenes's notoriously intense work ethic probably inspired the famous story that he practiced delivering his speeches on the beach with pebbles stuffed into his mouth, in order to build up strength of delivery. Unlike the clear and lucid style of Lysias, the style of Demosthenes owes much to Thucydides. He gets his point across with conciseness, even as the syntax is sometimes convoluted and involved, and he avoids parallel constructions wherever possible.

In the 350s, Demosthenes became alarmed at the growing power of Philip II of Macedon, the father of Alexander the Great. Athens was officially at war with Philip starting in 357, but there had been no concerted effort to stop his advances in Greece. So in 351, Demosthenes delivered the first of several speeches against Philip. These were called the *Philippics*, encouraging Greeks to unite against this threat. Let's look briefly at the *First Philippic*.

Demosthenes begins by apologizing for his youth; or rather his lack of experience, for not waiting to let others speak first, but this is a matter of utmost importance. The central theme of this and many of Demosthenes's speeches is that the Athenians must overcome their inaction and apathy, make concrete plans, and put them into action. He makes that point bluntly and forcefully. After talking about the aggression of Philip, then he directly addresses those in the assembly. Here's a section from it.

> Now, if you too, men of Athens, are willing to adopt a similar way of thinking now—even if you were not before— and if each of you stands ready to act where he is needed and can provide useful service to the city, casting off all pretense of incapacity, the man of means by paying the war-tax, the man of military age by serving—to put it all together in simple terms, if you are willing to become your own masters

and stop expecting that each of you can do nothing himself and his neighbor will do everything for him, then you will get back what is yours, God willing; you will recover what you have lost through neglect; and you will punish Phillip.

As Demosthenes goes on, even as he points out the dangers in Philip's approach, he emphasizes that Athens can indeed stop Phillip if the Athenians were to take action now. He offers a few concrete suggestions for the deployment of forces and some economic measures as well. But the importance is that Athens must take some sort of action. In one memorable passage, Demosthenes compares all previous Athenian actions against Phillip to the boxing of an untrained foreigner, responding to each blow as it falls.

> You fight Phillip exactly as barbarians box. When one of them takes a punch, he always feels for the blow, and if you hit somewhere else, there go his hands; as for blocking or looking you in the eye, he does not know how and does not want to. You do the same thing. If you hear that Phillip is in the Chersonese, you vote to send aid there; if he's at Thermopylae, there; if he's somewhere else, you run at his heels up and down, taking your orders from him. On your own, you have not come up with a single useful plan for the war…

Demosthenes closes this speech by saying that he might not be popular for what he's said, but that he has to say it. In fact, the Athenians did not follow any of Demosthenes's advice, but this speech is still generally recognized as a rhetorical, if not a tactical, masterpiece, and it seems to have launched Demosthenes's public career.

Now what I've given you here are some few examples from all of Greek rhetoric, some of the many ways that speeches play a role within other genres of literature, and looked at a few examples of free-standing speeches.

In the next two lectures, we move back to poetry, the poetry of the Hellenistic Age. It's a new world, in a new place, but the poetry, as we'll see, is very solidly grounded in the traditions we've been discussing, even as it breaks new ground.

Lecture Thirty-Four
Hellenistic Poetry I—Callimachus and Theocritus

Scope:

With the next two lectures, we move into a new world in many ways: away from mainland Greece to Alexandria in North Africa, from the democracy of the city-state to far-reaching monarchies, and from public forms of literature to works that demand of their audience more specialized forms of knowledge. Our focus is on Alexandria, a center of learning and the location of the great Library that held all we have been studying so far and much more. Callimachus worked at the Library, organizing its contents, and wrote both prose and poetry in a variety of genres. We discuss several examples of his poetry, noted for its highly refined, even scholarly qualities. The Syracusan Theocritus, who spent part of his life in Alexandria, was equally learned. We look here at selections from his *Idylls*, including those cited as the first examples of pastoral poetry.

Outline

I. We now move from mainland Greece to Alexandria in North Africa, from the city-state to monarchies, and from the Classical to the Hellenistic Period, in which we study the poetry of Callimachus and Theocritus.

II. First, some background about the Hellenistic Period is in order: Despite Demosthenes's best efforts, Philip of Macedon and his son Alexander did indeed incorporate Greece into their larger empire.

   A. At the death of Alexander in 323, his far-flung empire broke into several kingdoms, and fighting among those kingdoms continued for decades.

   B. Our focus is on one of those kingdoms, Egypt, under the rule of the Ptolemies, and its literary and cultural center in Alexandria.

   1. Alexandria's Library was a repository of texts, and we have stories about the ruthlessness of the Ptolemies in getting manuscripts for the Library. One of the achievements of Callimachus was to compose an

annotated catalogue of the Library holdings; unfortunately, it does not survive.

2. The Library also functioned as a research center.

3. Maybe because of all this activity at the Library, or maybe just arising at the same time, we see in the Hellenistic Period a new direction in literature, one that self-consciously looked back to works of the past even as it responded to its contemporary setting.

III. The literature of the 3rd century, as represented in this course by works of Callimachus, Theocritus, and Apollonius, is generally more erudite and polished than what we have seen so far, with a tendency to mix the lofty and the low in the same work.

A. Antiquarian lore, odd myths, geographical detail, and stories about origins threaten to give some of these works a pedantic feel.

B. Works are generally on a smaller scale than what we have seen (with the exception of Apollonius's epic), allowing for a greater attention to word choice and shifts in dialect.

C. Themes become less grandiose and more personal, with a penchant for burlesque and a new interest in romantic love.

IV. Callimachus (c. 300–c. 240) was a scholar-poet who worked in the Library at Alexandria and was said to have written some 800 works, of which very little survives.

A. His works included *Hekale*, a poem on an out-of-the-way story about Theseus, two poems on the causes of things, a collection of epigrams, and six hymns that recall, but diverge from, the Homeric Hymns.

B. His *Hymn 5: On the Bath of Pallas*, contains much that follows the pattern of the Homeric Hymns.

1. The focus is on a single deity, Athena (sometimes referred to as Pallas Athena), and as in the Homeric Hymns, we find cult names and places included.

2. Also like the Homeric Hymns, we often have at the center of Callimachus's hymns a mythical story associated with a god.

3. As well, certain words are deliberately archaic and

hearken back to Homer, if not the Homeric Hymns.

C. Athena is the focus of the hymn, which centers not just on her but on a ritual carried out for her, the bathing of an image of the goddess that was done regularly in the Greek city of Argos.

   1. The opening invocation is not to Athena but to the women carrying out the ritual.

   2. There is concrete reference to the sights and sounds of the ritual activity: The singer hears the neighing of the horses and the creaking of the chariot.

   3. The insistent commands make us feel part of the proceedings, as the singer gives instructions to those taking part; calls repeatedly on Athena to be present; and when she finally arrives, addresses the goddess directly.

   4. As the story progresses, we see that Teiresias, our old friend the Theban prophet, is still young, and he happens across Athena bathing in a secluded spring. Athena blinds him—those who see a naked goddess must be punished—but she is bathing with Teiresias's mother, who begins to cry over her son's blindness.

   5. Athena tells the weeping mother not to cry and gives Teiresias the gift of prophecy to make up for his lack of sight.

   6. The story about Teiresias—not a common version—increases the sense of urgency in the ritual: Athena cares about its proper performance and will punish those who transgress.

D. The poet thus strikes a balance between antiquarian archaizing and fresh immediacy.

   1. The details of the Argive ritual probably derive from a book in the Library.

   2. The learned would pick up on the many references to Homeric language and the contexts they invoke.

   3. But that learning does not slow the quick pace of the poem and its growing sense of urgency as the goddess approaches.

V. Theocritus (c. 300–c. 240) seems to have been born in Syracuse and spent at least part of his career in Alexandria. He is best known for his pastoral poems—those involving shepherds—but his corpus of 30 or 31 *Idylls* (depending on which edition you are looking at) is varied. His poems are often called *bucolics* after the Greek word for "shepherd."

A. *Idyll 1*, one of the pastoral poems, begins with a goatherd asking Thyrsis, a shepherd, to sing his famous song about a cowherd named Daphnis.

　　1. Here, as in other pastoral poems, the setting and characters are rustic, and the themes include love, loss, and song, but the language is often borrowed from epic and reveals the erudition of the city.

　　2. The set-up of the scene—with the whispering pine tree, the nearby spring, the immanence of Pan, and the midday heat—might remind us of the ideal rural setting outside Athens in Plato's *Phaedrus*.

B. In return for Thyrsis's song, the goatherd offers a wooden cup, which he describes at great length and in ways that have been seen as a commentary on pastoral poetry more generally: It is a rustic object taken to an unprecedented degree of perfection.

　　1. The action of the poem stops as the goatherd describes the cup in great detail. This *ekphrasis*, a description of an object within a poem, serves as a song in exchange for the song of Thyrsis.

　　2. The three scenes on the cup cover the ages of man, as well as his various emotional states.

　　　　a. At first, we see two adult males striving for the attentions of a woman; they are hollow-eyed from their love.

　　　　b. Then, we see an old fisherman who struggles with his catch, laboring mightily.

　　　　c. Finally, we come to a boy who neglects his duty of guarding a vineyard (and his own lunch) as he intently weaves a cricket cage. Like the bucolic poet, he is lost in his world of creation, making a beautiful object from his natural surroundings.

　　3. We are far from the shield of Achilles with this *ekphrasis*, but there is a certain completeness here: the three ages of man that echo the universal completeness of the shield.

C. Thyrsis agrees to sing his famous song about Daphnis, with which he has previously won a competition.

    1. The mention of a singing contest brings a note of professionalism and sophistication into this rustic scene.

    2. The song is full of strong emotional expressions, as the cowherd Daphnis wastes away, apparently because of love.

    3. The particulars of the story are not clear, but the tone throughout is higher than what preceded: We are in the realm of gods, muses, and references to Homeric heroes.

D. The poem ends with a return to the pastoral setting and concern for the sexual appetite of the goats; all is artificial, but there is a clear juxtaposition of high and low tone.

Essential Reading:

Callimachus, *Hymn 5: On the Bath of Pallas*, and Theocritus, *Idyll 1*.

Supplementary Reading:

Fowler, B., *The Hellenistic Aesthetic*.

Goldhill, *The Poet's Voice*, chapter 4.

Hutchinson, *Hellenistic Poetry*, chapters 2 and 4.

Questions to Consider:

1. Look back at the Homeric Hymns from earlier in the course. How does Callimachus's hymn hearken back to them? And how does it differ?

2. Theocritus's *Idyll 1* likewise looks back to earlier models even as it creates something new. What is Homeric about the poem, and what seems more influenced by lyric? What other influences do you detect?

Lecture Thirty-Four
Hellenistic Poetry I—Callimachus and Theocritus

Welcome back. In the last lecture, we completed our brief survey of Greek prose with a discussion of oratory, and now we return to poetry for two lectures. With these next two lectures, we move into a new world in many ways: away from mainland Greece to Alexandria in North Africa; away from the democracy of the city-states to far-reaching monarchies; and away from public forms of literature to works that demand of their audience more specialized types of knowledge. In short, we are moving from the Classical into the Hellenistic Period.

Alexandria, the center of our focus for this period, was a great center of learning and the location of the great library that held all the works we've been studying so far, and much, much more. In this lecture, I begin with a brief introduction of that period, and then turn to the work of two Hellenistic poets, Callimachus and Theocritus. In the next lecture, we'll continue with the epic poet Apollonius of Rhodes. Callimachus worked at the famous library in Alexandria, and he wrote both prose and poetry in a variety of genres. In this lecture we're going to discuss one of his hymns, written in a style that recollects, and also updates, the Homeric Hymns. The Syracusan Theocritus also spent part of his life in Alexandria. We look here at a selection from his *Idylls*, often cited as the first examples of pastoral poetry.

But first, the Hellenistic Period more generally: Despite Demosthenes's best efforts, and the efforts of others, Philip of Macedon and his son Alexander the Great did indeed continue their aggressive expansion, and Greece did become incorporated into an empire—an empire that stretched as far east as India and south into Egypt. In the year 323, Alexander died in Babylon, still only in his 30s, and that date, 323, traditionally marks the beginning of the Hellenistic Period. At his death, Alexander left no single heir, and his far-flung empire broke into several kingdoms. Fighting among those kingdoms continued for decades, with alliances shifting often, right up to the time of Roman expansion throughout the area in the 1st century B.C.E. In Egypt, there was relative stability under the rule of the Ptolemies.

But our purpose is not to sort out and analyze that tangled political and military web—thank goodness—but rather to look at the literary production of one of the kingdoms that was carved out after the death of Alexander—namely, Egypt, under the rule of the Ptolemy family. Even more particularly, our focus is on Alexandria, the city that was the literary and cultural center of Egypt and indeed of the Greek-speaking world. At the center of this literary and cultural life in Alexandria was the great Library. This was, on the one hand, a repository of texts, and we have stories about the ruthlessness of the Ptolemies in getting manuscripts for the library. Any visitor to the city, the story goes, had to relinquish all manuscripts in his possession. Scribes would then copy the manuscript, keep the original for the library, and give back the copy. This happened also for any ship that came into the port: searched for manuscripts, copies made, and sent back. The city of Athens once allowed the Ptolemies to have, only on loan, their prized copies of all the Athenian tragedians. Ptolemy took those, having paid high security, and agreed just to pay back that security and keep those texts for himself in the library. Now, we have no idea, after all this ruthless acquisition, how many actual volumes or scrolls the library contained, but it seems to have been a vast number indeed, with estimates ranging up to the hundreds of thousands of volumes. One of the achievements of Callimachus was to compose an annotated index to those library holdings—that does not survive.

But this library was more than a repository: it functioned as a research center, with librarians editing texts, correcting them, commenting on them, and writing new works about them. Maybe because of all this activity at the library, or maybe just arising at the same time out of similar impulses, we see in the Hellenistic Period a new direction in literature, one that self-consciously looks back to works of the past even as it responds to its contemporary setting.

Thus, there are certain qualities that characterize the literature of this period, at least as represented by our authors, Callimachus, Theocritus, and Apollonius. There is a large amount, a vast amount, that's lost from this period. Now, there are exceptions to every generalization I'm about to make, but these are some general characteristics of the period. The poetry is generally more learned, more polished than what we have seen so far. There is a marked tendency in it to mix the lofty and the low in the same work. Antiquarian lore, odd myths, geographical detail, stories about origins—origins of customs, origins of names, origins of cities—all of these abound. They threaten at times to give these works something of a pedantic feel. At times we can imagine our poets researching out-of-the-way references in the vast library holdings, sprinkling their works with details that only the learned will understand. But the best of these poems and this poetry, as we'll see, manage to remain fresh, even unpredictable, seeming new even in the midst of so much learning.

Works from this period are generally on a smaller scale than what we have seen—with the exception of Apollonius's epic, that we'll get to in this next lecture—and this smaller scale allows for a greater attention to word choice, to shifts in dialect, and here's where we saw a lot of particular, very particular references back to earlier works through that word choice. Themes become less grandiose, less heroic, and less political, and more personal and domestic. There's a tendency here toward parody and burlesque, and we find a new interest in romantic love. Alexandria itself was a cosmopolitan city, a crossroads for travelers from around the Mediterranean, and the literature produced there could count on a fairly sophisticated audience. Now, these are general features. We'll see particular examples as we proceed.

Let's turn now to Callimachus, who lived roughly from 300 to about 240. He was a scholar-poet who worked in the library at Alexandria and was said to have written some 800 works, but very little of that massive output survives. Unfortunately for Callimachus, that title "scholar-poet" too often gets emphasis on the first half, the scholar, and his work is remembered as learned and important, yes, rather than enjoyable, fun to read. It doesn't help that Callimachus does have a tendency to fill his poems with sometimes difficult references, lots and lots of proper names. It also doesn't help, and this is beyond his control, that so much of his work is only fragmentary now. The sands of Egypt, and the papyrus scraps found there, have helped us some in that latter area, but still we have very little of that massive output that we've heard about from Callimachus.

We know that Callimachus's works included a poem called the *Hekale*, on an out-of-the-way story about Theseus. This is when Theseus went to capture the bull of Marathon, one of his heroic deeds. On his way to do that he stayed with a poor old woman, Hekale herself, who took care of him. He went off, got the bull of

Marathon, came back to visit her, and she had died. In other words, it's a tangential way to get into a heroic story, not the central story itself. Callimachus also wrote two influential books of poems on the causes of things. He also wrote a collection of epigrams, many of which survive, and six hymns that recall, but also diverge from, the Homeric Hymns.

Now we're going to look at one of those hymns of Callimachus, the Fifth Hymn, *On the Bath of Pallas*. Let's look first, though, at some of the ways these hymns of Callimachus look back more generally to the Homeric Hymns. When Callimachus does refer to the Homeric Hymns, or recall them in some way, it is always with some twist—he is never slavish in following old models, but rather clever in reminding us of the old poems, even as he creates out of them something new. As in the Homeric Hymns, the focus in these hymns of Callimachus is usually on a single deity. Callimachus has hymns to Zeus, Apollo, Artemis, Demeter. The hymn *On the Bath of Pallas* centers on Athena, who's sometimes referred to as Pallas Athena, and only in one final hymn does he include more than one, the hymn to Delos, the birthplace of Artemis and Apollo.

As in the Homeric Hymns, we find cult names and places included in the hymns of Callimachus. Callimachus has some fun here with this listing of proper names, as in the *Hymn to Zeus*, where he refers to the two different stories about Zeus's birthplace, in Crete and in Arcadia. Within the poem, he asks: Which one of these stories is right? Well, he answers himself; we know that the Cretans are always lying, so it must be Arcadia. So, he proceeds with stories about Zeus's birth, his childhood, and his coming to power. It's as though Callimachus is reminding us that he knows all the possible versions of the story, but he's only going to put one in here. This is a theme, you might recognize, that's similar to what we saw in Hesiod's *Theogony*. Here it's much lighter in tone, witty, and the whole thing chock-full of proper names.

As in the Homeric Hymns, we often have at the center of Callimachus's hymns a mythical story associated with the god. Remember that for Aphrodite, in the Homeric Hymn, it was her affair with Anchises; for Hermes—the god Hermes—it was his childhood exploits. In Callimachus's *Hymn to Artemis*—similar to that methodology in the Homeric Hymns— in the *Hymn to Artemis* we have a story about the virgin huntress first obtaining her bow and arrows. She's only three years old, Callimachus tells us, and she dares to go confront the Cyclopes. She sits on their lap, these terrifying creatures who are forging her weapons for her. She plucks the chest hairs out of one of these Cyclopes, such that, forever after, his chest was always bare of hair in that spot. The *Hymn to Delos*, of course, has a story within it about the birth of Apollo and Artemis, and the trials and tribulations involved there. In our hymn *On the Bath of Pallas* we'll see that this story is about Teiresias.

Within these hymns, language also recalls the Homeric Hymns. We're going to have a hard time trying to catch this in translation, but Callimachus includes certain words that are deliberately archaic, no longer in common use, words that hearken back to Homer and the Homeric Hymns. There are also formal devices that we saw in the Homeric Hymns, especially the formal farewell to the deity, often expanded in Callimachus with a plea for prosperity, or at least a favorable reception for the poem.

Now, we find all of these features in the Fifth Hymn, *On the Bath of Pallas*—not always obviously. Athena is the focus of the hymn, the focal deity, but the whole thing centers not just on her, but on a particular ritual carried out for her, the bathing of an image of the goddess that was done on some regular basis in the Greek city of Argos. In a sense that image of Athena does become Athena, or at least their identities are closely linked, both in the ritual and in the hymn. The hymn opens, not with an invocation of Athena herself, but with an address to the women carrying out the ritual. Callimachus brings this all alive with concrete reference to the sights and sounds of the ritual activity. The singer hears the neighing of the horses, the creaking of the chariot. I'm going to skip around some in this poem, reading to you passages. Let me read you one now from the very beginning, and then another one from slightly later. Here's how the poem begins:

> All who pour water for the bath of Pallas,
> come out, come out! Just now I heard
> the mares of the goddess whinny: she, too
> is anxious to go! Hurry then,
> blond daughters of Pelasgia, hurry:…

Then skipping down:

> Come,

daughters of Achaia, and never mind bringing
perfumes or jars (listen:
that's the sound of axles grating),
no perfumes, attendants on the bath of Pallas,
no jars (Athena has no use for tinctured ointments),
and, please, no mirrors: she always looks beautiful.

There are insistent commands here; commands that are repeated throughout the hymn and make us in the audience, the readers of it, feel as though we are part of the proceedings, even as the singer gives instructions to those taking part within the ritual. He repeatedly calls on Athena to be present and when Athena finally arrives, he addresses the goddess directly. Let me read to you some of those many examples of these—these addresses, these ways of involving us more directly within the poem—more skipping around:

Bring her
something masculine, then: the pure olive ointment
Kastor prefers, the salve, too, of Heracles.
And bring her golden comb, so she may smooth
her hair back, shimmering now she has dried it.
Come out Athena! Here is a troupe
to your heart's liking, daughters
of the grand house of Arestor.

Skipping down:

Come out, Athena,
city destroyer, helmed in gold, thrilled
by the clash of horses and shields!

And then more briefly:

And now, Lady Athena,
do come out.

Then the poem concludes with another call for our involvement:

But here she is, here at last: Athena!
Receive the goddess, maidens
whose task it is: acclaim her,
call on her in prayer, cry your cries!
Hail, Goddess! Bless Argos of Inachos.
Hail to you, on your way out!
Return, driving your horses back again,

and preserve entire this land of Danaos!

Lots that will make us immediately involved in this hymn, in this ritual activity. We do find within this reconstruction of ritual activity, a myth that relates to our goddess: a story about Athena and Teiresias, our old friend the Theban prophet. But in this story, Teiresias is still young—hard to imagine a young Teiresias after we've encountered him so often in his age—and Teiresias happens across Athena bathing in a secluded spring:

> Alone
> but for his hounds, his chin
> darkened by his first beard, Teiresias
> happened on to the sacred spot. A burning
> thirst led him straight to the stream,
> poor fool: he saw, unwillingly,
> what he shouldn't have seen. Athena's anger
> blazed: 'Well, son of Eueres,
> who'll never leave this place with your eyes:
> what harsh power brought you here?'

Athena blinds Teiresias; those who see a naked goddess must be punished. But it just so happens that also there bathing with Athena is none other than Teiresias's mother; we didn't even know Teiresias had a mother. She—the mother—begins to cry over her son's blindness. "Don't cry," says Athena, "your son has gotten off easy, just think of what happened to Actaeon, and she goes into another mythical example: Actaeon, who saw Artemis bathing, and she changed him into a stag, and his own hunting dogs tore him to pieces. Teiresias got off lucky." And in addition, says Athena, "I will give him the gift of prophecy to make up for his lack of sight."

Now, this is not a very common version of how Teiresias won his prophetic gift. There is a more common version, one that involves copulating snakes, a couple of sex changes, and an argument about whether men or women get the most pleasure out of sex; that's not here.

Callimachus chooses this story, though, and not only because it's slightly arcane, out-of-way, familiar maybe only to the learned few. It's also effective. We're in the middle of a religious ritual in this poem, and this story increases the sense of urgency attached to its performance. Get the ritual right, the story suggests, because Athena does have a mean streak and will punish those who transgress; even as she can be merciful, as the story showed us. The poet thus strikes in this hymn a balance between antiquarian archaizing and a real, fresh immediacy. The details of the Argive ritual probably derive from some book in the Library, as do many of the references to mythical individuals or places. Also, the learned in the audience would pick up on the many uses of Homeric language in this hymn, and recollection of Homeric passages would enrich their experience of this poem. But not even all of those references, not even all that heavy learning can possibly slow the quick pace of the poem and its growing sense of urgency as the goddess approaches. As old as the references are, this poem, this hymn to Athena, like other poems by Callimachus, is remarkably fresh.

Let's move on now to Theocritus, who lived from around 300 to around 240 B.C.E. He seems to have been born in Syracuse and spent at least part of his career in Alexandria. He's best known for his pastoral poems, those involving shepherds, but his corpus of 30 or 31—depending on which edition you're looking at—his corpus of 30 or 31 idylls is varied.

Now, a couple of definitions: the word pastoral comes from a Latin root for shepherd; the Greek equivalent is *bucolic*, and you'll often find his poems referred to as "bucolics." The Roman poet Vergil wrote some poems in the Theocritean mode, and referred to them as Bucolics. The word "idyll" is from the Greek *eidullia*, and is the earliest name applied to these poems of Theocritus. It's a diminutive in form, and seems to mean something like "little types." And there are many types in this collection of idylls, not just pastoral poems. We have one of the idylls, for example, in which we see a woman casting a spell on a lover who has left her, trying to use magic to bring him back to her. We see another one in which two women go to a festival of Adonis, prattling on about all of the things that they see until they're interrupted by a beautiful hymn to Adonis within this poem.

But for the rest of this lecture, we'll look at the first idyll, one of Theocritus's pastoral poems. In form, it is a dialogue between a goatherd and a shepherd named Thyrsis. We don't have the goatherd's name. The goatherd asks Thyrsis to sing his famous song about a certain cowherd named Daphnis. Here, as in other pastoral poems, the setting and characters are rustic, and the themes include love, loss, and song; but, despite the rustic setting, the language is often borrowed from epic and reveals the erudition of the city. The setup of the scene—whispering pine tree, nearby spring, the imminent presence of Pan, and the midday heat—all of this might remind us of the ideal rural setting outside of Athens in Plato's *Phaedrus*. In the opening lines of this poem, we hear about that setting, as the two men involved, the goatherd and Thyrsis, compliment each other on their singing ability, and the prizes they would win in poetry contests. Thyrsis starts:

> There is sweet music in that pine tree's whisper, goatherd,
> There by the spring. Sweet too is the music of your pipe;
> You would win the second prize to Pan. If he takes as his
> Reward a horned goat, you will have the she-goat. If he
> Wins the she-goat as a prize, the kid will fall to you.
> The kid's meat is good, until the time it gives its milk.

And the goatherd responds:

> Shepherd, your songs sound sweeter than the water tumbling
> Over there from the high rock. If the Muses take a ewe
> As their prize, yours will be a stall-fed lamb. If they desire
> To take the lamb, then you will carry off the ewe.

The goatherd then asks Thyrsis to sing his song, his song—his famous song—about Daphnis, and he offers prizes of his own in return. Chief among those prizes is a wooden cup, which he describes at great length, and in ways that have been seen as a commentary on pastoral poetry more generally: This cup, like pastoral poetry, is something plain and rustic that's taken here to an unprecedented degree of perfection.

So the action stops—such as it is—the action stops as the goatherd describes the cup in great detail. This, we might recall, is an *ekphrasis*, a description of an object within a poem; and in a way this song, this *ekphrasis*, serves as another sort of payment for the song of Thyrsis: A song about the cup in exchange for the song about Daphnis. There are three scenes on the cup that, taken together, cover the ages of man, as well as his various emotional states. At first, we see two adult males striving for the attentions of a woman; they're hollow-eyed from their love. Each is offering a song, his own song, trying to win her attention. Second, an old fisherman struggles with his catch, laboring mightily to bring it in, his sinews standing out. Finally, a boy, who's neglecting his duty of guarding a vineyard and his own lunch, as he intently weaves a cricket cage. Like the bucolic poet, this boy is lost in this world of creation, making something beautiful from his natural surroundings. Here's a passage from that:

> Not far from this sea-beaten old man there's a vineyard
> Heavily laden with dark, ripe, grape-clusters. A little boy
> Watches over it, perched on a drystone wall.
> Two foxes lurk nearby; one prowls down the vine rows,
> Stealing the ripe fruit, while the other pits all her cunning
> Against the boy's satchel. No respite for him, she reckons,
> Till he has nothing left for breakfast but dry bread.
> But he is twisting a pretty cricket-cage of asphodel,
> Plaiting it with rushes, with never a thought for satchel
> And vines, absorbed as he is in his weaving task.

We're far from the shield of Achilles with this *ekphrasis*, but there is a certain completeness here, the three ages of man, that echoes the universal completeness of the shield. This is what the goatherd offers in exchange for the song; a song, he mentions, that Thyrsis has sung before in a poetry contest, winning a prize there. This mention of singing and prizes brings a note of professionalism into the poem that might intrude on the rustic scene. Thyrsis does sing the song, full of strong emotional expressions, as the cowherd Daphnis wastes away, apparently because of love. Here's a section of it:

> Now, you thorns and brambles, bring forth violets, and
> Let the lovely narcissus flower on the juniper. Let
> All things run contrary, since Daphnis is near to death.
> Let the pine tree sprout pears, let hounds be torn by stags,
> Let nightingales cry out to owls at the day's dawn.

The particulars of the story are not at all clear, but the tone throughout is higher than what preceded. We've left behind the animals in the field, left behind wooden cups, no matter how beautifully decorated; we have gods, Muses, even a reference to the Homeric hero, Diomedes. The poem ends, though, with a return to the pastoral setting, coming down from the heights of Thyrsis's song. The goatherd gives him the cup, and then turns his attention back to his goats and their sexual appetite:

> Look, my friend, here's the bowl, see how well it smells—

You could believe it had been washed in the Hours' spring.
Come over here, Ivy. You milk her, Thyrsis. Stop frisking,
You nannies, or the billy-goat will be up and after you.

All is very artificial here, but there's a clear juxtaposition of high and low tone. We've seen two examples in this lecture of highly learned poetry that still manages to be full of life and freshness. Can that same combination last throughout an entire epic?

We'll find out next time, when we complete our discussion of Hellenistic poetry with a look at the *Argonautica*, the epic poem about Jason and the Golden Fleece written by Apollonius of Rhodes.

Lecture Thirty-Five
Hellenistic Poetry II—Apollonius

Scope:

The single extant epic poem from the Hellenistic Period is Apollonius of Rhodes's *Argonautica*, an account of Jason's quest for the Golden Fleece. This lecture brings us full circle, taking us back to the Homeric epics that so clearly influence this work. While the *Argonautica* is very much a product of its own time, it borrows heavily from Homer in its language, the nature and role of the gods within it, and the focus on a single hero, but Apollonius often adapts his Homeric model to his own ends. In addition, Apollonius's epic draws heavily on its forebears in tragedy and lyric, especially in the treatment of the affair between Jason and Medea. Thus, as we discuss the qualities of this epic, we will necessarily go back to some of the masterpieces we have read earlier.

Outline

I. Many stories circulated about the life of Apollonius (c. 270–c. 210), but all we can say with any certainty is that he was a contemporary of Callimachus and Theocritus, connected in some way with the island of Rhodes, and at some point in his life, director of the Library at Alexandria.

   A. In addition to the *Argonautica,* Apollonius wrote a series of foundation stories, poems on the legends and the history of the founding of various cities.

   B. As head librarian, he is said to have written several interpretive works about the early poets, including Homer and Hesiod. All of those are lost.

II. In an Alexandrian world that favored the short and refined poem over the long epic, Apollonius wrote an epic, the *Argonautica*.

   A. Both Callimachus and Theocritus clearly revere Homer but make poetic statements against the writing of epic in their world.

      1. Callimachus says he prefers the slender muse and the clear drops of the spring rather than the muddy river.

And there is a fragment from Callimachus that finds fault with a *mega biblion*, a "big book."

    2. A character in Theocritus's seventh *Idyll* disparages houses as high as mountains and birds who try to crow as loud as Homer.

B. The tradition thus arose of an argument between Callimachus and Apollonius based on their different views of poetry. There is little evidence for it, and in fact, we have considerable evidence that all three of these poets were working in a similar tradition.

III. Apollonius's *Argonautica*, divided into four books, tells the story of Jason's voyage with the Argonauts to get the Golden Fleece in Colchis, at the eastern end of the Black Sea, and bring it back to Greece.

A. Books 1 and 2 tell of the gathering of the Argonauts and their adventures on the way to Colchis.

B. Book 3 describes events at Colchis, including the tests set for Jason before he could take the Fleece and the love between Jason and Medea, the daughter of the king.

C. Book 4 is devoted to the return to Greece of Jason, the Argonauts, and Medea and is filled with more adventure. It ends before the part of the story that Euripides tells in his *Medea*.

IV. Apollonius clearly knew Homer well and knew how to incorporate Homeric elements and how to alter them for his own purposes.

A. Even though the *Argonautica* is a studiously written epic, it retains Homeric language and some stylistic features of the oral epics, such as the catalogue of heroes at the start.

    1. The meter is dactylic hexameter. In addition, the syntax of the Argonautica is far more complex than what we find in Homer.

    2. We find descriptive epithets in Apollonius but none of the repetitions of scenes or speeches that we saw in Homer.

3. The vocabulary borrows clearly from Homer throughout, but Apollonius borrows from many other sources, as well

4. Apollonius retains certain structural devices we saw in Homer, such as the *ekphrasis*, the extended simile, and the catalogue.

B. We see the same divine interference as in the Homeric poems, but overall, the role of the gods is much diminished and we get a more domestic view of the gods than we usually see.

1. At the start of Book 3, for example, Hera and Athena decide to help Jason by asking Aphrodite to cause Medea, the daughter of the king, to fall in love with him.

2. Aphrodite is willing to help but fears that she cannot convince her wayward son Eros to do the job.

3. She finds him cheating at dice and bribes him with a golden ball.

C. Jason is at the center of the story, but the epic does not revolve around him, as Homer's do around Achilles and Odysseus, and he is a different sort of hero.

1. At the gathering of heroes, he is not the first choice to become leader, and he takes charge only after Herakles has supported him.

2. In all of the Argonauts' adventures, Jason is more likely to rely on the expertise of others than on his own abilities.

   a. At the beginning of Book 2, the boxer Polydeukes takes on the inhospitable Amykos, king of the Bebrykians.

   b. Later in Book 2, the winged Zetes and Calais scare away the flying Harpies from the blind prophet Phineus, who gives the heroes detailed information that is necessary for the completion of their voyage.

3. Jason's first adventure involves no military encounter but the romantic conquest of the Lemnian queen Hypsipyle. He girds himself for it with a beautifully woven red robe that reminds us in some ways of Achilles's shield.

D. Much of Book 4, the return to Greece, takes the Argonauts past Odyssean adventures, and in all cases, the treatment is different.

    1. Circe is Medea's aunt and poses no threat.

    2. They sail right past Calypso's island and the cattle of the Sun.

    3. Their resident musician, Orpheus, drowns out the sound of the Sirens.

V. Apollonius also draws on tragedy and lyric, especially in Book 3.

  A. As Medea falls in love with Jason, the force of her passion and its physical effects on her recall the poems of Sappho.

  B. The exploration of choices that characters face is reminiscent of what we saw in tragedies, especially Euripides's *Medea*.

    1. Medea is torn between her loyalty to her family and her desire to help Jason, with whom she is in love.

    2. Jason is often described as being at a loss, or uncertain, when faced with difficult situations, as when King Aeetes first tells him the tasks he must perform to win the Fleece.

VI. In many ways, the *Argonautica* is an appropriate epic for its time, and we can trace some of the changes that have led up to this Hellenistic epic.

  A. The heroic values of the *Iliad* seem best suited for a pre-*polis* setting, and Achilles questioned them even there.

  B. The *Odyssey*, with its emphasis on family, begins to reject some of the self-serving militarism of the *Iliad*.

  C. The tragedy of 5th-century Athens brought the Homeric world into contact with the *polis*, as in Sophocles's *Ajax* and Euripides's war plays, and revealed just how much the world had changed.

  D. Now, in the urban, urbane, and self-conscious setting of Alexandria, there is a more explicit call for something new.

    1. Herakles and his brute strength are left behind in Book 1; his immense strength and overpowering desires are at odds with the goal of the group.

    2. Some of the Argonauts hold on to old ideas of heroism and are unwilling to entrust their fate to women and their magic, thinking that shameful.

3. Jason, though, uses all tools at his disposal, including the abilities of the Argonauts, his own personal charm, and the love of the foreign sorceress.

Essential Reading:

Apollonius, *Argonautica.*

Supplementary Reading:

Beye, *Epic and Romance in the Argonautica of Apollonius.*

Goldhill, *The Poet's Voice*, chapter 5.

Hunter, *The Argonautica of Apollonius: Literary Studies.*

Questions to Consider:

1. Apollonius and Homer were composing in different ways, for different audiences and different occasions. Read any page of Homer and any page of Apollonius. How does the style of each reflect those differences?

2. Hellenistic literature is notable for its treatment and combination of earlier literary forms and styles. Some claim that makes the literature derivative, even stale in its reliance on old models. Others emphasize the innovation in the response to classics. What do you think?

Lecture Thirty-Five
Hellenistic Poetry II—Apollonius

Welcome back. In our last lecture, we introduced the Hellenistic Period, we talked about Hellenistic literature in general, and then looked at two representative poems from the period: Callimachus's hymn *On the Bath of Pallas* and Theocritus's first idyll. We turn now to another poem from the period, a much longer one. The single extant epic poem from the Hellenistic Period is Apollonius of Rhodes's *Argonautica*, an account of Jason's quest for the Golden Fleece. This lecture brings us full circle in some ways, taking us back to the Homeric epics that so clearly influence this work.

While the *Argonautica* is very much a product of its own time, it also borrows heavily from Homer in its language, the nature and role of the gods within it, and the focus on a single hero. But Apollonius adapts his Homeric model, adapts it to his own ends. In addition, Apollonius's epic draws heavily on its forebears in tragedy and lyric, especially in the treatment of the love affair between Jason and Medea. Thus, as we discuss the qualities of this Hellenistic epic poem, we'll necessarily go back to some of the masterpieces we've read and talked about earlier.

Apollonius of Rhodes seems to have been a native of Alexandria, and he lived from approximately 270 to 210 B.C.E.—we're not sure about either of those dates. Many stories have circulated about his life, but all we can say with any certainty is that he was a contemporary of Callimachus and Theocritus; as his name suggests, he was connected in some way with the island of Rhodes; and at some point in his life he was the director of the Library at Alexandria. In addition to the *Argonautica*, the epic poem we'll be talking about today, Apollonius wrote a series of foundation stories, poems on the legends and the history of the founding of various cities. We'll see some of that same interest in foundations in the *Argonautica*. Also, as head librarian, Apollonius is said to have written several interpretive works about early Greek poets, including Homer and Hesiod. All of those works are lost.

Now, those lost works fit well, or they seem that they would fit well, into the mainstream of Hellenistic literature; but this epic poem, Apollonius's *Argonautica*, seems something of a departure in a world that explicitly favored the short and refined poem over the long, grandiose epic. This, what we might call anti-epic sensibility, is apparent in the works of Callimachus and Theocritus. Now, it's obvious from their poetry that both of those poets clearly revere Homer; references to Homer abound in their works, and also work on the text of Homer was at the center of much of the activity at the library in Alexandria. But both of those poets, Callimachus and Theocritus, do make poetic statements against the writing of epic in their own world.

Callimachus, in the somewhat fragmentary prologue to his poems on origins, defends himself against some imagined critics. Critics who would have him write thousands of thundering and loud-resounding verses about kings and heroes. No, says Callimachus, he prefers the slender muse. He prefers clear drops of the spring rather than the muddy river. He'll travel the untrodden path rather than the broad highway. There's also a fragment from Callimachus that finds fault with a *mega biblion*, a big book. We have less of this sort of sentiment against epic in Theocritus, but a character in his seventh idyll, in the context of talking about songs and composing poetry, that character says that he hates the craftsman who tries to build his house as high as a mountain, and he hates those birds of the Muses who try to crow as loudly as Homer.

Out of these anti-epic tendencies if we can call them that, and especially from the comments by Callimachus, there arose the story—it's a story that continues to live on, despite being so often discredited—the story of a quarrel between Callimachus and Apollonius, a disagreement based on their different views of poetry. Some even claimed that Apollonius left Alexandria in disgrace after the unfavorable reception of his epic, and then ended up in Rhodes, hence his name, Apollonius of Rhodes. But we have no evidence for any quarrel and, on the other hand, considerable evidence that all three of these poets were working in a similar tradition: both Callimachus and Theocritus include in their poems stories that appear also in the *Argonautica*, stories about Jason and his various adventures, his travels, Golden Fleece stories. There are even some close verbal parallels between passages, in Apollonius and in Callimachus. The implication is that, despite the length of Apollonius's work, which sets him apart, all three of these poets were more similar than different in their poetic ideals.

Now, on to *Argonautica*, Apollonius's epic. It's divided into four books, and it tells the story of Jason's voyage with the Argonauts to get the Golden Fleece in Colchis, a city at the far eastern end of the Black Sea, and bring it back to Greece. Books 1 and 2 tell of the gathering of the Argonauts, and their adventures on the way to Colchis. Book 3 describes events at Colchis. Here we find the tests set for Jason before he can take the Fleece back with him, and even more memorably, here we find the onset of the love affair between Medea—the daughter of the king there in Colchis—and Jason. Book 4 is devoted to the return to Greece of Jason, the Argonauts, and now Medea, and it's filled with more adventures. The *Argonautica* ends before we learn or hear of Jason's further adventures back in Greece, in other words, before the part of the story that Euripides tells in his *Medea*.

Rather than moving through the epic in order, first book to fourth book, let's look at it in terms of its response to previous models, making sure that we do appreciate, as we go, the innovations of Apollonius even as we note his borrowings and his references to predecessors. Let's start with Apollonius's response to Homer's epics. He clearly knew Homer very well—backwards and forwards—and he knew how to incorporate Homeric elements into his epic, and also how to alter those elements for his own purposes. Even though the *Argonautica* is a studiously written epic, it does retain some stylistic and linguistic features of the orally composed Homeric epics. The meter for Apollonius is dactylic hexameter as for Homer, but we find that the single line of poetry does not as often contain a complete thought in Apollonius. More generally, the syntax of the *Argonautica* is far more complex than what we find in Homer, with more subordination of clauses within a single sentence.

We do find descriptive epithets in Apollonius, as in Homer, but much less frequently; and none of those repetitions of scenes or speeches that we saw in Homer, none of those are found in Apollonius. The vocabulary borrows clearly and often from Homer, one famous example of that, or well-noted example, is the vocabulary of sea and sailing that Apollonius seems to include almost wholesale into his epic from Homer. But Apollonius borrows from other sources as well; one thing we can say about the language is that the language of this epic is certainly not in the register of the speech of Apollonius's day.

Apollonius retains certain structural devices that we saw in Homer, such as the *ekphrasis*, that is, that description of an object within a poem; also the extended simile, the Homeric simile if you will, and the catalogue. Now, we'll see examples of the *ekphrasis* and the simile later in this lecture. But as for the catalogue, recalling Homer's catalogue of ships—that great long list of ships from the second book of the *Iliad*—Apollonius gives us the catalogue of heroes, that is, the *Argonauts*, almost immediately in Book 1, using the sort of language and description that owes much to Homer. What we find there in that catalogue of heroes, though, that's somewhat new, is a real pile up of proper names: place names, mythological names, family names, all these names that mark it as particularly Hellenistic. Some of the heroes that are introduced to us here: Orpheus, Heracles, the sons of the north wind, Zetes and Calais, the helmsman Tiphys, and on and on he goes. We'll meet some of these characters later as we look at other passages in the epic.

In Apollonius we have the same gods as in Homer and the same sort of divine interference in mortal affairs, but overall the role of the gods is much diminished. We have in Apollonius only two scenes where we see the gods on Olympus. Let's look at one of those, from the beginning of Book 3, where we get a more domestic view of the gods, we might say, than we're used to seeing. At the beginning of Book 3, Hera and Athena decide to help out Jason by asking Aphrodite to cause Medea—the daughter of the king—to fall in love with Jason. Now, we're used to seeing Athena help heroes; Jason is one of the few in mythology who's favored by Hera. Here's the mission, and the one to carry out this mission is Eros, the son of Aphrodite: Eros, who was frequently called upon to go among humans bringing love with his bow and his arrow, or else its opposite. Hera and Athena approach Aphrodite and ask her help. Aphrodite is willing to help Hera and Athena, but fears that she cannot convince her wayward son Eros to do the job. Here's how she answers Hera and Athena:

> My son will listen to you, Hera and Athena, much more than to me! Shameless though he is, for you a little shame at least will show in his eyes. To me he pays no heed, but he constantly provokes and disobeys me. Beset as I am on all sides by the misery of it, I have it in mind to break his bow and grim-sounding arrows right before his eyes.

Hera and Athena find this parenting problem amusing, and they go on to convince Aphrodite to approach her son. So she does. She finds Eros playing dice with Ganymede, the young cupbearer of the gods, and Aphrodite arrives on this scene just in time to catch her son cheating at dice. Aphrodite scolds him, not very severely we might think, and then she bribes him to get the job done. She offers her son a golden ball if he'll inflame Medea with love for Jason. What would Plato say about this representation of the gods, about Eros in particular? We might see echoes in this representation of the gods that go back to some of those Homeric Hymns, maybe even some sections of Homer.

But let's move now from the gods to the treatment of the hero. Jason is at the center of the *Argonautica*, but the epic does not revolve around him, at least not as closely as Homer's epics revolve around Achilles and Odysseus. Jason, as we'll see, is a different sort of hero. We see this different treatment of the hero early in Book 1, at the gathering of the Argonauts. After they have met, Jason addresses them, telling them they have to choose a leader, and in an embarrassing situation it seems, Jason is not their first choice. Here's his address to them at their response:

> '…therefore now without other thoughts choose the very best man as your leader—the man who will be concerned with every detail in conducting both our quarrels and our agreements with men of foreign lands.'

> So he spoke, and the young men immediately turned their eyes to the bold Herakles who was sitting in their midst, and with one voice they all urged him to take command. He, however, remained sitting where he was, raised his right hand and said:

> 'Let no one offer me this honour—I shall not accept it, and I shall not allow anyone else to put himself forward: let he who gathered our band together lead us on our way.'

> Such were Herakles' high-minded words, and they approved his instructions. The warrior Jason himself leapt up joyfully to address his enthusiastic crew:

'If you grant me the honour of being in charge of our expedition, let nothing, as before, stand in the way of our journey.'

Well Jason doesn't seem the least embarrassed, and with Herakles's support, he takes charge.

The Argonauts have many adventures on their travels, and throughout all of them we see more of this characterization of Jason. We see that he's more likely to rely on the expertise of others than on his own abilities. At the beginning of Book 2, the Argonauts meet the inhospitable Amykos, king of the Bebrykians, who challenges everyone who passes to a boxing match. Here is Amykos to the Argonauts:

'It is the law that no stranger who has come to the land of the Bebrykians may depart until he has lifted up his hands in combat against mine. Therefore choose the best man from among you all and set him to box against me here and now. If you choose to ignore and trample upon my laws, you will find that the consequences will be grim and violent.'

So he spoke in his haughtiness. Wild anger seized the Argonauts when they heard, and the threats struck Polydeukes most of all.

Not Jason, but Polydeukes. Heracles has already been left behind; he's no longer a part of this expedition. He's altogether too big for this adventure or else he would have stood up, but Polydeukes is the next best after Heracles. It's a brutal boxing match that Apollonius describes in some detail, and it's made more vivid by the pile up of some of these Homeric similes, similes that are long and involved. Finally Polydeukes prevails in the boxing match, kills Amykos The Bebrykians respond to the death of their king by attacking the Argonauts. We then hear about the valiant behavior of many of the Argonauts in response to this and, writes Apollonius, "with them, too, raced the warrior Jason," still not at the forefront.

Later in Book 2, the Argonauts meet the blind prophet Phineus, who gives them detailed information that is necessary for the completion of their voyage. He plays the in other words the same role, as Teiresias that other blind prophet, in Book 11 of the *Odyssey*. But before Phineus the prophet will give them that information, the Argonauts have to save him from flying Harpies. These are creatures that steal his food, they fly and they steal his food and what they leave behind they make unfit for human consumption. Jason can't help Phineus, but luckily he has with him the two winged sons of the North Wind, Zetes and Calais. When the Harpies next come, Zetes and Calais fly up after them, chase them away, saving Phineus, who then gives them all sorts of useful information about the continuation of their voyage. He gives them information, for example, about how to make it through the clashing rocks.

Now, this is one of the next adventures. As the Argonauts do make their way through the clashing rocks later in Book 2, Jason is still nowhere in sight, but the helmsman Tiphys rallies the Argonauts, calling on them to row even harder as they row through before these rocks come smashing back on what would have been the destruction of the Argo.

One more adventure, and this is the first one for the Argonauts on their journey, and it does involve Jason prominently. This one though involves no military encounter, but the romantic conquest of the Lemnian queen Hypsipyle. In the previous year—before Jason and the Argonauts arrived there at the island of Lemnos—in the previous year the Lemnian women had killed the entire male population, including husbands, sons, and fathers, all except for the old father of Hypsipyle. It seems that all those men had decided that instead of giving their attentions to their wives, they would turn to slave women, prostitutes, and others, and the Lemnian women took revenge. Anyway, these Lemnian women, now without men for a year, decide not to kill the Argonauts too, but to welcome them to their island. But danger still lurks, so Jason girds himself for the first meeting with the Lemnian queen by putting on a beautifully woven red robe, a gift from Athena:

> Around his shoulders Jason pinned the double cloak of purple, the work of the Itonian goddess, which Pallas had given to him when first she set up the stocks for the building of the *Argo* and issued instructions for measuring the cross-beams with the rule. You could cast your eyes more easily toward the rising sun than gaze upon the brilliant redness of the cloak. Its centre was bright red, the border all the way around purple, and along the full length of the edge had been woven many cunning designs in sequence.

The description of the robe continues at some length, reminding us, of course, of another subject of an *ekphrasis*, the shield of Achilles in the *Iliad*. But how different is this one; the context here romantic, rather than military. Jason makes a successful conquest of Hypsipyle, the queen of the Lemnians, and the Argonauts are safe and comfortable, even, among these women. Jason is indeed a different sort of hero.

In another nod to Homer, Apollonius has the Argonauts encounter many of the same obstacles that we saw in the *Odyssey*. Especially in Book 4, the return of the Argonauts to Greece, they see many of the Odyssean sights; and this is one generation before Odysseus does. Yes, the epic is being written so far after Homer, but it's about story that took place a generation before the Homeric heroes. In every case when the Argonauts encounter one of these Odyssean sights or experiences, the treatment is different. They meet Circe, but it turns out that Circe is Medea's aunt. So Circe and Medea speak together in their native language and there's no threat to the Argonauts despite the fact that all around there are these bizarre looking animals, half animal, half human; no threat to the Argonauts, though. As they move on they see Calypso's island, they see the island of the cattle of the sun, but they don't even stop at either of those places, they sail right past. As they approach the Sirens, those creatures that would lure sailors to their death with their deadly song, the resident musician of the Argonauts, Orpheus, drowns out that song with his own singing, and the Argonauts safely pass by.

We've seen that much in this epic comes from Homer, relies on Homer, looks back to Homer; but Apollonius also draws on tragedy and lyric, especially in Book 3, when Jason has arrived in Colchis and, thanks to the interference of Aphrodite and her son, Medea has fallen in love with him. As Medea falls in love with Jason, the force of her passion and its physical effects on her recall, perhaps, the poems of Sappho. You'll notice in this passage as well that there's a nice extended simile:

> Eros darted back out of the high-roofed palace with a mocking laugh, but his arrow burned deep in the girl's heart like a flame. Full at Jason her glances shot, and the wearying pain scattered all prudent thoughts from her chest; she could think of nothing else, and her spirit was flooded with a sweet aching. As when a woman heaps up twigs around a burning

brand—a poor woman who must live from working wool—
so that she might have light in her dwelling at night as she
sits very close to the fire, and a fierce flame spurts up from
the small brand and consumes all the twigs, just so was the
destructive love which crouched unobserved and burnt in
Medea's heart. At one moment her soft cheeks were drained
of colour, at another they blushed red, the control of her
mind now gone.

Medea is madly, painfully in love, but still uncertain about what to
do. In her anguished indecision, we see the Medea of Euripides's
tragedy. You remember Medea when she was trying to convince
herself whether she should in fact kill her children or not. Here,
Medea is torn between a loyalty to her family—her homeland; and
her desire to help Jason. But she soon makes up her mind; she throws
in her lot with Jason. It's a good thing for him, since Jason, too, is
often described in this epic as being at a loss, or uncertain, when
faced with difficult situations; as when King Aietes, the king in
Colchis, first tells Jason the tasks that he has to perform to win the
Fleece. He's told Jason he has to yoke these fire-breathing, bronzed-
hoofed oxen and plow a field, and carry on even further adventures.
Here's Jason's response to that.

> Jason sat silent where he was, his eyes fixed on the ground
> before his feet, unable to speak, at a loss as to how to deal
> with his wretched situation. For a long time he turned over
> and over what he should do: it was impossible to accept with
> confidence, as the challenge seemed overwhelming. At last
> he replied to the king:

> 'Aietes you have every right to place this hard constraint
> upon me. Therefore I shall risk the challenge, terrible though
> it is, even if I'm fated to die; for there is nothing worse for
> men than the cruel necessity which forces me to come here at
> the behest of a king.'

> Thus he spoke, distraught at the helplessness of his position.

We might be reminded here of that speech from Medea to Jason in
Euripides's play, when she argues that it was only because of Medea
and Medea alone that Jason was able to survive. He certainly seems
to need her help here.

We've been talking about some of the many ways the *Argonautica* builds upon, and yet differs from, earlier works—especially the Homeric epics—and most critics conclude that the *Argonautica* falls short of its models. But that's really not quite fair. In many ways, the *Argonautica* is an appropriate epic for its time. We can trace some of the changes that led up to it, up to this Hellenistic epic, from Homer. The heroic values of the *Iliad* seem best suited for a pre-*polis* setting, in which every man fights for himself in his own personal glory; and Achilles, you remember, questioned those values even there in the *Iliad*. Already in the *Odyssey*, with its emphasis on family and home, we begin to see a rejection of some of the, what we might call self-serving, militarism of the *Iliad*. Tragedy of 5th-century Athens brought the Homeric world into contact with the *polis*, as in Sophocles's *Ajax* and Euripides's war plays—and revealed just how much the world had changed, how out of place those Homeric values were in some ways.

Now, in the urban, and the urbane, and self-conscious setting of Alexandria in the Hellenistic Period, there's a more explicit call for something new. Heracles and his brute strength have been left behind in Book 1. Heracles had the opportunity to lead the whole expedition, and this would have been a different epic if he hadn't left and he hadn't gone away so early in the epic. Herakles's immense strength, overpowering desires would hardly fit well here in the *Argonautica*. Heracles is not what we might call a team player. Some others of the Argonauts hold on to old ideas of heroism, unwilling, for example, to entrust their fate to a woman, especially a woman like Medea who relied on magic: What self-respecting man would do such a thing? Well, Jason would, and he does. In fact, throughout this epic, he uses every tool at his disposal in order to succeed. He has collected a group of able associates in the Argonauts, and he takes advantage of the particular strengths of each one. His personal charm helps out with the Lemnian women, and again with Medea— with the help of the gods—and Jason is not above accepting the help of a woman, even if she is a foreign sorceress. This is indeed a new epic, with a new hero, for a new time.

We've come now to an end of our discussion of Hellenistic poetry. We've been emphasizing the many ways that this poetry, whether by Callimachus, Theocritus, or Apollonius, creates something new even as it looks back and builds on old models. It's time now for us, too, to look back, over the many works we've discussed in this course, and forward to the continuing survival and influence of these masterpieces. We'll do that in the next lecture, the final lecture, of the course.

Lecture Thirty-Six
Looking Back and Looking Forward

Scope:

The previous two lectures on Hellenistic literature serve well as an introduction to this concluding lecture on the survival and continued influence of Greek literature. It was largely through the Romans that Greek literature survived antiquity, and it was largely through the literary activity of the Hellenistic Period that the Romans accessed the Greeks. Vergil's *Aeneid* looks back to Homer by way of Apollonius, and his *Eclogues* owe clear allegiance to Theocritus; the Roman elegists look back to earlier Greek lyric through Callimachus; and the Library at Alexandria itself served as a focal point for the preservation (at least temporarily) and study of most of what remains. We conclude this series of lectures with a brief look at some of the paths of survival, mostly through the Romans, to the present.

Outline

I. In this lecture, we look at the influence of Greek literature beyond the Greek world and into the present.

    A. Most obviously, the collection of works in the Library at Alexandria ensured the survival of much of what we have.

    B. The Library did burn down, but even so, if a text made it into the Library, it had a better chance of survival.

II. Before we look at paths of influence, we need to look at the more general survival through the ages of these ancient Greek masterpieces.

    A. Roman military and political expansion throughout the Mediterranean took the Romans into both Greece and Egypt, the former coming under Roman power in 146 with the sack of Corinth and the latter in 30.

        1. Contact with Greeks in southern Italy and Sicily (*Magna Graecia*) led Romans to recognize and emulate the cultural sophistication of the Greeks.

2. Roman literature often traces its beginning to a translation of Homer's *Odyssey* into Latin by Livius Andronicus around 250.

3. Horace expressed the relationship most succinctly in his statement that captive Greece conquered the savage victor and brought art into rustic Italy (*Epodes* 2.1.156–157).

4. Vergil also recognized the different provinces of Greek and Roman ability. When his hero Aeneas travels to the Underworld, he hears from his father that others (implying the Greeks) excel in the arts, oratory, and astronomy, but the Roman art will be in ruling and bringing order to the world (*Aeneid* 6.1012–1018).

B. By the 6th century C.E., the Roman Empire had split into a Latin Western Empire and a Greek Eastern or Byzantine Empire.

1. As the Latin West was beset by marauding hordes, our Greek masterpieces were better treated in the East, where the Greek language was still used.

2. Also important for the preservation of some of our material in the East was the Arab interest in Greek thought, especially in Greek science, philosophy, and mathematics.

3. Things started settling down in the West in the 12th century C.E., and scholars began translating Greek texts into Latin.

C. It was only with the Renaissance that attention in the West turned to Greek literature.

1. Petrarch, the 14th-century-C.E. Italian Humanist, was one of the earliest to recognize the importance of reading the famous Greek authors in Greek.

2. In the 15th century C.E., Florence became a center of Greek learning in the West, supported by the ruling Medici family.

   a. Marsilio Ficino translated Plato into Latin and established an academy in Florence modeled on Plato's academy.

   b. Another of the great Florentine Humanists and Hellenists was Angelo Poliziano.

3. With the advent of the printing press in Europe at about this time, the world became safer than ever for the preservation of our Greek masterpieces.

D. We still continue to add to the body of ancient Greek literature on a fairly regular basis.

1. Papyrus scraps continue to yield new treasures, such as the Sappho poem we read earlier in this course.

2. New technologies allow us to get more out of texts we already have. One example is the famous *Archimedes Palimpsest*.

III. Now we turn to the influence of Greek literature. Vergil's *Aeneid*, unfinished at the author's death in 19, is the most Roman of all poems, telling of the mythical founding of the city from the ashes of Troy. But it shows obvious allegiance to its Greek ancestors, especially Homer and Apollonius.

A. The epic begins with a statement of its dual focus: "I sing of arms and the man."

1. Vergil thus refers both to the *Iliad*—and prepares for the militaristic part of the epic—and to the *Odyssey*, in his focus on the wanderings of one man, Aeneas.

2. The epic is in 12 books, the first 6 narrating the journeys of Aeneas from Troy to Rome and the last 6 concerned with the battles that awaited him upon arrival at the site of Rome.

3. During his wanderings, Aeneas has Odyssean adventures, including a trip to the Underworld, and rescues one of Odysseus's men left behind on the island of the Cyclops.

4. In his battles, there is a constant reference to Homer's Trojan War heroes: Is Aeneas now a new Achilles because he is the attacker, or has he met a new Achilles in the form of his opponent, Turnus, in Italy?

B. Throughout, the language, meter, and style recall the Homeric model.

C. But there is also a clear nod to Apollonius (and, through him, to Greek tragedy) in Aeneas's tragic romance with the Carthaginian queen Dido in Book 4.

    1. Blown off course to the city of Carthage in North Africa, Aeneas is welcomed by Queen Dido, at least in part because Venus has caused Dido to fall in love with him.

    2. Aeneas eventually leaves Dido, driven by his mission to found Rome; she curses him and the Roman race and kills herself.

D. Vergil's reading of Homer and Apollonius formed the basis of the European epic tradition that has led through Dante's *Divine Comedy* and Milton's *Paradise Lost* and, more recently, to James Joyce's *Ulysses* and Derek Walcott's Caribbean interpretation *Omeros*.

E. Thus, epic poetry, at one time the dominant narrative genre, has yielded to another narrative mode in recent centuries, the novel.

    1. The *Odyssey*, in particular, has been referred to as the first novel.

    2. The *Iliad*, on the other hand, is considered the source of all that is tragic.

IV. In lyric and pastoral poetry as well, the Romans looked back to and built upon their Greek predecessors, from both the earlier period and from the Hellenistic Period.

A. Greek lyric has found translators, imitators, and admirers in almost every Western poetic tradition. Catullus (1ˢᵗ century) wrote poems in a variety of meters and styles, many of them immediately topical but clearly influenced by Greek models.

    1. His poem 51 is a translation, with an added stanza, of Sappho's poem on the effects of love.

    2. In his own love poetry, he adds a further nod to Sappho by calling his very Roman lover Lesbia.

    3. His sometimes vituperative attacks on public officials recall both Archilochus and Aristophanes.

    4. His corpus also includes a translation from Callimachus—a poem that served as inspiration for Pope in his "Rape of the Lock"—and echoes the Callimachean preference for the small and refined over the epic.

B. Horace (also 1ˢᵗ century) explicitly models himself on Alcaeus in his meters and his poetic themes.

C. Theocritus's bucolic poems influenced the European pastoral tradition through Vergil's *Eclogues*, written in 37. In the English pastoral tradition, we might think of Milton's *Lycidas*, the poems of Spenser and Sidney, and even some of Shakespeare's comedies.

V. Now, we turn to the influence of ancient Greek drama.

    A. Roman comedians Plautus and Terence translated and reworked the plays of Menander; the spinier Aristophanes does not seem to transplant as well.

    B. Romans did write tragedy—the works of Seneca in particular were influential—but without the sublime power we saw in Athens.

        1. Since then, tragedy has flourished only temporarily, most notably in Elizabethan England and 17th-century C.E. Paris.

        2. And certainly, the genre continues in the works of Ibsen and the American playwrights Eugene O'Neill, Arthur Miller, and Tennessee Williams.

    C. Greek drama still graces our stages but not in any form the ancients would recognize. Recent decades have seen a phenomenal revival of ancient theater onstage, very often heavily adapted, as playwrights and producers recognize the timeless force of these plays.

VI. Historians look back to Herodotus and Thucydides as the founders of their genre.

    A. One tendency in the centuries after these two was to write universal histories, or histories of an entire people or city.

    B. Historians continue to ask the same questions and confront the same problems as Herodotus and Thucydides, for example, how best to handle sources or how to strike a balance between accuracy and entertainment.

    C. Thucydides, in particular, has been influential outside of the field of history. We all can see his continuing relevance, especially to questions of foreign policy.

VII. Rhetoric, especially as practiced by Demosthenes, heavily influenced the greatest Roman orator, Cicero, from the 1st century.

    A. Cicero's style, in turn, was influential throughout the

Renaissance.

B. But contemporary rhetoric bears little resemblance to the ancient speeches, perhaps because of changed legal and political contexts, perhaps because of reduced attention spans.

VIII. We will not try to assess the influence of Plato's thought, but what about his philosophical style?

A. His student Aristotle wrote treatises, and that is certainly the most prevalent format for philosophical writing through the ages, right up to the present.

B. But the tradition of the philosophical dialogue has persisted in the works of Cicero and some of the early Christian writers and down to the 20th century with Santayana's *Dialogues in Limbo*.

IX. All of the works we have read are still with us in one way or another.

A. All of them have shaped who we are because each has, in some way, shaped the world we come from, and that alone is a good reason to read these masterpieces.

B. The best reason to read these masterpieces, however, is because they are compelling, engaging, and enjoyable, every one of them, each in its own way.

Supplementary Reading:

Easterling, *The Cambridge Companion to Greek Tragedy*, part III, Reception.

Fowler, R. L., *The Cambridge Companion to Homer*, part 5, Homeric Receptions.

Goldhill, *Love, Sex, and Tragedy: How the Ancient World Shapes Our Lives*.

Questions to Consider:

1. Consider any contemporary adaptation—literary, musical, theatrical—of a Greek work we have discussed. What has the artist retained of the original, what has the artist changed, and with what effect?

2. Looking back over all we have discussed, which of these works is most immediately meaningful to you, and why? Which will you return to and reread? Which do you like less? In all cases, whether the work engages you or not, do you think it merits being called a literary masterpiece?

Lecture Thirty-Six
Looking Back and Looking Forward

Welcome back. The previous two lectures on Hellenistic literature serve well as an introduction to this, the concluding lecture of the course, on the survival and the continuing influence of the masterpieces of ancient Greek literature we've been reading. Throughout the course we've been commenting on the way that later works respond to and build upon earlier ones, even within the Greek world, that is. That sort of adaptation of the past is nowhere more evident than in the Hellenistic Period, and in Hellenistic poetry. In this lecture, we take that same practice one step further, looking at the influence of Greek literature beyond the Greek world, sometimes even into the present.

It was largely through the Romans that Greek literature survived antiquity, and it was largely through the literary activity of the Hellenistic Period that the Romans had access to Greek literature at all. Most obviously, it was the collection of works in the library at Alexandria that ensured the survival of much of what we have. The library did burn down in antiquity—we're not sure when, we're not sure how, there are many theories, many suspects—but even so, if a text once made it into the library it did have a better chance of survival overall. In addition, it was the Hellenistic poets who provided a stepping stone of sorts to the Roman literary world for much of what we've been reading. Vergil's *Aeneid*, for example, looks back to Homer by way of Apollonius, and Vergil's *Eclogues* owe clear allegiance to Theocritus. Many Roman elegists look back to earlier Greek lyric through Callimachus.

But before we look at some of these more particular paths of influence, let's sketch out, in the broadest terms, the more general survival through the ages of these ancient Greek masterpieces. Military and political expansion throughout the Mediterranean took Romans into both Greece and Egypt, including Alexandria. Greece came under Roman rule in 146 B.C.E. with the sack of Corinth, and Egypt became a Roman province in 30 B.C.E. Long before that political takeover, though, Greeks and Romans were in contact with one another, especially since so many Greeks had settled in southern Italy and Sicily—the area known as *Magna Graecia* because there were so many Greeks there. The Romans recognized and emulated the far older and more firmly established Greek culture. In fact, Roman literature often traces its beginning to a translation of Homer's *Odyssey* into Latin by Livius Andronicus around the year 250 B.C.E.

The Roman poet Horace, writing in the 1st century B.C.E., expresses the relationship between the two peoples most succinctly in his statement that captive Greece conquered the savage victor and brought art into rustic Italy: *Graecia capta ferum victorem cepit et artes intulit agresti Latio.* The Roman poet Vergil, also writing in the 1st century B.C.E., says more or less the same thing, in a different way, about the relationship between Greeks and Romans. When his hero, Aeneas, travels to the Underworld, he meets his father and learns of the future grandeur of Rome. Aeneas's father tells him there that others—referring to the Greeks—others will excel in the arts, in oratory and astronomy, but that the Roman art will be in ruling and bringing order to the world; that's in the sixth book of the *Aeneid*.

Given this recognition and appreciation of Greek culture, the direct knowledge of Greek and of Greek literature remained fairly safe throughout much of the Roman Empire. By the 6th century, though—C.E., that is, of the Common Era; and again, these are broad historical trends I'm describing—by the 6th century the Roman Empire had split into two halves. A Latin Western Empire and a Greek Eastern Empire—and that Eastern Empire became to be known as the Byzantine Empire from its center in Byzantium, the city that would later be called Constantinople and still later Istanbul. As the Latin West was beset by marauding hordes, our Greek masterpieces were better treated in the East, where the Greek language was still used and the texts themselves were preserved and recopied. Also important for the preservation of some of our material in the East was the Arab interest in Greek thought, especially in Greek science, philosophy, and mathematics. Arab scholars of the Middle Ages translated great quantities of these Greek texts into Arabic. To this very day, some of the materials written by the ancient Greeks, particularly in the fields of science and mathematics, those texts survive only in Arabic, some of them still never translated into any other language.

Things started settling down in the West in the 12th century, and with that stability there arose a new interest in the sort of learning that had been preserved in the East, Greek learning. There was communication between East and West, so there was a recognition in the West of what was going on in the East. Scholars began translating these Greek texts into Latin, some of them going directly from Arabic into Latin since the Greek originals had been lost. Still, the interest was primarily in such practical subjects as science, math, and philosophy. Greek philosophy was indeed practical since it was so useful as the basis for theological discussion, for both Christians and Muslims.

It was only with the Renaissance that attention in the West turned, in any concerted way, toward Greek literature. Petrarch, the 14th-century Italian Humanist, was one of the earliest to recognize the importance of reading these famous Greek authors in Greek. He tried to learn Greek, but failed; blame it on bad teaching. His successors had better luck. In the 15th century, a steady stream of Greek teachers came into Italy from the East, bringing with them not only the Greek language, but also the motivation to collect Greek manuscripts in the West. We hear stories about Italian collectors returning from these grand collecting trips with hundreds of manuscripts at a time.

In the 15th century, the Italian city of Florence, in particular, became a center of Greek learning in the West, supported in large part by the ruling Medici family. Marsilio Ficino translated Plato into Latin, and he established an academy in Florence, modeled on Plato's Academy, complete with symposia in Greek dress if the stories are to be believed. One of Ficino's great projects was to work out the connections between Greek philosophy, especially Plato's, and Christian theology. Even so, his work with the pagans got him into some trouble with the Pope. Another of the great Florentine Humanists and Hellenists was Angelo Poliziano, often called Politian. His tomb is now in the church of San Marco in Florence, and there you can see on it an inscription that says that he, Poliziano, tried to recreate in Florence under Lorenzo de'Medici, something of the glory of Athens under Pericles. Such was his admiration of many of the works we've been reading. When you go see his tomb there in San Marco, you'll notice an irony: It's somewhat hidden behind a bust of the Dominican monk, Savonarola, the man who was so interested in burning so many of these books.

Now with the advent of the printing press in Europe at about this time, the world became a much safer place, safer than ever for the preservation of our Greek manuscripts, our Greek masterpieces. So we won't trace their survival any farther. It's true, though, that we still continue to add to the body of ancient Greek literature on a fairly regular basis. Papyrus scraps continue to yield new treasures, such as the Sappho poem we read earlier in this course. New technologies now allow us to get more out of texts we already have. One example of that is the famous Archimedes Palimpsest. Now, a palimpsest is a manuscript that's been written over with another text; this over-writing was often done because of the scarcity of writing materials. In this case, a text of the Hellenistic mathematician Archimedes had been obscured under some prayers written in about 1200. Very interesting prayers I'm sure, but we want to get at the Archimedes. In the late 1990s, innovative lighting methods made new portions of this Archimedes legible, both text and diagrams, underneath those prayers.

But enough on survival, let's turn to questions of influence, and briefly trace the afterlife of as many of our masterpieces as we can. So, let's start with Homer and epic more generally. I won't even try to summarize the extensive influence of those epics within the Greek world; we've been talking about those all along. Rather, let's turn to the Roman world, and the greatest of the Latin epic poems: Vergil's *Aeneid*. That epic, unfinished at the author's death in 19 B.C.E., is the most Roman of all poems, telling of the mythical founding of the city of Rome from the ashes of Troy as it were. But this poem, the *Aeneid*, shows obvious allegiance to its Greek ancestors, primarily Homer, but also Apollonius.

The epic begins with a statement of its dual focus: I sing of arms and the man. *Arma virumque cano*. In that one line—or rather those three Latin words, Vergil tells us that he will be making reference to both the *Iliad*—that's the "arms" part—and to the *Odyssey*, the man. Remember that the first word of the *Odyssey* in Greek is *andra*, the man. Vergil's one man is his hero, Aeneas, the son of Anchises and Aphrodite, and one of the survivors of the Greek destruction of Troy. Vergil's epic is in 12 books, the first six narrating the journeys of Aeneas from Troy to Rome—reflecting there the *Odyssey*; and the last six, the Iliadic six, about the battles that awaited Aeneas upon his arrival at the site of Rome. During his wanderings, Aeneas has Odyssean adventures, including a trip to the Underworld in Book 6; and he even stops by the island of the Cyclops, and he rescues one of Odysseus's men who had been left behind.

Once Aeneas has arrived in Italy and is engaged in battle with the natives, and especially with the Italian hero Turnus, there is regular and explicit reference to the fighting at Troy: has Aeneas now become a new Achilles, since he is the attacker, having invaded Italy; or has Aeneas met a new Achilles in the form of his opponent, Turnus, in Italy? Throughout, the dactylic hexameter meter, the repeated epithets, the similes, and other features of style all recall the Homeric model. But while we're in Vergil's epic, we have to leave Homeric influence for a moment and look at the nods to Apollonius and, through Apollonius, to Greek tragedy. These are most obviously in Book 4, where Aeneas has a tragic romance with the Carthaginian queen Dido.

Blown off his course to the city of Carthage in North Africa, Aeneas is welcomed by queen Dido, at least in part because Venus—that is Aphrodite to the Greeks, and this is Aeneas's mother—Venus has caused Dido to fall in love with him, and Vergil describes that love vividly, as a wound, an illness, a fire that consumes Dido. This all sounds very familiar. But Aeneas soon leaves Dido, driven by his mission to found the city of Rome; like a good Roman, he places public welfare; duty above his own personal pleasures and preferences and sails away. Dido curses Aeneas, curses the Roman race, then kills herself.

The recollections of Jason and Medea, from the third book of the *Argonautica*, are clear here, but altered. Vergil's considerable adaptation of Homer and Apollonius formed the basis of the European epic tradition that includes—in different ways and with different degrees of influence—such works as Dante's *Divine Comedy*; Milton's *Paradise Lost*. Early English translations of Homer, by Chapman, Dryden, and Pope, are considered masterpieces in their own right. In the 20th century, James Joyce, in *Ulysses*, translates Odysseus to 20th century Dublin, changing characters around, making Penelope unfaithful; and Derek Walcott, in his poem *Omeros*, gives us a Caribbean slant on the epics.

Examples of epic influence abound, but it is true that epic poetry, at one time a dominant narrative genre, has yielded to another narrative mode in recent centuries: It's yielded to the novel. Still, some critics argue for the influence of Homer even there. the *Odyssey* in particular has been referred to as the first novel, and it lays the foundation not only for adventure stories, but also for domestic dramas, with characters from a wide variety of classes and backgrounds. The *Iliad*, on the other hand, is the source of all that is tragic.

We'll have little to say here about Hesiod, and didactic poetry in general. Vergil, again, is the Roman inheritor of the tradition, this time in his *Georgics*—four books of dactylic hexameters modeled closely on the *Works and Days*. The subject is rural life and farming, but also with moral lessons as in Hesiod, lessons that stretch far beyond this farming life.

But let's move on now to other forms of poetry, putting the Homeric Hymns together with lyric and pastoral poetry. Chapman, the translator of Homer, also translated the Homeric Hymns, as did the Romantic poet Shelley, a great lover of the Greeks and all things Greek. Greek lyric has found translators, imitators, and admirers in almost every Western poetic tradition. We can start with the Roman Catullus from the 1st century B.C.E.—Catullus, who wrote poems in a variety of meters and styles, many of them immediately topical, many of them clearly influenced by Greek models. His poem 51, the one that begins *Ille mi par esse deo videtur*, is a translation, with an added stanza, of Sappho's poem on the effects of love. In this poem—and throughout his love poetry—Catullus adds a further nod to Sappho by calling his very Roman lover by the name Lesbia. Catullus's sometimes vituperative attacks in some other of his poems recall in some other of his poems both Archilochus and Aristophanes. Some of his venom is reserved for other lovers, or suspected lovers, of his Lesbia, but he also mentions Julius Caesar and Cicero. Catullus's poetry also includes a translation from Callimachus, a poem that serves as inspiration then for Pope in his *The Rape of the Lock*. Elsewhere Catullus explicitly echoes the Callimachean preference for the small and the refined over the epic.

Horace, also from the 1st century B.C.E., explicitly models himself on any number of Greek lyric poets, especially Alcaeus, in his meters and his poetic themes. His brilliant treatments of the Greek models deserve close attention, closer than we can get into here, so let's move on.

What about pastoral? Theocritus's poems influenced the European pastoral tradition through Vergil's *Eclogues*, written in 37 B.C.E. In the English pastoral tradition, we might think of Milton's *Lycidas*; the poems of Spenser and Sidney; and even some of Shakespeare's comedies. All of that can be traced back to Theocritus, if not to that pastoral setting we saw in Plato's *Phaedrus*.

Let's turn now to drama. We've already mentioned the way that comedy changed after Aristophanes, becoming tamer, less politically topical, less fantastic in its plots. The Greek New Comedian Menander paved the way for the two great Roman comedians, Plautus and Terence, who actually staged lightly reworked translations of some of Menander's comedies, as well as their own work in similar style. Aristophanes for the most part has not transplanted as well. He has not been as much of an influence on later comedy, and modern productions of Aristophanes tend to take considerable liberties with staging, often in admirable attempts to retain the punch of the comedy; the original force of Aristophanes's comedy, while making it intelligible to its audience and funny.

Tragedy: Romans did write tragedy, and the works of Seneca in particular were influential in the European tradition; but those works are rarely seen to match the sublime power of what we saw in Athens. They were not, it seems, the sort of public manifestations of civic ideals as we saw in Athens with the tragedies there. After the Roman Period, tragedy has enjoyed a number of discrete flowerings: in Elizabethan England with Shakespeare and Marlowe; 17th-century France with Corneille and Racine; and even into the modern period. Playwrights looking back to the tragic tradition include Ibsen, the American playwright Eugene O'Neill, who very explicitly and consciously modeled some of his plays on Greek tragedies. We can include here also Arthur Miller, Tennessee Williams, writing in the tragic tradition.

Greek comedies and tragedies still do grace our stages, in great numbers, but they're often not in any form that the ancients would recognize. That's okay; they don't have to be museum pieces if they're alive. The late 20th century, and the early 21st, has seen a strong revival of ancient theater onstage and in the movie theaters. These are very often heavily adapted, but what that shows is that playwrights, producers recognize the timeless force of these plays. In this same period, the formerly and still sometimes stuffy field of Classical scholarship has started taking increasing notice of this new use of our material.

The genre of tragedy in general has attracted considerable notice from a broad spectrum of critics. What exactly are the defining features of tragedy? In the ancient world, we can define tragedy in formal terms, but what makes a later work tragic, or not? Critics often wonder: What it is that makes tragedy so enjoyable, why it seems to flourish? Related to that question, why it seems to flourish at certain periods, in certain places, and not in others, whether in the writing of new tragedies or the new production of old ones. I make no guesses about that here, but the ongoing questions do suggest the continuing influence of the genre.

Moving on to history now: historians have always looked back to Herodotus and Thucydides as the founders of their genre. This began within the Greek world, and continued into the Roman. One tendency, in the centuries after our two historians Herodotus and Thucydides, was to write universal histories, or histories of an entire people or city. For Rome, for example, there was Livy's *History since the Founding of the City*. Livy's basic narrative structure follows Thucydides's in setting out events year by year; but Livy also includes what we might call Herodotean digressions. Historians continue to ask the same questions, and confront the same problems as Herodotus and Thucydides: For example: How best to handle sources? We might remember the story of a biography of the American president Ronald Reagan; it was filled with speeches, direct quotations, conversations that turned out to originate nowhere else than in the author's imagination. But it was an informed imagination, and one that produced all the things that were in his opinion demanded by the various occasions and following the general sense of what he really said. That explanation—Thucydidean as it might be—was not well received.

Other questions about history: How to strike a balance between accuracy and entertainment? Thucydides addressed this one. Now in a good academic bookstore you can find scholarly histories and popular histories; sometimes the two overlap, but not always. Sometimes we do assign bestsellers as textbooks for our classes, but rarely. What's the difference between those two types of histories? Is it a given that an accessible and bestselling history has to sacrifice accuracy? Thucydides might have said so. Or is such a history simply better written?

Thucydides, in particular, has been influential outside of the field of history. The philosopher Thomas Hobbes translated the *History of the Peloponnesian War* into English, and he seems to have found in it support for his own low opinion of human nature. The British critic and poet of the Victorian Age, Matthew Arnold, famously said that Thucydides's work can be called ancient history only to the extent that the events it describes happened a long time ago. In a more enlightened age, debates in Parliament and Congress made frequent reference to our historian; and we all, I think, can see his continuing relevance, especially to questions of foreign policy.

We're left now with oratory and philosophy. Oratory, particularly as practiced by Demosthenes, heavily influenced the greatest Roman orator, Cicero, from the 1st century B.C.E. There was a great interest in oratory of all sorts in the period known as the Second Sophistic, or the second flourishing of Sophism, in the 2nd and 3rd centuries C.E.— that is, our era, the Common Era. Cicero's style, in particular, was influential then and throughout the Renaissance. But contemporary rhetoric bears little resemblance to the ancient speeches, perhaps because of changed legal and political contexts, perhaps because of reduced attention spans. We don't look to Demosthenes for the sound byte.

How to assess the influence of Plato as we turn to philosophy? I won't even try to assess his thought, however we might determine exactly what that thought is. But what about his philosophical style? His student, Plato's student, Aristotle did not use the philosophical dialogue, but wrote treatises, and that is certainly the most prevalent format for philosophical writing through the ages, right up to the present. But the tradition of the philosophical dialogue has persisted as well, already in the works of Cicero—we're calling his name often today, in some of the early Christian writers; and into the 20th century with, for example, Santayana's *Dialogues in Limbo*. Some of Plato has persisted.

But now, for a grand conclusion. All of the works we've read, I would argue, are still with us in one way or another, whether their influence is still directly or indirectly felt. All of them have shaped who we are, simply since each one has, in some way, shaped the world we come from. That alone is a good reason to read these masterpieces: to know who we are by understanding what has shaped our world. That's a good reason to read these masterpieces, but I have to admit, I don't think it's the best reason. The best reason to read these masterpieces, I think, is because they're compelling, they're engaging and enjoyable—every one of them, each in its own way. We all have our favorites, and those are the ones we go back to again and again, but I hope you agree that each one them is well worth your time and your attention. Now I thank you for your time and your attention throughout this course.

Timeline

Note: All dates in this timeline are B.C.E.

2000–1100 .... **Bronze Age.**

1100–800 .... **Dark Age.**

800–490 .... **Archaic Period.**

c. 750 .... Homeric epics written down; Hesiod's poems written down; some Homeric Hymns written down.

c. 638 .... Birth of Solon.

Late 7th century .... Archilochus, Sappho, Alcaeus flourish.

558 .... Death of Solon.

535–510 .... Tyranny of Peisistratus and his sons in Athens.

c. 534 .... Thespis produces first tragedy.

525 .... Birth of Aeschylus.

c. 505 .... Democratic reforms of Cleisthenes in Athens.

496 .... Birth of Sophocles.

490–323 .... **Classical Period.**

490 .... Battle of Marathon.

c. 484 .... Birth of Herodotus.

480 .... Battles of Thermopylae and Salamis; birth of Euripides.

479 .... Battle of Plataea; defeat of Persians.

472 .... Aeschylus, *The Persians.*

c. 460 .... Birth of Thucydides.

458 .... Aeschylus, the *Oresteia.*

456 .... Death of Aeschylus.

454 .... Delian League treasury moved to Athens.

c. 450..............................Birth of Aristophanes.

447–433 ....Construction of the Parthenon in Athens.

c. 445..............................Sophocles, *Ajax*; birth of Lysias.

c. 440..............................Sophocles, *Antigone*.

431–404 ....Peloponnesian War.

431 ....Euripides, *Medea*.

c. 429..............................Birth of Plato.

428 ....Euripides, *Hippolytus*.

c. 425..............................Death of Herodotus; Sophocles, *Oedipus the King*; Aristophanes, *The Acharnians*.

c. 420..............................Euripides, *Electra*.

c. 419..............................Aristophanes, *The Clouds* (extant version).

415 ....Euripides, *Trojan Women*.

411 ....Aristophanes, *Lysistrata*.

409 ....Sophocles, *Philoctetes*.

408 ....Euripides, *Orestes*.

406 ....Death of Euripides; death of Sophocles; Euripides, *Bacchae*.

405 ....Aristophanes, *The Frogs*.

401 ....Sophocles, *Oedipus at Colonus*.

c. 400..............................Death of Thucydides.

399 ....Execution of Socrates.

c. 385..............................Death of Aristophanes.

384 ....Birth of Demosthenes.

c. 380..............................Death of Lysias.

351 ....Demosthenes, *First Philippic*.

347 ....Death of Plato.

323–31 ....Hellenistic Period.

Glossary

analysts: Homeric critics who argue that the poems are compilations of several different stories or songs, discrete parts that we can distinguish from one another.

Areopagus council: A council established early in Athenian history, probably with particular oversight of murder trials; it was reformed in 462 and figures prominently in Aeschylus's *Oresteia* of 458.

aristeia: A hero's moment of glory on the battlefield, especially seen in the *Iliad*, when he reveals himself as best, or *aristos*.

aulos: A double-reeded instrument akin to our oboe, used in accompaniment to some lyric poetry.

City Dionysia: Annual Athenian festival in honor of Dionysus. The celebration included dramatic competitions, perhaps as early as 534.

Delian League: Established as a defensive alliance after the Persian Wars, it gradually turned into an Athenian Empire, as evidenced, for instance, by the transfer of the treasury from Delos to Athens in 454.

deliberative oratory: Also known as political oratory, this refers to the speeches delivered in public assemblies in the *polis*.

Delphi: Site of the oracle of Apollo, where pilgrims came from all over Greece to learn the future from Apollo's human mouthpiece, the Pythian priestess.

deus ex machina: Latin for "god from the machine," the term for the sudden appearance of a god or hero at the end of a play; used to bring resolution to a plot.

ekkyklema: The rolling platform used in Greek drama to bring out before the spectators an interior scene or tableau.

ekphrasis: The description within a literary work of a physical object.

elegiac poetry: Poems written in elegiac couplets, not necessarily mournful or funereal.

epideictic oratory: Oratory for show; a large category of speeches that includes those delivered at funerals, festivals, or other public occasions—outside of the courtroom and the assembly.

epinicians: Poems celebrating athletic victories, composed for public performance by a chorus.

ethopoeia: The ability of a speechwriter to create with language a distinct and sympathetic persona for each of his clients.

forensic oratory: Courtroom speeches, for both prosecution and defense.

Homeric question: Actually, a series of questions about the authorship of the Homeric epics: Was there a single author? If so, who? When? And by what mechanism?

iambic: Poems that are often (but not always) in iambic meter, marked by erotic themes and sometimes harsh invective.

kleos: Glory or fame, especially after death.

Lesbos: Island in the eastern Aegean; home of the lyric poets Alcaeus and Sappho.

Library of Alexandria: Founded in the 4th century, this was not only the largest collection of books in the ancient Greek world but also a center of scholarly and literary activity.

Marathon: Site north of Athens of a battle in 490. There, the Athenians, with little help from other Greeks, turned back the attack of the Persians under Darius.

mechane: Greek word for the crane used in the Greek theater to lower gods and others onto the stage or the stage building. The Latin translation is *machina*, hence, *deus ex machina*.

melic poetry: Any poetry that was sung; from the Greek *melos*, "song."

metatheater: A theatrical convention wherein actors call attention to a play's own theatrical status, commenting on the necessities and practices of the stage; a self-referentiality or awareness of theater as theater.

nostos: Greek for "return," this term is applied to those stories, such as Homer's *Odyssey* or Aeschylus's *Agamemnon*, that involve the return of a hero to his home after a long absence.

oral-formulaic composition: According to a theory developed in the 20th century, this is the means by which the Homeric poems were produced. Generations of singers passed along the poems orally, with additions, deletions, and modifications appearing in every retelling.

parabasis: The choral song in a Greek comedy during which the chorus comes forward and addresses the audience directly, often on behalf of the playwright.

parodos: The opening choral song of a Greek tragedy, during which the chorus proceeds into the orchestra, where it will operate for the remainder of the play.

Parthenon: The temple of Athena Parthenos, the patron deity of Athens, situated on the Acropolis above Athens and destroyed by the Persians in 480; the one we see now was built from 447–433 during the height of Athenian imperialism.

Peloponnesian War: The war between Athens, with her allies, and Sparta, with her Peloponnesian allies; it lasted from 431–404 and ended with the defeat of Athens.

Persian Wars: The wars between the Greeks and Persians fought in two stages: Darius invaded and was turned back in 490; his son Xerxes invaded in 480 and, after a victory at Thermopylae, was defeated at Salamis in 480 and Plataea in 479.

Plataea: Site in northern Greece of the Greek victory over Xerxes's land forces in 479.

polis: Greek political unit in the 5th century, often translated as "city-state."

Potiphar's wife story: The name taken from the story in Genesis 39 and applied to any story that follows the same pattern: a love triangle in which a woman tries unsuccessfully to seduce the son (or younger friend) of her husband.

priamel: A poetic device in which the author emphasizes a point by contrast, starting with what others think about a particular subject and leading up to the climax of what the author thinks.

Salamis: Island near Athens, off the shores of which the Greeks, led by an Athenian contingent, defeated Xerxes's Persian navy in 480.

Sicilian expedition: The Athenian invasion of Sicily in 415–413, which took place during a break in the Peloponnesian War (the Peace of Nicias). A large Athenian fleet was completely destroyed.

stichomythia: A rapid-fire verbal exchange in a drama, with each character speaking only one line; often used at moments of heightened tension.

symposium: A semi-formalized male gathering for eating and drinking.

Telemacheia: The name given to the first four books of Homer's *Odyssey*, because they describe, in part, the coming of age of Odysseus's son, Telemachus.

Thermopylae: Site of a battle in 480 between the Persians, under Xerxes, and the Greeks, led by a select group of Spartans under King Leonidas. Every Spartan died in the failed attempt to defend a pass.

timē: Honor, especially as measured by outward manifestations, such as war prizes.

Titanomachy: The battle described by Hesiod between the Titans and the Olympians, led by Zeus. The Olympian victory was an essential step toward establishing Zeus as the chief god.

unitarians: Homeric critics who argue that the poems are the unified products of a single poetic genius.

xenia: Greek for hospitality, an important social bond, often lasting for generations between the families of guests and hosts, and overseen by Zeus in his role as the protector of guests.

Biographical Notes

Legendary, Mythological, and Fictional Figures:

Achilles: The best of the Greeks fighting at Troy. Homer's *Iliad* centers on his decision to leave the fighting and later return to it to avenge the death of his friend Patroclus.

Aegisthus: Cousin of Agamemnon, son of Thyestes; he has an affair with Agamemnon's wife, Clytemnestra, while Agamemnon is at Troy. Killed by Clytemnestra's son Orestes.

Agamemnon: Leader of the Greek forces at Troy. Killed upon his return from the war by his wife, Clytemnestra.

Agave: Daughter of the Theban king Cadmus, mother of a son, Pentheus. She kills her son in a Dionysian frenzy after refusing to acknowledge the divinity of Dionysus.

Ajax: A Greek warrior at Troy noted for his physical prowess. After losing to Odysseus in a contest for the dead Achilles's arms, he tries to kill the leaders of the Greek force, then kills himself.

Anchises: A Trojan prince, who, seduced by Aphrodite, becomes the father of the Trojan hero Aeneas.

Andromache: Wife of the Trojan hero Hector.

Antigone: Daughter of Oedipus; she insists on proper burial for both of her brothers, even after an edict from King Creon forbidding the burial of Polynices. She is caught in the act and sent to her death.

Aphrodite: An Olympian goddess associated with erotic love.

Apollo: An Olympian god associated with health, music, and prophecy. Mortals learned of the future through an oracle devoted to him at Delphi.

Artemis: A virginal Olympian goddess, sister of Apollo; associated with the hunt and protectress of hunters.

Astyanax: Son of Hector and Andromache, he was thrown to his death from the walls of Troy after the Greeks won the war.

Athena: A virginal Olympian goddess, born full-grown and armed from the head of Zeus. She was associated with warfare, wisdom, and womanly crafts, such as weaving.

Atreus: Father of Agamemnon and Menelaus, who are thus referred to as the Atreidae. He tricked his brother Thyestes into eating a stew of his own children.

Cadmus: Founder and king of Thebes; father of Semele, Agave, and others; grandfather of Pentheus.

Calypso: A goddess living on the island of Ogygia, known almost exclusively for her "hosting" of Odysseus for several years during his trip home from Troy.

Cassandra: Daughter of King Priam of Troy, she was given the gift of prophecy by Apollo, but after rejecting his advances, she received another "gift": No one would ever believe her. After the fall of Troy, she became Agamemnon's war prize and died with him upon their return to Greece.

Circe: A divine sorceress who turned many of Odysseus's men into pigs but was unable to get the better of Odysseus. He spent one year with her during his return from Troy.

Clytemnestra: Wife of Agamemnon, sister of Helen; she killed Agamemnon when he returned home from Troy, mostly because he had killed their daughter Iphigeneia. Her son Orestes avenged his father by killing her.

Creon: A generic name for a king. One was the brother of Iocasta, the mother/wife of Oedipus. He ruled in Thebes after the expulsion of Oedipus and again after the death of Oedipus's two sons. Another Creon was king in Corinth when Jason and Medea were there.

Demeter: An Olympian goddess associated with fertility, especially of grains. One center of her worship was at Eleusis, near Athens, where Greeks celebrated a highly influential and secretive set of rites in her honor.

Dikaiopolis: Hero, if you will, of Aristophanes's comedy *The Acharnians*. We might call him a low-life everyman, desperate for peace, but largely so that he can satisfy his many personal appetites.

Diomedes: One of the greatest of the Greek warriors at Troy, he won particular glory when Achilles sat out of the fighting.

Dionysus: An Olympian god, son of Zeus and the Theban princess Semele; he was associated with wine, exuberant behavior, and fertility. Myths about him often involve an initial resistance to recognizing his divinity.

Electra: Daughter of Agamemnon and Clytemnestra; she plotted with her brother Orestes the deaths of Clytemnestra and her lover, Aegisthus.

Eros: Love and the personification of love. Sometimes seen as a son of Aphrodite (think Cupid with his bow), sometimes as an elemental force in the creation of the universe.

Eteocles: Son of Oedipus and Iocasta, ruler of Thebes until he died in battle with his brother Polynices.

Eumaeus: Odysseus's swineherd, loyal to Odysseus during his 20-year absence. Odysseus stayed with him when he first returned to Ithaca.

Furies: Translation of the Erinyes, chthonic goddesses (that is, living under the Earth rather than on Olympus) whose particular job was to take vengeance on those who shed kindred blood. In Aeschylus's *Oresteia*, we see them transformed into Eumenides, or "Kindly Ones."

Gaia: Earth, the mother of all through her mating with Ouranos, the Sky. Hesiod gives her a personality and a role in the downfall of Ouranos as ruler of the universe.

Hector: Son of Priam, husband of Andromache, greatest of the Trojan heroes; killed by Achilles.

Helen: Most beautiful woman in the world, she was the wife of Menelaus, then taken to Troy by Paris; hence, the Trojan War.

Hephaestus: An Olympian god associated with the forge and things made there. He was lame, the only physically imperfect god.

Hera: An Olympian goddess, primary consort of Zeus, most active in myth as a foil to Zeus in his various plans and dalliances.

Hermes: An Olympian god associated with trickery, fast talking, and the ability to cross boundaries, as between gods and mortals, life and death. As such, he was useful as a messenger.

Hippolytus: Son of the Athenian king Theseus, he was a devoted follower of the virginal huntress Artemis, whom he emulated in his hunting and in his rejection of all things associated with love. Aphrodite punished him for that.

Iocasta: Mother, then wife of Oedipus; she hanged herself when she realized she had been married to her own son.

Iphigeneia: Daughter of Agamemnon, who killed her at Aulis in order to win from the gods favorable winds for the voyage to Troy.

Jason: Hero whose quest took him after the Golden Fleece on the eastern shores of the Black Sea. He completed the quest with the help of Medea, whom he subsequently left for another woman.

Kronos: A son of Ouranos and Gaia, he plotted with his mother to castrate and, thereby, overthrow his father. He was subsequently overthrown by his son Zeus.

Laertes: Father of Odysseus.

Laius: King of Thebes and father of Oedipus; he was killed by Oedipus in a scuffle at a crossroads.

Medea: A regal sorceress from the East; after helping Jason retrieve the Golden Fleece, she punished him for trying to marry another in her place.

Menelaus: Brother of Agamemnon, husband of Helen, and hence, one of the principals in the Greek expedition against the Trojans.

Nausicaa: Phaeacian princess who first encountered Odysseus when he washed up on her shores. She had marriage on her mind but proved invaluable in helping Odysseus on his way back to Ithaca.

Neoptolemus: Son of Achilles, he was instrumental in bringing Philoctetes to Troy, where his presence was required for Greek victory.

Odysseus: Cleverest of the Greeks fighting at Troy; his return to Ithaca took 10 years, and there, he was faced with a household of suitors for the hand of his wife, Penelope.

Oedipus: Son of Laius and Iocasta, king and queen of Thebes, he was exposed on a mountain soon after birth; he survived to kill his father, marry and bed his mother, and eventually come to realize what he had done.

Orestes: Son of Agamemnon and Clytemnestra, he plotted with his sister Electra the deaths of Clytemnestra and her lover, Aegisthus.

Ouranos: The Sky, married to Gaia, the Earth, and the first dominant male in Hesiod's creation story. He stuffed their many children back inside Gaia in an attempt (failed) to avoid overthrow by his children.

Paris: A Trojan prince, son of Priam, and brother of Hector. For choosing Aphrodite as the fairest (above Hera and Athena), he was given Helen. Given that she was already married to Menelaus, the Trojan War ensued.

Patroclus: Close companion of Achilles. His death at the hands of Hector spurred Achilles to return to the fighting in the *Iliad*.

Penelope: Wife of Odysseus, she remained faithful to him throughout his 20-year absence and used her cleverness to hold off the suitors.

Pentheus: Young king of Thebes, grandson of Cadmus; he was torn to pieces by a crazed group of Theban women, including his own mother, Agave, because he and they refused to recognize the divinity of Dionysus.

Phaeacians: Odysseus's final stop before Ithaca was with these people. They hosted him graciously, and after he narrated to them the story of his wanderings, they took him safely home.

Phaedra: Wife of Theseus and stepmother of Hippolytus. As punishment for Hippolytus's avoidance of sex, Aphrodite caused Phaedra to fall in love with him, thus starting a sequence of events that led to the deaths of both Phaedra and Hippolytus.

Philoctetes: A Greek who was abandoned on the way to Troy because of a festering foot wound. When it became known that he and the bow of Herakles he possessed were needed by the Greeks in order to take Troy, Odysseus and Neoptolemus brought him to Troy.

Phoenix: Father figure of Achilles at Troy, he was unable to persuade Achilles to return to the fighting with his speech in *Iliad* 9.

Polynices: Son of Oedipus and Iocasta, he brought an army against Thebes in an attempt to claim rule from his brother Eteocles. Both brothers died in the battle, and Polynices's body was left unburied until his sister Antigone performed a ritual burial.

Polyphemus: The Cyclops who hosted Odysseus and his men in *Odyssey* 9. Odysseus's cleverness won the release of most of the men, but his boasting allowed the Cyclops to call down a devastating curse on him.

Priam: King of Troy, he visited Achilles in *Iliad* 24 to ask for the body of his son Hector.

Prometheus: Son of a Titan, he tried to trick Zeus on behalf of mortals and was punished: chained to a rock, where an eagle ate at his liver daily.

Pylades: Close companion of Orestes, he supported him in his plot to kill his mother. He made a surprising and central proclamation to motivate Orestes in Aeschylus's *Libation Bearers*.

Rheia: A Titan, daughter of Ouranos and Gaia and consort of Kronos. She ensured that their last son, Zeus, was not swallowed down by Kronos. Zeus thus went on to overthrow Kronos.

Semele: Daughter of Cadmus of Thebes, mother of Dionysus by Zeus. Hera tricked her into asking Zeus to appear as he did to the gods; when he did so, she burned, and Zeus was able to save only the unborn baby, who gestated within his thigh.

Sirens: Half-woman, half-bird creatures who tempt mariners to their deaths by singing. Odysseus and Jason both survived their charms, in different ways.

Sphinx: A creature that has the head of a woman, the body of a lion, and the wings of an eagle. She tormented the city of Thebes until Oedipus answered her riddle and caused her to destroy herself.

Strepsiades: Hero of Aristophanes's *Clouds*; the embodiment of old-fashioned, rural Athenian values, as opposed to the newfangled intellectual developments of Aristophanes's own day.

Teiresias: Blind Theban prophet, he appears in Sophocles's Theban plays, in Euripides's *Bacchae*, in Callimachus's Hymn 5, and in the Underworld in *Odyssey* 11.

Telemachus: Son of Odysseus and Penelope, he came of age in the opening books of the *Odyssey* and later helped his father defeat the suitors.

Theseus: Early king of Athens (after his adventures in Crete with the Minotaur), he cursed his son Hippolytus after reading a false message from his wife, Phaedra. He was also known for welcoming to Athens outsiders, such as Oedipus.

Thetis: Sea nymph, mother of Achilles, she persuaded Zeus in *Iliad* 1 to honor her son by causing the Trojans to succeed while Achilles sat out.

Thyestes: Brother of Atreus, father of Aegisthus, recipient of the grisly feast of Thyestes, where his own children were served to him by Atreus.

Titans: Children of Gaia and Ouranos; overthrown by Zeus and his sibling Olympians in the Titanomachy; described by Hesiod.

Typhoios: Monstrous son of Gaia, he challenged Zeus after the Titanomachy. Zeus defeated him, thereby securing his place as chief god.

Zeus: King of the Olympian gods, associated with the sky, the weather, and such matters as justice and the proper treatment of guests.

Historical Figures:

Note: All dates are B.C.E. unless otherwise indicated.

Aeschylus (525–456): The oldest of the three great Athenian tragedians; a veteran of the battle of Salamis, he wrote between 70 and 90 plays, of which 7 survive, or only 6 if, as many suggest, he did not write *Prometheus Bound*.

Alcaeus (late 7th century): With Sappho, one of the two great lyric poets from the island of Lesbos. His verses include both amatory and political themes.

Alcibiades (c. 450–404): An Athenian general during the Peloponnesian War, famous as a student of Socrates and a bon vivant. He agitated in favor of the Sicilian expedition but was recalled from it on charges that he had smashed statues of Hermes. One of the most brilliant and controversial figures of the period, he was in and out of favor in Athens for the rest of his life.

Alexander (356–323): A Macedonian king; called "the Great" because of his military conquests around the Mediterranean and far beyond. He founded Alexandria in Egypt, the city that became the center of Greek culture in the Hellenistic Period.

Apollonius (c. 270–c. 210): Called Apollonius of Rhodes because of an association with that island late in life. He was a librarian at Alexandria, where he wrote the epic about Jason, the *Argonautica*.

Archilochus (mid-late 7th century): One of the earliest of the lyric poets, his range included elegiac and iambic poetry of considerable grace and power.

Aristophanes (c. 450–c. 385): The author of the only surviving examples of Old Comedy, highly successful during a career that began in 427. He claims to have run afoul of certain politicians with his outspoken criticism, but we know little about his life, and most of that is suspect.

Aristotle (384–322): Prolific and tremendously influential Greek philosopher; student and critic of Plato; and author of treatises on a wide variety of subjects, including ethics, physics, politics, and poetry. His writings come to us in an unpolished form, possibly notes rather than finished works.

Callimachus (c. 300–c. 240): A prolific scholar and poet who worked in the Library of Alexandria. He wrote some 800 works, very few of which survive, and some of those only in fragments.

Croesus (c. 550): Lydian king who ruled over eastern Greeks; he was famous for his wealth.

Darius (d. 486): Persian king who put down the Ionian Revolt, then made an expedition against the Greeks; defeated at Marathon in 490.

Demosthenes (384–322): Greatest of the Greek orators, his career began with forensic speeches as he tried to defend himself against unscrupulous guardians. He called, vociferously but unsuccessfully, for a union of Greeks against the growing threat of Philip II of Macedon.

Euripides (480–406): The youngest of the three Athenian tragedians and the most obviously influenced by the intellectual innovations in the 5th century. His plays (of which 18 are extant) did not often win first prize in his lifetime but became more popular after his death.

Herodotus (c. 484–c. 425): From Halicarnassus in modern Turkey, he traveled extensively and spent some time in Athens. For his history of the Persian Wars, he is referred to as the Father of History.

Hesiod (c. 700): Author of *Theogony* and *Works and Days*, he gives us some biographical information about himself in his poems, but most of that is suspect.

Homer (c. 750): This is a name we give to the poetic tradition that culminated in the two epics the *Iliad* and the *Odyssey*. Maybe there was an individual by this name, maybe a blind bard from Asia Minor, as the ancients thought.

Lysias (c. 445–c. 380): One of the greatest of the orators, he has been celebrated through the ages especially for the clarity of his style and, in his forensic speeches, his ability to create and convey the character of the speaker for whom he was writing.

Menander (344–292): An Athenian comic playwright, leading representative of the so-called New Comedy. His work comes to us primarily through Roman adaptations of his plots and, more recently, papyrus finds.

Nicias (c. 470–413): An Athenian general known for his caution and his great wealth, he negotiated the so-called Peace of Nicias with Sparta, a 50-year peace that actually lasted from 421–414. During that peace, he became a reluctant general of the Athenian forces that went to Sicily, where he died.

Peisistratus (c. 607–528): Tyrant of Athens from 535–528, he was a supporter of the arts and institutionalized several of the religious festivals, such as the Dionysia, at which tragedies were performed. His sons succeeded him in the tyranny until 510.

Pericles (c. 495–429): Leading Athenian politician of the mid-5th century, from roughly 461 until his death from the plague. He was behind the rebuilding program on the Acropolis, and it was his strategy that guided Athens through the early years of the Peloponnesian War. He was a student of philosophy, the greatest orator of his day, and even won the praise of Thucydides for his leadership.

Phaedrus (c. 444–393): A follower of Socrates, Plato includes him as a major character in both the *Phaedrus* and the *Symposium*. He was implicated in the sacrilegious behavior of 415 that led to Alcibiades's recall from Sicily.

Philip II (382–336): King of Macedonia, to the north of Greece, from 359 until his death. He expanded his country considerably, eventually seizing power throughout the Aegean. He thus bequeathed a strong position to his son Alexander, later called "the Great."

Pindar (c. 518–c. 438): From Thebes, the author of 17 books of choral songs, from which almost all that survives is a group of epinicians, songs in honor of athletic victories.

Plato (c. 429–347): A follower of Socrates, he composed dialogues in the form of Socratic conversations, gradually inserting more of himself and less of Socrates as he developed his own ideas. Although he never speaks in his own voice, he is often referred to as the Father of Western Philosophy.

Sappho (late 7th century): With Alcaeus, one of the two great lyric poets from the island of Lesbos; her works survive largely in fragments, giving us just a glimpse of what made her so famous in antiquity as one of the greatest of the lyric poets. Her themes are largely amatory.

Schliemann, Heinrich (1822–1890 C.E.): A German businessman with a passion for Homer, he spent a portion of his fortune on excavating at Troy and Homeric sites in Greece in an attempt to prove the historicity of the Homeric epics.

Socrates (470–399): The gadfly that stirred up the sluggish Athenian citizenry. He wrote nothing himself, but according to the accounts of Plato, Xenophon, and Aristophanes, he spent his life questioning his fellow citizens. His fellow Athenians put him to death, but his methods and his interest in ethical questions formed the basis for all subsequent Western philosophy.

Solon (c. 638–558): Athenian statesman and poet, he described his political innovations and tribulations in verse and offered moral reflections.

Sophocles (496–406): An Athenian who was successful in his political career, held an important religious position, and wrote nearly 120 tragedies, often winning with them at the dramatic festivals.

Theocritus (c. 300–c. 240): Probably from Sicily but later working in the circle of Callimachus and Apollonius in Alexandria; he is best known as the inventor of pastoral poetry, but his *Idylls* also include urban mimes, vignettes from the streets of Alexandria.

Thucydides (c. 460–c. 400): Athenian from a wealthy family, he suffered and survived the plague; he was elected general in 424 and was exiled from Athens soon after that. In his *History of the Peloponnesian War*, he traces events that led up to the war and takes us through the events of 411. The work is notable not only for its attention to accuracy but also for its insightful treatment of power and morality.

Vergil (70–19): Roman poet, much influenced by the epics of Homer and Apollonius, as well as Greek tragedy and lyric, in his epic the *Aeneid*. His pastoral poems, *The Eclogues*, show the influence of the *Idylls* of Theocritus.

Xenophon (c. 427–355): Author of Socratic reminiscences, as well as a history that picks up where Thucydides's left off. His style is remarkably lucid, but he has the misfortune to be compared to Plato in his Socratic writings and Thucydides in his histories.

Xerxes (r. 486–65): Son of Darius, he led the second great Persian invasion of Greece in 480. After a victory at Thermopylae, his navy was defeated at Salamis and his land forces at Plataea.

Bibliography

Essential Reading:

Note: Many translations are available for all of these works. Those listed here work well for this course. Others have other attractions: closer to the Greek, more poetic, more colloquial, already on your bookshelf, and so on. Some are even available on tape. If you have the luxury, sample a few to see what suits you best.

Aeschylus. *The Complete Greek Tragedies: Aeschylus I* and *II: The Complete Greek Tragedies*. Edited by D. Grene and R. Lattimore. Chicago: University of Chicago Press, 1953 (I) and 1956 (II).

Apollonius. *Jason and the Golden Fleece* (*The Argonautica*). Translated by R. Hunter. Oxford: Oxford University Press, 1993.

Aristophanes. *Aristophanes: Lysistrata, The Acharnians, The Clouds*. Translated by A. Sommerstein. New York: Penguin, 1973.

———. *The Frogs, Four Plays by Aristophanes*. Translated by W. Arrowsmith, R. Lattimore, and D. Parker. New York: Meridian, 1994.

Callimachus. *The Poems of Callimachus*. Translated by F. Nisetich. Oxford: Oxford University Press, 2001.

Demosthenes. *Philipic 1*, in *Athenian Political Oratory, 16 Key Speeches*. Translated by David D. Phillips. New York: Routledge, 2004.

Euripides. *Euripides I, II, III, IV,* and *V: The Complete Greek Tragedies*. Edited by D. Grene and R. Lattimore. Chicago: University of Chicago Press, 1955, 1959.

Herodotus. *The Histories*, rev. ed. Translated by A. de Sélincourt and John M. Marincola. New York: Penguin, 2003.

Hesiod. *Works and Days* and *Theogony*. Translated by S. Lombardo. Indianapolis: Hackett, 1993.

Homer. *The Iliad*. Translated by R. Fagles. New York: Penguin, 1990.

———. *The Odyssey*. Translated by R. Fagles. New York: Penguin, 1996.

The Homeric Hymns. Translated by A. N. Athanassakis. Baltimore: Johns Hopkins University Press, 1976.

Lysias. *On the Killing of Eratosthenes*, in *The Murder of Herodes and Other Trials from the Athenian Law Courts*. Translated by K. Freeman. Indianapolis: Hackett, 1963.

Miller, A. N., translator and commentator. *Greek Lyric: An Anthology in Translation*. Indianapolis: Hackett, 1996.

Plato. *Republic, Phaedo, Ion, Symposium*, and *Phaedrus*, in *Plato: Complete Works*. Edited by J. M. Cooper. Indianapolis: Hackett, 1997.

Sophocles. *Ajax* and *Philoctetes*, in *The Complete Greek Tragedies: Sophocles II*. Edited by D. Grene and R. Lattimore. Chicago: University of Chicago Press, 1957.

————. *Oedipus the King, Oedipus at Colonus*, and *Antigone*, in *Sophocles: The Three Theban Plays*. Translated by R. Fagles. New York: Penguin, 1982.

Theocritus. *Idylls*. Translated by A. Verity. Oxford: Oxford University Press, 2002.

Thucydides. *The Peloponnesian War*. The Crawley Translation, revised by T.E. Wick. New York: Random House, 1982.

Supplementary Reading:

Asmis, E. "Plato on Poetic Creativity," in *The Cambridge Companion to Plato*, edited by R. Kraut, pp. 338–364. A good discussion of the many and seemingly contradictory references to poetry in Plato's dialogues.

Beye, C. R. *Epic and Romance in the Argonautica of Apollonius*. Carbondale, IL: SIU Press, 1982. A clearly written study of the literary techniques of the entire epic, with regular reference back to earlier models.

Burnett, A. P. *Catastrophe Survived: Euripides' Plays of Mixed Reversal*. Oxford: Oxford University Press, 1971. An influential study of the seven so-called "happy-ending plays," including *Orestes*.

Cairns, D. L., ed. *Oxford Readings in Homer's Iliad.* Oxford: Oxford University Press, 2001. A collection of excellent essays, ranging from general discussions of origin and background to readings of specific passages.

Carey, C. "Observers of Speeches and Hearers of Action: The Athenian Orators," in *Literature in the Greek and Roman Worlds*, edited by O. Taplin, pp. 192–216. A wide-ranging overview of Greek rhetoric, from Homer through Demosthenes.

Clay, D. *Platonic Questions: Dialogues with the Silent Philosopher.* University Park, PA: The Pennsylvania State University Press, 2000. An insightful and engaging study of the dialogues as philosophical dramas, with readings of several dialogues.

Clay, J. S. *Hesiod's Cosmos.* Cambridge: Cambridge University Press, 2003. A detailed interpretation of both *Works and Days* and *Theogony*, with comments on the interaction between them.

———. "The Homeric Hymns," in *A New Companion to Homer*, edited by I. Morris and B. Powell, pp. 489–507. A useful overview of the genre, with brief comments about each of the major hymns.

Cohen, B., ed. *The Distaff Side: Representing the Female in Homer's Odyssey.* Oxford: Oxford University Press, 1995. A collection of 11 essays on various aspects of women and their role in the epic.

Conacher, D. J. *Aeschylus' Oresteia: A Literary Commentary.* Toronto: University of Toronto Press, 1987. A scene-by-scene discussion of the trilogy, clearly written and argued. A good introduction.

———. *Aeschylus: The Earlier Plays and Related Studies.* Toronto: Toronto University Press, 1996. A treatment similar to the one below of Aeschylus's other plays, including *Persians*.

Connor, W. R. *Thucydides.* Princeton: Princeton University Press, 1984. An excellent and fairly brief treatment of many of the aspects of Thucydides's work considered in this course.

Corrigan, K., and E. Glazov-Corrigan. *Plato's Dialectic at Play: Argument, Structure, and Myth in the Symposium.* University Park, PA: The Pennsylvania State University Press, 2004. A detailed discussion of the literary aspects of the dialogue and the ways in which the literary and philosophical interact.

Crane, G. *The Blinded Eye: Thucydides and the New Written Word.* Lanham, MD: Rowman & Littlefield Publishers, 1996. A reading of Thucydides's work that focuses on his manipulation of the genre of prose history, not only to record events but to fashion a new civic ideology.

Dodds, E. R. *The Greeks and the Irrational.* Berkeley: University of California Press, 1951. A seminal corrective to the view of Greeks as sterile intellectuals.

————. "Introduction," in *Euripides: Bacchae*, 2nd ed., edited and commented by E. R. Dodds. Oxford: Oxford University Press, 1960. Even though this is an introduction to a Greek edition of the play, it is accessible to those with no Greek (yet) and highly informative on a broad array of topics.

————. "On Misunderstanding the *Oedipus Rex*," in *Oxford Readings in Greek Tragedy*, edited by E. Segal, pp. 177–188. In this seminal essay, the author responds, often amusingly, to student attempts to understand the play. Clearly argued and well written.

Dover, K. J., ed. *Ancient Greek Literature*, 2nd ed. Oxford: Oxford University Press, 1997. A good, brief survey of the material in this course, with essays by highly regarded experts.

————. *Aristophanic Comedy*. Berkeley: University of California Press, 1972. A useful and well-written introduction to Aristophanes's plays and Old Comedy more generally.

Easterling, P. E., ed. *The Cambridge Companion to Greek Tragedy*. Cambridge: Cambridge University Press, 1997. Very good essays on tragedy in general, its context, interpretation, and afterlife, rather than on particular plays.

Edwards, M. *Homer: Poet of The Iliad*. Baltimore: The Johns Hopkins University Press, 1987. Good background information, as well as excellent and readable commentaries on several of the central books of the epic.

Emlyn-Jones, C. "The Reunion of Penelope and Odysseus," in *Homer*, edited by I. McAuslan and P. Walcot, pp. 126–143. A good study of the protracted recognition scene that extends from Book 17 through Book 23.

Foley, H. *Female Acts in Greek Tragedy*. Princeton: Princeton University Press, 2001. Good treatments of several of the key female characters in tragedy.

————. "Tragedy and Politics in Aristophanes's *Acharnians*," in *Oxford Readings in Aristophanes*, edited by E. Segal, pp. 117–142. The author emphasizes the connection between Aristophanes and Dikaiopolis, both of them questioning the wartime policies of Athens.

Fowler, B. *The Hellenistic Aesthetic*. Madison: University of Wisconsin Press, 1989. A readable introduction to the period, useful in bringing together literature and the visual arts.

Fowler, R. L., ed. *The Cambridge Companion to Homer*. Cambridge: Cambridge University Press, 2004. A recent collection of essays covering considerable thematic ground. It closes with eight essays on receptions of the poems.

Goldhill, S. *Aeschylus: The Oresteia*, 2nd ed. Cambridge: Cambridge University Press, 2004. An excellent, brief introduction to the trilogy, organized thematically.

————. *Love, Sex, and Tragedy: How the Ancient World Shapes Our Lives*. Chicago: University of Chicago Press, 2004. A wide-ranging and engaging exploration of the many ways in which the ancient Greeks have shaped the modern West.

————. *The Poet's Voice*. Cambridge: Cambridge University Press, 1991. An investigation of the place of the poet's own voice in ancient Greek poetry, with chapters on Homer, Pindar, Aristophanes, Theocritus, and Apollonius.

Griffin, J. *Homer: The Odyssey*, 2nd ed. Cambridge: Cambridge University Press, 2004. An excellent, brief introduction to the production of the poem, its themes, and some aspects of its reception.

Griffin, J., and M. Hammond. "Critical Appreciation: *Iliad* 1.1–52," in *Homer*, edited by I. McAuslan and P. Walcot, pp. 65–82. A close reading of these lines, with good discussion of the ways in which the poet uses them to introduce the entire epic.

Griffith, M. *The Authenticity of Prometheus Bound*. Cambridge: Cambridge University Press, 1977. The most influential presentation of the arguments against Aeschylean composition of this play. The book assumes knowledge of Greek and some understanding of Greek metrics.

————. "Introduction," in *Sophocles: Antigone*, edited and commented by M. Griffith. Cambridge: Cambridge University Press, 1999. An introduction to a Greek edition of the play but accessible to all; an excellent and fairly brief treatment of many of the central issues of the play.

Harrison, T. *The Emptiness of Asia: Aeschylus' Persians and the History of the Fifth Century*. London: Duckworth, 2000. A study of the value of the play as a historical document, as a source for events, for the Athenian attitude toward the Persians, and for their attitude about their own expanding power.

Henderson, J. *The Maculate Muse: Obscene Language in Attic Comedy*, 2nd ed. Oxford: Oxford University Press, 1991. A catalogue and explication of the many obscenities in Aristophanes's comedies. The first three chapters, on the place and use of obscenity in comedy, are accessible to the Greek-less.

Hesk, J. *Sophocles: Ajax*. London: Duckworth, 2003. A fairly brief general introduction to the play that focuses on some of the more difficult scenes, as well as some aspects of context and reception.

Hornblower, S., ed. *Greek Historiography*. Oxford: Oxford University Press, 1994. A collection of essays about several Greek historians, with interesting articles on Herodotus and Thucydides.

———. "Narratology and Narrative Technique in Thucydides," in *Greek Historiography*, edited by S. Hornblower, pp. 131–166. A study of how Thucydides's narrative technique underscores his claims to objectivity.

Hunter, R. *The Argonautica of Apollonius: Literary Studies*. Cambridge: Cambridge University Press, 1993. Essays on the epic by one of our foremost experts on Hellenistic poetry.

Hutchinson, G. *Hellenistic Poetry*. Oxford: Oxford University Press, 1988. A good overview of the period that includes separate chapters on each of the Hellenistic poets considered in this course.

Kitto, H. D. F. *Form and Meaning in Drama: A Study of Six Greek Plays and of Hamlet*. London: Methuen, 1960. An eminently readable treatment of the *Oresteia*, *Philoctetes*, *Antigone*, and *Ajax*, with a chapter on Greek and Elizabethan drama and one on *Hamlet*.

Knox, B. M. W. *The Heroic Temper: Studies in Sophoclean Tragedy*. Berkeley: University of California Press, 1964; reissued, 1983. An influential treatment of the particularly Sophoclean tragic hero: a figure who refuses to yield no matter what the odds or result.

———. "Introduction," in *Homer: The Iliad*, translated by R. Fagles. Excellent coverage of topics and themes, well written, and in places, even compelling in its own right.

———. *Oedipus at Thebes*. New Haven: Yale University Press, 1957. An influential study of Sophocles's *Oedipus the King* as a reflection of 5th-century Athenian values

———. *Word and Action: Essays on the Ancient Theater*. Baltimore: The Johns Hopkins University Press, 1979. Some of Knox's best-known essays and reviews are conveniently collected here.

Kraut, R., ed. *The Cambridge Companion to Plato*. Cambridge: Cambridge University Press, 1992. Essays by leading scholars, all introductory in nature, many of them with a more purely philosophical approach than I take in this course.

Kurke, L. "Charting the Poles of History: Herodotos and Thoukydides," in *Literature in the Greek and Roman Worlds*, edited by O. Taplin, pp. 133–155. A survey of the works of the historians, especially as they relate to their historical milieu.

———. "The Strangeness of 'Song Culture': Archaic Greek Poetry," in *Literature in the Greek and Roman Worlds*, edited by O. Taplin, pp. 58–87. A good treatment of the lyric poets we discuss, as well as their context.

Lamberton, R. *Hesiod*. New Haven: Yale University Press, 1988. An even-handed and concise introduction to the author and his works.

Lateiner, D. *The Historical Method of Herodotus. Phoenix* Supl. Vol. 23. Toronto: University of Toronto Press, 1989. A detailed study of many of Herodotus's literary and historiographical techniques.

———. "*The Iliad*: An Unpredictable Classic," in. *The Cambridge Companion to Homer*, edited by R. L. Fowler, pp. 11–30. A synoptic consideration of the plot of the epic, this essay achieves its goal: orienting new readers to the story and provoking returning readers into considering it afresh.

Luce, T. J. *The Greek Historians*. London: Routledge, 1997. This book contains good introductions to the historians read in this course, with discussions of their place within the larger context of Greek historical writing.

Marincola, J. "Introduction," in *Herodotus: The Histories*, translated by A. de Sélincourt. New York: Penguin, 1996. A relatively brief and helpful introduction to the historian and his work.

Mastronarde, D. "Introduction," in *Euripides: Medea*, edited and commented by D. Mastronarde. Cambridge: Cambridge University Press, 2002. An introduction to a Greek edition of the play, this is a storehouse of information and insight on many aspects of the play and its mythical background.

McAuslan, I., and P. Walcot, eds. *Homer. Greece and Rome Studies*, vol. IV. Oxford: Oxford University Press, 1998. A collection of essays on Homer, all of them insightful and accessible to those without Greek.

Miller, A. "Introduction," in *Greek Lyric: An Anthology in Translation*, translated and commented by A. Miller, pp. xi–xvi. Read together with the introductions to each of the poets in this volume, this very brief introduction helps put the poems into context.

Mills, S. *Euripides: Hippolytus*. London: Duckworth, 2002. A readable general introduction to many aspects of the play.

Morris, I., and B. Powell, eds. *A New Companion to Homer*. Leiden, Netherlands: Brill, 1997. A large collection of scholarly articles on a broad array of topics related to the production, appreciation, and afterlife of the Homeric poems.

Mossman, J., ed. *Euripides: Oxford Readings in Classical Studies*. Oxford: Oxford University Press, 2003. A useful collection of articles on Euripidean tragedy, including treatments of several individual plays.

Nightingale, A. "Sages, Sophists and Philosophers: Greek Wisdom Literature," in *Literature in the Greek and Roman Worlds*, edited by O. Taplin, pp. 156–191. A focus on the performance of wisdom, both written and oral, that takes into account the original audiences and the historical context.

Pelling, C. *Literary Texts and the Greek Historian*. London: Routledge, 2000. An interesting examination of the ways that literature can be historically useful and vice versa. Good sections on Thucydides, Aeschylus, and Aristophanes.

Press, Gerald. A., ed. *Who Speaks for Plato? Studies in Platonic Anonymity*. Lanham: Rowman & Littlefield Publishers, 2000. A collection of essays by distinguished contributors. All essays approach the problem of finding Platonic doctrine within his dialogue format.

Reinhardt, K. "The Adventures in *The Odyssey*," in *Reading The Odyssey*, edited by S. Schein, pp. 63–132. A detailed examination of the adventures, with the goal of assessing their relation to the larger work.

Romm, J. S. *Herodotus*. New Haven: Yale University Press, 1998. A general introduction to the author and his work, organized thematically. The author's goal is to inspire his readers to read Herodotus himself.

Rosen, R. "Homer and Hesiod," in *A New Companion to Homer*, edited by I. Morris and B. Powell, pp. 463–488. A good treatment of the two authors that notes similarities; particular attention is given here to the question of priority and influence.

Rutherford, R. B. *The Art of Plato: Ten Essays in Platonic Interpretation*. Cambridge: Harvard University Press, 1995. Studies of several of the dialogues, focusing on the ways in which the literary and philosophical aspects of the dialogues interact.

———. "From *The Iliad* to *The Odyssey*," in *Oxford Readings in Homer's Iliad*, edited by D. L. Cairns, pp. 117–146. An essay on the relationship between the two epics, with comments about authorship, overlap between the two, and the views of the ancients.

Schein, S., ed. "*The Iliad*: Structure and Interpretation," in *A New Companion to Homer*, edited by I. Morris and B. Powell, pp. 345–359. A good overview of the structure of the epic and the significance of that structure for the epic's meaning.

———. *Reading The Odyssey*. Princeton: Princeton University Press, 1996. A collection of 10 influential essays on many aspects of the epic, several appearing only here in English.

Schenker, D. "The Strangeness of the *Phaedrus*." *American Journal of Philology* 127.1 (2006). A literary reading of the dialogue that addresses many of its traditionally problematic aspects.

Segal, C. "Aristophanes' Cloud-Chorus," in *Oxford Readings in Aristophanes*, edited by E. Segal, pp. 162–181. While the focus is on the chorus in *Clouds*, this essay ranges more broadly through critical interpretations of many aspects of the comedy.

———. *Dionysiac Poetics and Euripides' Bacchae*. Princeton: Princeton University Press, 1982. A sophisticated appreciation of the play that begins with fundamental information about cult and myth.

———. *Oedipus Tyrannus: Tragic Heroism and the Limits of Knowledge*, 2nd ed. Oxford: Oxford University Press, 2001. An in-depth analysis of the play, intended for the nonspecialist. Good comments on the context of the play, as well as its later reception.

Segal, E., ed. *Oxford Readings in Aristophanes*. Oxford: Oxford University Press, 1996. A collection of 16 articles on Old Comedy in general and on specific plays.

———. *Oxford Readings in Greek Tragedy*. Oxford: Oxford University Press, 1983. A convenient collection of many excellent articles on tragedy in general, the tragedians, and individual plays.

————. "The *Physis* of Comedy," in *Oxford Readings in Aristophanes*, edited by E. Segal, pp. 1–8. A brief treatment of the place of Old Comedy in the overall development of comedy.

Shapiro, H. A. "Coming of Age in Phaiakia: The Meeting of Odysseus and Nausikaa," in *The Distaff Side*, edited by B. Cohen, pp. 155–164. A discussion of various artistic representations of the meeting, this essay exemplifies well how we might gain insight into a scene from the reactions of those closer in time to its production.

Silk, M. *Homer: The Iliad*, 2nd ed. Cambridge: Cambridge University Press, 2004. A very good and brief general introduction to questions of production, to the poem itself, and to its afterlife.

Stokes, M. *Plato's Socratic Conversations: Drama and Dialectic in Three Dialogues*. Baltimore: The Johns Hopkins University Press, 1986. A good literary treatment of *Laches*, *Symposium*, and *Protagoras*.

Storey, I. C., and A. Allen. *A Guide to Ancient Greek Drama*. Oxford: Blackwell Publishing, 2005. An excellent introduction to all matters dealing with the production of both tragedy and comedy, with biographical notes about each playwright and brief summaries of each extant play.

Taplin, O. "Fifth-Century Tragedy and Comedy," in *Oxford Readings in Aristophanes*, edited by E. Segal, pp. 9–28. The author compares the two genres in terms of the relation of the world of the play to the world of the audience. Excellent comments on the significance of theatrical self-referentiality.

————, ed. *Literature in the Greek and Roman Worlds: A New Perspective*. Oxford: Oxford University Press, 2000. The first half is an in-depth survey of the material covered in this course, with essays by leading scholars. The focus is on the literature within the world that produced it, with special attention to the receivers or audience of the literature.

————. "The Shield of Achilles within *The Iliad*," in *Homer*, edited by I. McAuslan and P. Walcot, pp. 96–115. A discussion of the long description of the shield as it relates to the rest of *The Iliad* and even *The Odyssey*.

————. "The Spring of the Muses: Homer and Related Poetry," in *Literature in the Greek and Roman Worlds*, edited by O. Taplin, pp. 22–57. A good introduction to Homer and Hesiod, with an emphasis on their performance contexts.

Tracy, S. *The Story of The Odyssey*. Princeton: Princeton University Press, 1990. In this engaging book-by-book treatment of the poem, the author sets out to describe what Homer has done and to suggest why what he has done makes one of the best tales ever told.

Vernant, J. P. "A 'Beautiful Death' and the Disfigured Corpse in Homeric Epic," in *Oxford Readings in Homer's Iliad*, edited by D. L. Cairns, pp. 311–341. An exploration of some of the central themes of *The Iliad*, focusing on the role of death in defining the lives of the heroes.

Vickers, B. *Towards Greek Tragedy: Drama, Myth, Society*. London: Longman, 1973. An excellent introduction to the nature of tragedy in general and Greek tragedy in particular, with detailed treatments of the *Oresteia* and the Electra plays.

West, M. L. "Other Early Poetry," in *Ancient Greek Literature*, edited by K. J. Dover, pp. 29–49. A good overview of the great variety of lyric poems.

Whitmarsh, T. *Ancient Greek Literature*. Cambridge: Polity Press, 2004. Not a chronological survey but a thematic consideration of the literature. The first section addresses the difficulties inherent in talking about literature of another culture that might not share our idea of what literature is.

Willcock, M. "The Search for the Poet Homer," in *Homer*, edited by I. McAuslan and P. Walcot, pp. 53–64. An argument for single authorship of *The Iliad* that builds on the theory of oral composition. A brief introduction to many of the arguments about compositional methods.

Winkler, J. J. *The Constraints of Desire*. New York: Routledge, 1990. A collection of seven intriguing essays on sexuality in the ancient world, with good treatments of Sappho and Homer's Penelope.

Worthington, I., ed. *Persuasion: Greek Rhetoric in Action*. New York: Routledge, 1994. A wide-ranging collection of essays on all aspects of ancient rhetoric and oratory, particularly as they relate to the historical and literary contexts.

Zeitlin, F. "The Closet of Masks: Role-Playing and Myth-Making in the *Orestes* of Euripides," in *Euripides: Oxford Readings in Classical Studies*, edited by J. Mossman, pp. 309–341. An intriguing treatment of an intriguing play, arguing for layers of allusion throughout, both to other versions of the Orestes story and to other plays by Euripides.

———. "The Dynamics of Misogyny in the *Oresteia*." *Arethusa* 11 (1978): 149–184, reprinted in *Playing the Other: Gender and Society in Classical Greek Civilization*, F. Zeitlin, pp. 87–119. Chicago: Chicago University Press, 1996. A seminal treatment of the many aspects of the trilogy that center on male-female conflict.

Internet Resources:

Crane, G., ed. *Perseus: An Evolving Digital Library*. Tufts University. www.perseus.tufts.edu/. A comprehensive collection of searchable texts from Greek and Roman antiquity, along with commentaries, lexica, maps, images, and much more.

Didaskalia. www.didaskalia.net/. An electronic journal and resource dedicated to the study of ancient Greek and Roman drama in performance.

Martin, T. *An Overview of Classical Greek History from Mycenae to Alexander*. Tufts University. www.perseus.tufts.edu/cgi-bin/ptext?doc=Perseus:text: 1999.04.0009. This is a particularly useful link on the Perseus site, a searchable history of the period covered in this course.

Scaife, R. *The Stoa Consortium*. www.stoa.org/. An excellent and ever-evolving collection of classical links.

Notes

Notes